PRAISE FOR *THE LONG GAME*

✩✩✩

"From Alabama country boy bedridden for two years with polio to majority leader of the US Senate is a remarkable journey. Mitch McConnell tells this quintessentially American story with lucid prose and refreshing candor. A most valuable historical contribution to the politics of our time."

—Charles Krauthammer, author of *Things That Matter*

"Mitch McConnell's impressive career in the US Senate demonstrates the power of strong leadership coupled with patience and perseverance. *The Long Game* is a fascinating and enjoyable read that vividly depicts the origins of McConnell's tenacity and commitment to public service, and shares how-to secrets from an American statesman."

—Arthur Brooks, president of the American Enterprise Institute

"With candor and a sure sense of history—both of the nation's and of the Senate—Mitch McConnell has written an engaging and compelling memoir of a life spent in the arena. Readers seeking to understand where we are, how we got here, and what might come next will find this book at once entertaining and essential."

—Jon Meacham, author of *Destiny and Power*

"Mitch McConnell's *The Long Game* is a warm, candid, and captivating story of a young boy who conquered polio, loved the Brooklyn Dodgers, and set his sights on becoming a ballplayer before finding his life's calling in politics. The steady upward climb from high school president to office boy in the Senate mailroom, from county judge to majority leader, is told with insight, humor, and telling detail."

—Doris Kearns Goodwin, presidential historian

"Mitch McConnell's absorbing memoir arrives at a moment when the nation needs and deserves what his book provides—a mature defense of the political profession by one of its best practitioners. His career in one of America's most complex institutions demonstrates that politics is both an individual craft and a team sport. His readers will acquire deepened respect for him, for the Senate, and for the patience that politics requires and rewards."

—George F. Will, political commentator and author of *A Nice Little Place on the North Side*

"Senator McConnell has been a tough foe of President Obama and the Democrats, but in this revealing memoir he also takes on the Tea Party and other purists for engaging in futile gestures and preferring to make a point rather than a difference. Even if you don't agree with his politics, you'll find a wealth of valuable lessons to learn from his journey."

—Walter Isaacson, author of *Steve Jobs* and president and
CEO of the Aspen Institute

THE LONG GAME

Mitch McConnell

THE LONG GAME

A Memoir

Sentinel

SENTINEL
An imprint of Penguin Random House LLC
penguinrandomhouse.com

First published in the United States of America by Sentinel 2016
This paperback edition with a new foreword and afterword published 2019

Most Sentinel books are available at a discount when purchased in quantity for sales promotions or
corporate use. Special editions, which include personalized covers, excerpts, and corporate imprints,
can be created when purchased in large quantities. For more information, please call (212) 572-2232
or email specialmarkets@penguinrandomhouse.com. Your local bookstore can also assist with
discounted bulk purchases using the Penguin Random House corporate Business-to-Business
program. For assistance in locating a participating retailer, email B2B@penguinrandomhouse.com.

PHOTOGRAPH CREDITS
Insert page 4 (top): From *The Courier-Journal*, November 7, 1999, © 1999
Gannett-Community Publishing; page 5 (bottom): From *The Courier-Journal*,
June 23, 1996, © 1996 Gannett-Community Publishing. All rights reserved.
Used by permission and protected by the copyright laws of the United States.
The printing, copying, redistribution, or retransmission of this content
without express written permission is prohibited.

Credits for other photographs appear adjacent to the respective images.

Library of Congress Cataloging-in-Publication Data
Names: McConnell, Mitch, author.
Title: The long game : a memoir / Mitch McConnell.
Description: New York, New York : Sentinel, 2016.
Identifiers: LCCN 2016017709 | ISBN 9780399564109 (print) |
ISBN 9780399564123 (ebook)
Subjects: LCSH: McConnell, Mitch. | United States. Congress.
Senate—Biography. | United States—Politics and government—1989– |
United States—Politics and government—1981–1989. | Legislators—United
States—Biography. | Conservatives—United States—Biography. |
Politicians—Kentucky—Biography.
Classification: LCC E840.8.M3325 A3 2016 | DDC 328.73/092aB—dc23
LC record available at https://lccn.loc.gov/2016017709

ISBN 9780399564116 (paperback)

Printed in the United States of America
1 3 5 7 9 10 8 6 4 2

Designed by Amy Hill

Penguin is committed to publishing works of quality and integrity.
In that spirit, we are proud to offer this book to our readers; however,
the story, the experiences, and the words are the author's alone.

To my mom and dad

Contents

Contents

Foreword

By President Donald J. Trump

During my 2016 presidential campaign, I spent a lot of time talking about the need for public policy to be made by the American people through their elected representatives, not by unelected judges. As part of this effort, I was proud to work with the Federalist Society to assemble a list of individuals who shared my vision, people I thought merited consideration for the Supreme Court. I wanted the American people to know up front the legal minds who represented the constitutional principles I value. And the American people responded favorably; the issue of judges proved to be a major reason for my big win over Hillary Clinton.

Yet filling slots on the federal bench is not the president's job alone. The Constitution requires Senate advice and consent before a nominee can join the federal bench. Therefore, my efforts to restore the federal judiciary to its proper role in our society required an effective partner, someone who shared my commitment to transforming the judiciary. That person was Senate majority leader Mitch McConnell. I couldn't have asked for a better partner. Mitch recognized, as did I, that since judges enjoy life tenure, the impact of judicial nominations can be felt for thirty years or more. *Transforming the federal judiciary is the ultimate long game!*

When I was sworn in as president in January 2017, there was a vacancy on the Supreme Court. It was the seat held by the great justice Antonin Scalia. The reason the seat was vacant was not an accident. It was vacant because Mitch had announced eleven months earlier that Scalia's seat would be filled by the newly elected president, not by the lame-duck Barack Obama.

Therefore, one of the first major decisions of my new administration in 2017 was to name someone to fill that vacancy. I was proud to nominate Judge Neil Gorsuch of the Tenth Circuit, who was on the list I had made public during the campaign. Gorsuch was highly qualified; no one could question his credentials. But the Democrats could not seem to accept the reality of my electoral triumph, and they were still upset about not being able to fill the Scalia slot. They made clear that they were going to filibuster anyone I put forward. And so they filibustered Gorsuch. But I had an "ace in the hole"—my partner Mitch.

Senate Democrats had changed the rules of the chamber in 2013 to permit virtually all nominees to be confirmed by a majority vote. They did that to get liberal Obama nominees onto the federal courts. The only exception the Democrats made was for Supreme Court justices. With the Democrats filibustering Gorsuch, Mitch realized that the only way this administration would ever be able to name a justice to the high court would be to make Supreme Court nominees subject to a majority vote as well. And he set out to convince his fellow Republican senators to do just that. Mitch and his Republican colleagues succeeded in changing the Senate rules, and Neil Gorsuch was confirmed to the court. It was a big win for our nation.

As hard as it is to believe, the Democrats' treatment of my next Supreme Court nominee made my first appointment look like a walk in the park! When Justice Anthony Kennedy decided to step down in 2018, I was pleased to have the opportunity to nominate another wonderful jurist: Brett Kavanaugh. However, the Democrats and their allies pulled out all the stops to try to block Kavanaugh. It was a midterm election year, and the Democrats believed they had a good chance that November to win back control of the Senate. The Democrats thought that if they could delay a final vote on Kavanaugh until after the election and then vote him down, the Senate would not have enough time to approve a replacement. Mitch and I were in close coordination throughout the Kavanaugh nomination process; we made sure that didn't happen. And in the end, once again, a highly qualified jurist was appointed to the Supreme Court.

Mitch and I worked closely on confirming not only Supreme Court justices but also lower-court nominees. With Mitch and the Republican Senate's support, I was proud to appoint thirty judges to the federal appellate courts during the first half of my term—more than any other president in a comparable period since the federal circuit courts were established, more than 125 years ago. As of mid-2019, I had already named almost one out of every four circuit court judges. A historic achievement in just two and a half years!

The effort to transform the courts is one that will benefit the American people far into the future. It is a legacy of which I am immensely proud and one for which Mitch McConnell deserves great credit. Confirming judges has been a key part of making the past two and a half years one of the most productive and conservative periods in our nation's history.

THE LONG GAME

Introduction

Over the three decades I have been a US senator, I've been the subject of many profiles. I usually play the villain, according to the standard good guy/bad guy accounts favored by most Washington reporters. The more positive ones tend to focus on my ability to broker deals with supposed adversaries, keep my head when others don't, and win elections I'm not supposed to. Until now, though, no one has ever tried to write the story as I see it, which is really my doing. I only talk to the press if it's to my advantage, and I always discourage my staff from revealing details of my meetings with presidents and other public figures. It's rare that I attend the kind of social events where people tend to engage in the gossip and intrigue for which Washington is famous. I've only been to Nantucket a few times, and I didn't like it. My idea of a good time is a quiet evening at home with my wife, Elaine Chao, or—although I may hardly strike people as the tailgating type—gathered with friends in the parking lot of the University of Louisville's Papa John's stadium, before a Cardinals football game, a tradition I've enjoyed for decades.

Beyond that, the place I feel most at ease is the Senate, an institution that rewards patience and confounds those who lack it. Every serious student of the institution, from Tocqueville to my late colleague Robert Byrd, has viewed the Senate as uniquely important to America's stability and flourishing. In their view, as well as in mine, it has made all the difference. Why? Because during the most contentious and important battles throughout our nation's history—from the fierce early fights over the shape and scope of the federal government, to those that preceded and followed a nation-rending Civil War, to those surrounding the great wars of the twentieth century, or a decades-long Cold War, or the war on terror—the Senate is the tool that has enabled us to find our footing almost every time.

At its best, the Senate exists to keep the government from swinging between extremes as one party loses power and another gains it. The Senate is the only legislative body on earth where a majority is not enough—most things require sixty votes to pass. Without this moderating effect, today's majority passes something and tomorrow's majority repeals it; today's majority proposes something, tomorrow's majority opposes it. We see that in the House of Representatives all the time. But when the Senate is allowed to work the way it was designed to—meaning a place where nothing is decided without a good dose of deliberation and debate, as well as input from both the majority and minority parties—it arrives at a result that is acceptable to people all along the political spectrum.

In recent years, however, we've lost our sense for the value of slow and steady deliberation, for the type of work that depends more on patient diplomacy than on power plays and media manipulation. Under Democratic leader Harry Reid, the Senate Chamber frequently became little more than a Democratic campaign studio. Many of the bills that Reid allowed for consideration were bills his party did not intend to pass. And none of us—no senator, no American—should be at peace with that. Because if America is to face up to the challenges we face in the decades ahead, she'll need the Senate the Founders in their wisdom intended, not the hollow shell of the Senate created in recent years under Reid.

No better example exists of this than the story behind the passage of Obamacare. When Democrats in the Senate couldn't convince even one Republican that this bill was worth supporting as written, they decided to do it on their own and pass it on a party line vote. And now we're seeing the result. The chaos this law has visited on our country isn't just deeply tragic, it was entirely predictable. That will always be the case if you approach legislation without regard for the views of the other side. Without some meaningful buy-in, you guarantee a food fight. You guarantee instability and strife. It may very well have been the case that on Obamacare, the will of the country was not to pass the bill at all. That's what I would have concluded if Republicans couldn't get a single Democratic vote for legislation of this magnitude. But Democrats plowed forward anyway. They didn't want to hear it and the results are clear. It's a mess.

The problem, admittedly, originates not solely from the Left alone, but also, disappointingly, from a very few on the Right. Just as the Democrats have used every gimmick to push through radically liberal policies, some on the Right have demanded that if they don't get every single thing they want, we may as well burn the place down, even if it means scorching the reputation and future success of our own party. People are not elected to the Senate to get everything they want. This is not an all-or-nothing place. And these are not the type of people we want to be the leaders in the Senate, or of anything else.

A big part of the problem with the Senate today is the way many politicians on both sides of the aisle style themselves as saviors. It's not only self-serving nonsense in most cases, it's exploitative of the voters. And it reflects a fundamentally un-American view of how our political institutions were meant to function. The proper basis of government, James Madison believed, was human frailty. That's why it was just as important to Madison, in devising the government we have, not only to protect the people from their own worst impulses, but also to protect them from the worst impulses of those they put in office. And that's also why the moment we conclude that our political institutions are no longer up to the task of resolving the challenges we face is the moment we give up on the American project altogether. Why? Because in the end it's the institutions, not the flawed men and women who pass through them, that will save us from ourselves *and* from the politicians we're all so fond of criticizing.

All these things have always seemed obvious to me, to the point that I never felt the need to unburden myself of any of it in a book, let alone tell my own story. But I've come to realize that those ideas—and many other constitutional principles—are anything but obvious to most people today. And when I was reelected in 2014, winning by a fifteen-point landslide against all odds and attracting a level of attention I could only find amusing, I realized it was time for me to write this book.

From the moment I made that decision, I was determined to make it true to who I am. So much of politics today is about artifice and obfuscation, and that extends to the standard political memoir, many of which seem artificial to me. They're either cloyingly grandiose, or dishonest about what usually motivates people in my business. I didn't want my book to be either. The truth is that very few of us expect to be at the center of world-changing events when we first file for office, and personal ambition usually has a lot more to do with it than most of us are willing to admit. That was certainly true for me, and I never saw the point in pretending otherwise. It doesn't mean we don't bring deep and abiding concerns to the job. It does mean that the standard story of the humble idealist who unexpectedly finds him- or herself in Washington, carried by a wave of encouraging friends in a selfless pursuit of justice and truth, is largely a fable. We're all the flawed politicians Madison worried about, and the hero pose isn't a good look for anyone.

I'm free to say all this because, unlike so many other senators, I've never had an interest in running for president. And since trashing the Senate seems to be a prerequisite for a presidential run these days, it falls on people like me to write books like this, defending this precious institution and telling the true story of what politics in America is actually like.

Anybody can enter politics, but I believe that being good at it—meaning winning elections so that you can impact policy—comes only as a result of an extraordinary amount of preparation. My ascension as leader of a new Republican majority was years in the making. Depending on how you look at it, preparation like the kind I've practiced seems either admirable or overly calculating. But it happens to be the new reality of politics in America. Unless you are blessed with extraordinary gifts of charisma or step into the national spotlight at a particularly opportune moment, making it in the world of politics today frequently involves incredible feats of preparation and endurance. Fortunately for me, that's the only way I have ever approached life. Maybe that's because I learned at an early age that nothing worthwhile comes easy. Maybe it's because I've had to work hard to overcome obstacles of birth and circumstance. Whatever the reason, I have never had to quarrel with the realities of life as a senator. Success in politics is a lot of work, and pretending otherwise isn't just pointless, it never seemed right to me.

This is a big, boisterous, complex country. Getting to the top in any field should be tough. The reward for that effort is the knowledge that you have truly earned your place at the table, and that, in politics at least, the privilege of serving your fellow citizens is something that's been hard-won, and for that reason, worth the effort, before and after the votes are counted. This book is the story not of one particular campaign, but a lifetime of campaigns. It is the story of how patience and perseverance have been the keystone of my four decades in public life, and why I think both qualities are needed now more than ever if we are to meet our greatest challenges as a nation. It is the story of how a little kid from Alabama found his purpose in life and pursued it with everything he had.

It's the story of the long game, and it begins in a small hospital room in Warm Springs, Georgia.

CHAPTER ONE

A Fighting Spirit

You can walk but you can't walk. That's what my mom would say to me after I was struck with polio at the age of two, to explain why she wouldn't let me get up on my feet.

It was the summer of 1944, ten years before Jonas Salk developed the polio vaccine. The disease was sweeping the nation, prompting full-blown hysteria not only in urban communities in the Northeast, but in rural towns like Five Points, Alabama, in a house like ours. Our real home was about two hundred miles north, in Athens, Alabama, a town of fewer than six thousand people, but my mom and I had come to Five Points to live with my mother's sister, Edrie Mae, while my dad was off fighting World War II. Without even a single stop sign, there was little reason to slow down on your way through Five Points. Edrie Mae, who we called Sister, ran a country store she and her husband, Julius, owned. It was in their house, just after I turned two, and not long after my dad left for basic training, that I first came down with what my mother thought was the flu. But when she took me to see the local doctor, hoping for something to make me feel better, she learned the diagnosis was far more grim.

The thing about polio—a virus that invades the nervous system and can, within a matter of hours, cause total paralysis—was how unpredictable it was. Some kids might get it and be permanently paralyzed; others might never see any effects. The disease struck and weakened my left leg, the worst of it my quadriceps. It's one of my life's great fortunes that Sister's home was only about sixty miles from Warm Springs, Georgia, where President Franklin D. Roosevelt had established a polio treatment center and where he'd often travel to find relief from the polio that paralyzed him at the age of thirty-nine. My mother took me there every chance she had. The nurses would teach her how to perform exercises meant to rehabilitate my leg while also emphasizing her need to make me believe I could walk, even though I wasn't allowed to.

"If he tries to walk, his leg will stiffen and we won't be able to help the muscle," they told my mother. "So do not, under any circumstances, let him walk. But if he comes to believe he's crippled, that'll be just as bad."

It was a distinction lost on me at two years old. All I knew was that as other kids my age were easily learning to run, jump, and climb, I was fighting from the confines of my bed for the chance to one day do the same. Four times each day—fiercely determined to keep me, her only child, from experiencing any disadvantage—my mother would lead me in long, aching exercises to stretch and tone my leg muscles. This went on for two very long years. She was both strict and emboldening, watching me like a hawk to keep me off my feet, and yet reminding me to deeply believe that this was temporary; that one day I would, in fact, walk.

My mom managed this with tremendous patience and grace, which was her way. She was from a little town called Wadley, Alabama, in a dirt-poor county about twenty miles from the Georgia border. She was the youngest of seven, born into a family of subsistence farmers in a region where the land was too dry to yield very much. Her mother died when she was five months old, leaving the job of raising her to Edrie Mae, just eight years old at the time. With the help of his five sons, my grandfather Shockley lived off the land: feeding his family with what they grew in the spring, and canning what they could for the winter. I was nineteen when Grandpa Shockley died in 1961, and unlike my patient and often reserved mother, I knew him to have a feisty, often angry, temper. Of course, I think he had good reason. As he was the youngest of seven kids, his parents never got around to giving him a name. After his birth, they called him Babe, and it stuck. The fact that he was never officially named made him mad as hell.

While her own parents didn't make it out of grade school, my mother graduated from Wadley High School in 1937. Soon after graduation, she found her way out of rural Alabama and into Birmingham, where she moved in with a brother who worked in a factory there. She'd been known her whole life not by her first name, Julia, which she loved, but by her middle name, Odene, which she detested. So in Birmingham she began to call herself Dean, and with no thought of ever returning to Wadley, she took a job as a secretary at CIT, a finance company. It was here that she met A. M. McConnell II.

My dad was born in Limestone County, Alabama, near the Tennessee line, to a long line of hardworking and often colorful McConnells. James McConnell, from County Down, Ireland, who came to this country as a young boy in the 1760s, went on to fight for the colonies in the American Revolution. My dad's grandfather was a circuit-riding Calvinist preacher who sermonized at a different church every Sunday, carrying his Bible in the saddlebags I still have.

When my dad was born in 1917, his parents—known to me as Big Dad and Mamie—harbored high expectations for him, their youngest son. They sent him to Darlington, a respected prep school in Rome, Georgia, where he was good enough at football to go on to play for Wake Forest. He transferred to Auburn his sophomore year, but stayed only a year before dropping out of college.

My dad was known to be stubborn, at times impetuous, and was extremely outgoing—open, bold, and often unfettered. At CIT, he found a job to match his personality and physical brawn: repossessing cars from customers who hadn't paid their loans. But he held greater ambitions than this job and soon left for the so-called oil patch of Baytown, Texas, just south of Houston. Arriving in Texas, he had quite a difficult time forgetting about Dean Shockley, the pretty twenty-one-year-old secretary he'd left behind. The fact that she was already engaged to another man didn't discourage my father's pursuit of her one bit. Luckily for him, she was mutually enchanted; by his warmth and good-natured obstinacy, not to mention his promise to do everything he could to provide her a stable and happy life. On September 19, 1940, she boarded a train to Houston with the few possessions in her hope chest—some bedding and dishes, an apple corer, and a can opener—and the next day, in a simple dress and fur stole, she married my father.

I was born two years later, in 1942, at Colbert County Hospital, about forty miles from Athens, Alabama. In another two years, my dad left for the war. He was exempt from fighting on two accounts: having a child, and his job as a civilian employee for the army at Huntsville Arsenal. But like so many men of his generation, he felt a duty to participate. He was an able-bodied man, and a citizen who deeply loved his country. The idea that he had taken the out offered to him, while millions of others wore the uniform—and many he knew had been killed—ate away at him. He wouldn't ignore that nagging for long. Just after I turned two years old in 1944, he enlisted in the army at the age of twenty-six.

On top of having to care for a baby sick with polio, my mother also had to deal with my father's absence, and her fear he wouldn't survive the war. Every day she'd check for one of his letters, in which he'd write of the things he was allowed to share: about the ham and eggs he ate at midnight in a German home, his first home-cooked meal in a long time; the wool underwear that didn't keep him warm enough; the flowers on people's lawns that made him miss spending time tinkering in my grandparents' backyard. What he didn't write about was the experience of being "in the thick of it," as he later described it, like the night his company lost two-thirds of its men.

It was only much later, after I became a husband and father myself, that I could appreciate what this time must have been like for my mother, how vast her worry for both my dad and me. There are simply no words to describe how grateful I am for her commitment to our family, and to me. Without it, I never would have had the experience that remains not only my first vivid memory, but one of the most significant moments of my life: stopping at a shoe store in LaGrange, Georgia, on the way out of Warm Springs, where she bought me my very first walking shoes—a pair of low-top saddle oxfords. The nurses had just told my mother that our two years of hard work had paid off and we'd won the fight. I could walk. Without a brace, without even a limp. We had beaten polio, and because of my mother's tenacity and patience, I was given the promise of a happy, normal childhood.

✩✩✩

Which, for the most part, it was. On May 8, 1945, my father wrote a letter to my mom, and for the first time since he'd left for the war, he was able to say where he was: Pilsen, Czechoslovakia. It was VE Day, and the war in Europe was over. "I'm in a large city," he wrote, "and the people have literally gone wild. When we went through the towns coming here, every man, woman and child lined the streets, waving flags, throwing flowers, giving us cognac, wine, cake, cookies, etc. And kissing us and shaking hands with us. It has not been easy here until today but now we are the victors."

He boarded the USS *Monticello* in Le Havre, France, on July 13, 1945, and made it home a little over a week later. We were all extraordinarily relieved he was back, unscathed other than a nick on his chin where he'd been hit by shrapnel. He was then issued jungle gear, and given orders to head to the Pacific. But to the substantial relief of our family, President Truman dropped the A-bomb on Japan. Knowing the potential suffering this saved my dad, and the great number of lives spared by bringing an end to the war, there's never been any second thoughts in our family about the wisdom of that decision.

I was too young at the time to know the pride I'd later feel about my dad's service in Europe, or to fully appreciate his bravery. He didn't offer a lot about his experience, although he would later tell me he'd been a scout, meaning he walked ahead of his squad as it advanced. What a dangerous and courageous thing to do. As time passed and I got older, I noticed subtle ways in which the war had impacted him. Where he once enjoyed hunting a great deal, he took me squirrel hunting just once after returning home from the war. As we roamed the field together in the early dawn of a perfect spring day, just like so many southern fathers and sons before us, my father put his rifle to his side and said we were going home.

"I think I'm done with shooting anything for a while," he said. He never hunted again, and nor would I.

My mom and I both grew very close to my dad's parents, Big Dad and Mamie. They owned a funeral parlor in Athens and Big Dad's real name was Robert Hayes McConnell. He was born in 1877, a month before Rutherford B. Hayes was sworn in as the nineteenth president. The 1876 race between Hayes and Samuel J. Tilden had been exceptionally close. Tilden had won the popular vote by a small majority, and after some ballot counts were disputed, Congress created an electoral commission to decide the election. The haggling began, and a deal was eventually cut between the Hayes forces and the electors in Louisiana, South Carolina, and Florida: they would give Hayes their votes, and thus the presidency, if he ended Reconstruction. Hayes kept his word and shortly after taking office, he withdrew federal troops from Louisiana and South Carolina, bringing an end to the era of Reconstruction. I'm sure that my grandfather was given his middle name after the president. It surely couldn't be a coincidence that he was born February 23, 1877, and Hayes was sworn in ten days later, especially since this name doesn't appear to have been used at any time in our family history. And nearly a hundred years after Big Dad's birth, I would pass the same middle name on to my firstborn daughter.

Having lost her own mother as an infant, my mom came to think of

Mamie as her own, and I don't think there could have been two people that either of us loved any more. I'd spend every Friday night sleeping in the spare bedroom in their big yellow house with the wide porch at 201 East Bryan Street, waking up the next morning to meet my friends at the picture show, as we called it then. My dad would give me fifteen cents—ten for admission and five for popcorn. The main attraction was usually a Roy Rogers or Gene Autry cowboy movie, but it was the short serial they'd play following the movie that I liked best. The hero would be left hanging from a cliff by his fingernails, forcing me to wait an entire week to see what happened. On the weekends, I'd join the other kids in my neighborhood for a game of cowboys and Indians or, more frequently, Civil War. Of course, in the South of the early 1950s, it was nearly impossible to find a single boy—many who, like me, had great-grandparents who fought under Robert E. Lee, whose grandmothers belonged to the United Daughters of the Confederacy—willing to be a Yankee. At night, I'd join my parents in front of the radio to listen to *The Shadow*, *Amos 'n' Andy*, and Jack Benny.

It was a simple but happy childhood. As their only child, I never wanted for my parents' attention, and while they were never too strict or severe, there was no question that when offered the choice, I must always choose right over wrong. They taught me, both in what they said and in how they lived their lives, about personal responsibility and hard work, and it was here in Athens that I learned many lessons that would serve me well throughout my life. Like, for instance, how to stand up to a bully. His name was Dicky McGrew, and he lived across the street from us. His dad owned the local newspaper, and Dicky was as big as he was bossy. I was thoroughly intimidated. He had an annoying tendency to push me around while we played together, and sometimes I'd notice my dad silently watching from our lawn. But he didn't remain silent for long. One afternoon, my father stopped his yard work and called me home from Dicky's.

"Son, I've been watching the way you interact with him," he said. "That's got to change, and it's got to change right now."

"What do you mean?" I asked.

"That kid's been pushing you around for too long. You're going back across that street, and you're going to beat up Dicky McGrew."

I felt my stomach drop. "Dad," I protested, "he's bigger than I am. And older."

"Well, I'm bigger and older than you too," my dad responded. "And I've had enough of this. It's time you showed him who's boss. Now go."

There I was: torn between my father and Dicky McGrew. Not being a foolish child, I decided I had a far better (if still highly unlikely) chance at winning a fight with Dicky than I did with my father. Steeling myself, I crossed the street, approached Dicky, and started swinging. I don't know if it was because my punches were on point or Dicky was too startled to defend himself, but I won the fight. I even bent his glasses. From that moment forward, Dicky never bullied me again.

This experience made a lasting impression on me, teaching me a few lessons I'd return to again and again throughout my life: standing up for myself, knowing there's a point beyond which I can't be pushed, and being tough when it's important to be tough. In the line of work I would choose, compromise is key, but I'd come to find that certain times required me to invoke the fighting spirit both my parents instilled in me. Every time I've had to be tough, I've gotten a lot of criticism, but it's almost always worked, just like bending Dicky McGrew's glasses.

CHAPTER TWO

From Baseball to Politics

I got my first baseball glove the summer of 1954, when I was twelve years old. My father and I split the cost of it, with my share coming from money I'd earned cutting my neighbors' lawns in Augusta, Georgia, where, four years earlier, my family had moved. My father had continued to work with the army after his discharge from the military, and in 1950, just after I turned eight, he was transferred to Camp Gordon, now Fort Gordon, in Augusta. It was not easy to leave Athens, Alabama, having to say good-bye to Big Dad and Mamie, but as we settled into life in Georgia, we all tried to make the best of it. For me, this meant finding baseball.

I'm not sure what, exactly, drew me so strongly to the sport. Maybe it was my way of trying to find someplace to feel at home at a time I otherwise felt so uprooted. Or that even by the age of twelve, I had come to realize that I'd never truly gain the respect of my peers if I didn't excel in something athletic. Or that the polio, which left me unable to run for long distances, narrowed my choices.

It was probably a mix of all those things, but either way, I loved the game. So did my father. The summer of 1955, he took me to see the Augusta Tigers, a Detroit Tigers farm team, no less than thirty-five times. We'd sit in the bleachers, filling up on hot dogs and popcorn, and then race home. Before the screen door even slammed shut behind us, we'd be in front of the radio, turning the dial to the Brooklyn Dodgers game. The Dodgers were my team, and 1955 was their year. It was the fifth time in nine years they'd gone up against the Yankees in the World Series. They'd lost every time, but I believed their day had come. The Yankees won the first two games but the Dodgers came back. The series was tied at 3–3. Just before the seventh and final game, my family and I traveled back to Athens, Alabama, to attend the funeral of my great-uncle Ad. While everyone gathered somberly in the kitchen, I was in the living room, trying to pick up the game on the radio. I had to press my ear against the speaker and constantly jiggle the dial to try to hear the game over the static, wishing the whole time I were at home watching on TV, listening to the commentary offered by Vin Scully, the famous voice of the Dodgers. In one of the final plays, Yogi Berra hit a line drive to Sandy Amoros in left field. Amoros threw it to Pee Wee Reese on second for an out, and then Reese to Gil Hodges at first, for a double play. This would be the play that decided the game, which ended 2–0 Dodgers, handing them the series for the first time in the franchise's history. Trying to respect the mourning adults in the next room, I jumped up and down as quietly as I could.

This was all well and good, but when it came to my own attempt at the sport, I had a serious problem. I was terrible at baseball. I picked up a bat to find I couldn't hit; nor could I throw particularly well. It was a dampening realization, to say the least, but I also knew I had a choice: I could accept my limitations and move on, or I could work hard to overcome them. I chose the latter, and the summer I turned twelve—a summer that saw Hank Aaron hit his first home run, the polio vaccine get introduced in the United States, and the Supreme Court pass down the historic *Brown v. Board of Education* decision—I approached my goal of getting good at baseball as if it were the most important task in the world.

Our house at the time—2311 Neal Street—was the first home my parents owned, after almost ten years of marriage, and I bet they didn't pay any more than $8,000 for it. It was a modest house, made more modest by the telephone pole that, for some reason, had been erected right smack in the middle of our front lawn. It was a little embarrassing. My parents looked into having it removed, but were told it would cost more than they'd paid for the house. (The telephone pole would remain.) One of the best things about this house is that we were just two doors down from the home of Bernie Ward, the principal at my elementary school. Before he became our principal, Bernie played professional baseball in the minor leagues, and he certainly knew a lot about the game. Often, when he saw me practicing with my friends in our backyard, he'd stop by to offer some instruction—showing me how to grip the ball to get a more accurate pitch; how to throw a curveball. We worked on my batting and fielding, and after he'd gone home, I'd convince the other kids to stick around, to practice with me a little longer.

To my amazement, the effort paid off. I started hitting the ball well. My pitches were good. It seemed to happen suddenly, as if something had clicked. By the end of the summer, I'd found that with nothing other than persistence and hard work, I had turned myself from a crummy ballplayer into a pretty darn good one.

It was extremely gratifying, and by the time I was thirteen, playing in the local Little League, I was feeling very confident in my baseball abilities. I was no longer just a student of the sport; I was now a serious competitor. In fact, I'd say I was even feeling a little full of myself. Maybe I had a future in the sport, I thought. Maybe I was going to even play in the big leagues. And then the all-star game came along and with it another important life lesson.

At the end of the summer, I was chosen as a county all-star, which meant I got to play in the exhibition game against the city all-stars. All season I'd hoped for the chance to play in this game, and had been looking forward to it for weeks. But that excitement gave way to fear the moment we arrived at their field.

They were bigger than we were. They had better uniforms. Their field was nothing like the dusty, pebbled patch behind Wheeless Road Elementary where we played, but an actual baseball field with freshly cut grass, a pitcher's mound, and a home-run fence.

The game was seven innings, and the other pitcher on my team was slated to pitch the first three and a half innings, and I'd pitch the last. This gave me plenty of time to sit on that hard wooden bench, gripping my glove and realizing how overmatched we were. Come the fourth inning, I made my way to the mound on shaky legs, praying my nerves wouldn't show themselves in my pitches. I wasn't so lucky.

I walked the first guy. And then the second. And then the third and the fourth. That was one run in. As the next batter approached the plate, I reminded myself of how hard I'd worked, how good I was, how I had every reason to be confident. I was going to get that ball in the strike zone, the way I had hundreds of other times.

Well, I did, only to watch the batter knock it over the fence and out of the park. Needless to say, we lost the game. Afterward, my dad knew enough to allow me the car ride home in silence. I kept my head pressed against the glass so my dad couldn't see my disappointment, and knew I'd just learned another important lesson. As soon as you start to believe there's nobody smarter or stronger or better than you, you will undoubtedly come up against the kid who's going to clear the bases with a home run, knocking the ball far over the fence, and taking your overconfidence right along with it.

☆☆☆

Just as I was finally growing accustomed to life in Augusta, Georgia, my dad came home with an unexpected announcement: we were moving to Louisville, Kentucky. Three years earlier, he'd left his job with the army to work for the DuPont company, which was building the Savannah River nuclear plant in Aiken, South Carolina, right across the Savannah River. The company had offered him a promotion in Kentucky. It was a step up, with a higher salary, and he couldn't turn it down. Before I even had the chance to protest, we were once again packing our things into boxes, and loading Button and Cookie, our two Boston bulldogs, into our 1956 Chevy for the eight-hour drive north. We arrived in January of 1956. Big Dad was concerned about our move. Not because it brought us even farther from Mamie and him in Athens, but because in his view, as a man who felt a lot of pride and patriotism to have spent his whole life in the Deep South, moving as far north as Kentucky meant moving to Yankee territory.

We rented a small house in a middle-class neighborhood in the southern end of Louisville. Having to uproot our lives for the second time in six years was hard on my mother. She missed Big Dad and Mamie, and with her roots in rural Alabama, Louisville felt too urban and unfriendly. It was hard on me as well. I was halfway through the eighth grade, preparing to enter high school. The idea of starting over in a wholly unfamiliar place made this already daunting transition feel even more so. I enrolled at duPont Manual High School, housed in an ornate Gothic building across from the University of Louisville. The only thing that excited me about this new school was that it was the alma mater of Louisvillian Pee Wee Reese, a member of my beloved Brooklyn Dodgers, who had captained the team to its 1955 World Series victory.

It was the biggest high school in the state, and I didn't know a soul. With my southern accent and tendency to be on the quiet side among so many strangers, I didn't make friends easily. While most other kids were discovering Elvis and cruising downtown's Fourth Street, looking for girls to ask to the next YWCA dance, I spent most of my time with my mom, both of us battling homesickness. I'm pretty sure we survived that winter thanks largely to the pleasure we found watching the University of Louisville basketball team, which, under all-American Charlie Tyra, went on to win the 1956 NIT championship.

The one bit of good news was that Louisvillians took their youth baseball far more seriously than we had in Augusta. The local Beechmont League played on nice fields and wore impressive uniforms, and boys had to first try out. The team managers came to watch the tryouts, attended by at least three hundred kids, and after a few days, a draft was held. I was the number one pick, and was placed on a team called the Giants. I was exceedingly proud, and really wanted to live up to this honor, but after my experience in Augusta, I knew I shouldn't allow my highs to be too high or my lows too low, and I remained cautious. This ended up being a wise decision. After a good year with the Giants—hitting over .300, pitching well—I was not chosen as an all-star player, passed over for one of the manager's sons. By tenth grade, I wasn't even good enough to make the Manual High School team.

It wasn't easy, but I accepted it: if I was going to excel at something, it wasn't sports. And the more baseball faded, the more something else was beginning to entice me, something that shared the same sense of competition, the team spirit, the need for endurance: politics.

☆☆☆

When I was quite young, my father shared with me the story of how his father, Big Dad, had first explained politics to him.

"Sit down, son," Big Dad said. "This won't take long." My dad did as he was told. "Okay," my grandfather continued. "The Republican Party is the party of the North. The Democratic Party is the party of the South. You can go now."

From what I could tell, my grandfather's words remained true. In Athens, I'd sometimes tag along with Big Dad to the funeral parlor he owned, where the men from the neighborhood would gather on the comfortable leather chairs in the large front foyer to talk politics. I heard the story of one local election. This was back in the days of paper ballots, and when the polls closed, the election officials counted the ballots back at the courthouse. It was pretty routine: Democrat, Democrat,

Democrat. But once, a ballot for the Republican appeared. Then, after a while, another was pulled from the box.

"What do we make of this?" one official asked the others.

"Throw it away," someone said. "The poor son of a bitch voted twice."

When my dad voted for Dwight Eisenhower in the 1952 presidential election, it's therefore very likely he was the first McConnell ever to support a Republican. But he'd fought the war under Ike, who served as the supreme commander of the Allied Forces in Europe. I greatly looked up to my dad, and if he was loyal to Eisenhower, then so was I— so much so that in my fifth-grade class photo, attached to the wide lapel of my button-down shirt, is a pin reading "I Like Ike."

The election of 1956 four years later, a rematch between Eisenhower and Adlai Stevenson, was the first to capture my attention. Both the Democratic and Republican national conventions were broadcast on television, taking over several hours of programming, replacing shows like *As the World Turns* and *The Johnny Carson Show*. The broadcast was nothing more than a view of the podium, with intermittent observations offered by Chet Huntley and David Brinkley or Walter Cronkite. In other words, it was deadly boring and I would venture a guess that I was probably the only fourteen-year-old boy in America interested enough in politics to watch both conventions, gavel to gavel.

Watching these conventions helped to move me beyond simply adopting my father's political loyalties to feeling sure of my own. It may have been unusual to identify as a Republican in Kentucky at the time, but it didn't feel that way when considered from a wider lens and a longer view. Americans have always tended to be a fairly conservative bunch. The colonists overthrew the English not because they wanted to create some radically new political order, but because they liked the country they had put together here and wanted to preserve a way of life they had come to enjoy. Even as a boy I could see that the Constitution was meant to limit government, reserving power for the people. And I was proud to call myself a member of the party created on February 28, 1854, when about fifty opponents of slavery got together in a little white schoolhouse in Ripon, Wisconsin.

The year 1956 would sure turn out to be an exciting one for a budding Kentucky Republican like me. Eisenhower won a second term, and not one but two Republicans were elected to the US Senate from Kentucky: Thruston Ballard Morton, who beat the Democratic incumbent; and John Sherman Cooper, who was elected in a special election to fill the seat made vacant by the death of former majority leader Alben Barkley. In the vicinity of these unlikely successes, it was not only a lot easier to form my party affiliation, it also led me to think that holding elected office might be something I could do—an idea that I'd first attempt to put into practice at Manual High School.

✫✫✫

I'd been a student at Manual for a few hours when the teacher announced it was time to head to the convocation, an all-student assembly that customarily took place once a week. I joined the other students in the vast auditorium, and surrounded by hundreds of strangers who all seemed to have grown up together, I took a seat toward the back, where I could hide in a poorly lit corner. Sitting there, I felt a pang of homesickness. When my dad had first told us we were moving to Louisville, it was a moment just like this that I had most dreaded: being an outsider. I was overwhelmed by how big this school was—so much so that I think that while I might have once been considered outgoing, I immediately became an introvert. But, although I couldn't know this at the time, these first uneasy months at Manual, and this day in particular, would spur me to set a clear, if seemingly out-of-reach, goal that would set the course of my life.

The convocation was presided over by the president of the student council, a boy from the senior class. I found the idea of public speaking to be utterly daunting, and the confident ease with which he spoke impressed me. He didn't seem the slightest bit intimidated. After school that afternoon, I rode the city bus back to my house, where my mom was eagerly waiting to hear about my first day. I couldn't help but share every detail of the convocation, and how in awe I had been of the student council president. It wasn't just that he himself had particularly impressed me, but it was also the fact that one person could have the envy of everyone at the school. What teenage boy didn't desire that?

"That would be something," I said. "Getting to be president of that big school, and having the respect of your peers and an influence over the direction of the school."

She must have sensed what was behind my words. "I bet you could do that."

"I doubt it," I said. "I don't know a soul at that school. I don't have even one friend."

"That won't always be the case," my mom said. "Later, if it's something you want to do, I'm sure you could make it happen."

Her words stayed with me, and by the time I was a junior at Manual, things had improved. My grades were good, I'd made a few friends, and I even had a steady girlfriend, Annell Samuels, who was sweet and as pretty as can be. Her mother would drive us to the dances, and then out for a burger at the Ranch House drive-in. Annell and I would sit in the backseat, trying to forget Mrs. Samuels sitting silently in the front. I liked Mrs. Samuels, but was very happy when I got my driver's license at sixteen, and could take Annell out on my own.

At the end of my junior year, my desire to lead the school and know I'd earned the respect of my classmates had not abated. If I was going to do it—put myself out there and make a run for it—it was now or never. I walked into school one morning and entered my name into the race, feeling proud, excited, and pretty sure I was going to lose. My opponent, Terry McCoy, was by far the odds-on favorite. He was a better student than me, and enjoyed the obvious support of the student council adviser, Mr. Purnell. My mom's advice was to stay positive, my dad's: to work hard.

"You can't be one of those kids who puts your name on the ballot, sits back, and hopes for the most votes," my dad told me. "You have to be smart and focused about this."

I agreed. To win the election, I needed to run a better campaign. Because I was not particularly well known, I needed the support of those who were. Just like Kentucky candidates today seek the endorsement of the Louisville *Courier-Journal*, I began to seek the endorsement of the popular kids, like Janet Boyd, a well-known cheerleader; Bobby Marr, the best high school pitcher in the state; and Pete Dudgeon, an All-City Football player. I was prepared to ask for their vote using the only tool in my arsenal, the one thing teenagers most desire. Flattery.

I'd find them in the hallway or lunchroom. "People follow your lead," I told Janet and the others. "If you vow to vote for me, I think others will too." Not one person said no, and others quickly followed suit. I designed a pamphlet entitled "We Want McConnell for President" and listed the names of the popular students whose endorsements I'd secured. A classmate convinced her father to make copies. During my time between classes, or after school, I walked the long, tiled halls, sliding a pamphlet into the locker of every single student, even the underclassmen, often overlooked in these campaigns.

A few weeks before the election, it was anybody's win, and I went at it full-on. Enlisting my parents and some friends for help, we gathered in my basement and painted "McConnell for President" onto a twenty-five-foot-long banner. I carried it to school under my arm, and hung it on the wall of the school's central stairwell, where it was impossible to miss.

The day of the election, the school administrators set up three voting booths, and later, Terry and I went to Mr. Purnell's office to receive the results. I'll never forget the surprised and somewhat disappointed look on Mr. Purnell's face as he handed me the returns.

"Congratulations, Mitch," he said. "You've won."

I rode the bus home with Terry after school, exhilarated. Although I did feel a bit sorry for him, I'd simply outworked him. Of course, my jubilation over winning was sobered a few days later, when I felt the pressure to prove to my fellow students that they had made the right choice in electing me. On the first day that I took the stage as the leader of my school—the same stage from which I'd watched the student council president speak a few years earlier as I hid in the back of the auditorium—I vowed to work hard over the next year to show they had. Walking onto that stage was a proud moment. I'd been tireless and smart and had run a better campaign. I knew that I'd earned that win.

And I knew something else too: having had my first taste of the responsibility and respect that came with holding elected office, I was hooked.

CHAPTER THREE

Seeing Greatness

Soon after moving to Louisville, I had made a vow to myself: if I ever got used to Kentucky, I was never going to leave. The two moves I'd made as a child were downright traumatic, and I wasn't interested in going through that again. In 1960, I enrolled at the University of Louisville. I remained living with my parents, and my dad bought me a little red Corvair to drive back and forth to campus each day.

Whereas it had taken me a few years to find my footing at Manual High School, I immediately felt at home at U of L. I joined Phi Kappa Tau, a highly respected fraternity, and quickly made a group of close friends. Although I lived at home with my parents, I spent most of my free time at our frat house. Greek life provided the epicenter of social activities at our college, and every weekend, I was on campus, attending a party or dance. I became a rabid fan of the U of L Cardinals football and basketball teams, rarely missing a home game. This was the beginnings of a love that endures to this day.

At the insistence of my college girlfriend, I attempted to expand my interests beyond politics. I signed up for an art appreciation class, and committed to take it seriously. For our first assignment, we were asked to write a paper on a painting of our choosing. I put a great deal of effort into that paper, and felt quite proud of it. It earned a D. Somebody's trying to tell me something here, I thought, accepting the idea that I was probably never going to be a Renaissance man.

Instead, I happily focused my studies on political science and, perhaps my favorite subject, American history. Later, as a law student at the University of Kentucky, my love of history was so great that I briefly considered dropping out to pursue a doctoral degree in history, and an eventual position as a history professor. I obviously thought better of this idea, but I've been interested in history since I was very young, especially in learning about the lives of great men and women who stood strong in their beliefs regardless of popular opinion. People like John Marshall Harlan, the Kentucky-born Supreme Court justice who is best known as the lone dissenter in the 1896 case *Plessy v. Ferguson*, which upheld segregation. And another fellow Kentuckian, Senator Henry Clay, the so-called Great Compromiser. I'd spend my senior year at U of L studying Clay for my honors thesis, admiring his efforts to hold the union together in the years prior to the Civil War. Learning about Clay, seeing what he was able to accomplish from his place in the US Senate, was the first time I began to feel the stirrings of hope that I might, in my very wildest dreams, follow in Clay's footsteps and serve as a US senator myself. Learning about great men like Harlan and Clay—coupled with the experiences I would have with contemporary political leaders over the next few years, as I finished my undergraduate degree and went through law school—only crystalized this ambition.

✧✧✧

At U of L, I was fortunate to fall under the tutelage of Grant Hicks, a political science professor who inspired me, on a more personal level, to practice my own independent thinking, especially about the type of government that can best serve our country. In a university where most professors were liberal Democrats, Grant Hicks was the lone conservative.

The poor guy probably had to eat lunch by himself, but unlike most other political science teachers I had, Hicks didn't give conservative thinking short shrift. In learning about both sides of the political coin, I had a way to make a comparison, allowing me to further cement my conservative views. In Democrats, I saw a party more concerned about prioritizing the state over the individual and whose playbook was filled with plans to bloat government, enact out-of-control spending, and then raise taxes to pay for it all. My studies greatly confirmed my growing skepticism about big government. Whereas Democrats wanted to place their trust in the government and its agents to guide our institution and direct our lives, I felt it far wiser to put our trust in the wisdom and the creativity of private citizens working voluntarily with each other and through more local mediating institutions, guided by their own sense of what's right and fair and good.

A Barry Goldwater enthusiast, Hicks turned me on to Goldwater's *The Conscience of a Conservative*. Reading this book made me excited about Goldwater and what he meant for the future of my party. Since FDR, cowed by the success of the New Deal, Republicans had sacrificed a lot of their ideology and essentially went along with Democrats. In fact, the liberal orthodoxy was so entrenched in the middle of the century that William F. Buckley, one of the nation's leading intellectuals and the founder of the *National Review*, often reminded people of the prevailing idea at the time, first espoused by a prominent liberal intellectual—that there were no conservative ideas in general circulation in America at this time. None.

But here was Goldwater, moving Republicans away from the "me too" way of thinking embraced by Dewey and Eisenhower, advocating more conservative policies, emphasizing the need to rail against the ever-increasing concentrations of authority in Washington. He pledged to present voters "a choice, not an echo" of the way it had been.

I was so inspired by Goldwater, in fact, that Grant Hicks encouraged me, in my role as the president of the College Republicans, to invite him to speak on campus. I was proud, and more than a little surprised, when Goldwater accepted, and prouder yet to be the one to introduce him before the speech he gave to the large crowd that had gathered on the university's main quad.

That day, a reporter snapped a picture of the moment I met Goldwater. It appeared in the *Courier-Journal*, and if you walk into my office in the Russell Senate Office Building today, an office once inhabited by Ted Kennedy, you'll find that photograph, which Goldwater later signed for me, hanging prominently on the wall. I like this image immensely, as it helps to remind me how far I've come since that day in 1962 when, even at that young age, I was beginning to harbor hopes about a political future of my own.

My staff, however, likes this photo for an entirely different reason: with one look at me then, all crew-cut and earnest, wearing a jacket and tie, you can put yourself at ease over the question of whether I ever smoked pot in college.

☆☆☆

If I was serious about holding elected office someday, I needed to get some real experience and I set my sights as a college student on getting that experience both through elected office myself as well as real-life experience in Washington, DC. Fortunately, I achieved both. After two unsuccessful runs for office at U of L my sophomore year—both of which I lost by exactly one vote—I was elected my junior year to be the president of the Arts and Sciences student council. Then, that summer, I was, happily, the first student chosen in the U of L political science congressional internship program, and went to work for Kentucky congressman Gene Snyder, an ultraconservative Republican who was elected the previous year to the House of Representatives.

Arriving in Washington, DC, for my first political job was a truly proud moment. The last time I'd been to DC was the summer I turned ten, when my parents and I spent two weeks driving in our 1953 Chevy through the mountains of North Carolina and Virginia. We visited Mount Vernon, and then went up to Washington, where we toured the Smithsonian and every monument up and down the mall. This time, it wasn't a 1953 Chevy that brought me to DC, but a two-seat 1961 MG that certainly made me feel as if I was something else. I moved into Hartnett Hall at Twenty-First and P Street NW, where I had my own small room, and shared a bathroom with the other tenants on my hall.

Snyder was an interesting guy—he once suggested, somewhat tongue-in-cheek, that a way to help the struggling Kennedy Center was not to throw tax dollars at it, but to host wrestling matches on Friday nights—and I was his only intern. For six hours of college credit and $200 a month, I was assigned the work of reviewing hearings of the House Appropriations Committee to find areas of excessive government spending, and mailing cookbooks to ladies' groups. The most rewarding part of the experience was being there at such an interesting time—no day more interesting than August 28, 1963, when Martin Luther King Jr. delivered his "I Have a Dream" speech.

That day, I left Snyder's office and walked outside, overcome by the sight of the crowd, which stretched from the Lincoln Memorial to the Washington Monument. I was too far away to hear Dr. King, but I knew I was witnessing a pivotal moment in history. Growing up in the Deep South, I had lived with segregation. At the movie theater in Athens, Alabama, there were separate entrances for blacks and whites; public water fountains were clearly marked with "For Colored Only" signs. The first time I attended school with African American students was my freshman year of high school, two years after the passage of *Brown v. Board of Education*.

But my parents had instilled me with a deep-seated belief in equal and civil rights, which, given their own upbringing in the Deep South, was quite extraordinary. My great-grandfather had been a Confederate soldier, enlisting in 1863 at the age of seventeen, and the only African

Americans we'd known well were Texie and Archie, a married couple who worked at Big Dad and Mamie's house. But on this issue, my parents were far ahead of their time and years beyond their peers. From an early age, they'd taught me that everyone deserved equal opportunities and the right to vote.

As my dad would write to me a few years later, in expressing his joy over the passage of the Civil Rights Act of 1964, "As you know, I sincerely wish we didn't need such a law but we do and I'm glad it's done. I hope and pray it will all work out with little violence. God gave a man certain dignity and rights and I wish we didn't have to fight over it. I hope you never forget the importance of every single one of us. In my view each man has their right to stand up and be counted where he sits . . . A lot of us went to battle because some people didn't believe in the 'one man, one vote' rule. As much as I hate violence I would fight over a man's rights quicker now than I did twenty years ago." This certainly stayed with me, greatly impacting my own thinking on civil rights. The final semester at U of L, I'd help to organize a march on the state capitol in Frankfort, in support of a state public accommodations law that would end discrimination in businesses and all other facilities open to the public.

Unfortunately, even as I stood on those steps watching the march go by, I knew that the man I worked for opposed its cause. Snyder would later go on to vote against the civil rights bill of 1964, and our opposing views on this issue quietly strained our relationship. But my experience working with him included learning at least one critical lesson. In 1966, three years after my internship, he was running for office, and I very publicly supported his primary opponent. Snyder was mad about this, and he should have been. It was a mistake. Snyder had given me an important opportunity by allowing me to come to Washington and intern for him, and for that, I owed him some degree of allegiance. My decision was one that caused me regret, and it was an important early lesson in loyalty that I would never forget.

Many years later, when Snyder's wife asked me to deliver his eulogy, after his death in 2007, I was deeply honored, and also a little relieved. It meant that he had gotten over the insult, and for this I was equally grateful.

✩✩✩

"The president's been shot." It was Friday, November 22, 1963, my last year of college. I had just finished watching an intramural football game on the quadrangle in front of the administration building. I don't remember who said those words to me, but they are words I'll never forget. My first thought was, I hope he will live, but it wasn't too long after arriving at the Student Center to have lunch that we all learned Kennedy had died. I was utterly devastated. I was an ardent supporter of Richard Nixon in the 1960 race. At the time, Kentucky allowed voting at eighteen and my vote for Nixon was the first for a president that I'd cast. I was disappointed with the results of that election, but I couldn't believe that something like this—something this violent and tragic—could happen in our country. My parents were spending the weekend visiting relatives, and I drove home to an empty house. I was happy to be alone, to sit with my grief without having to speak.

For the next few days, I remained planted on the couch watching the news, trying to grasp what had happened. Come Sunday morning, I had to remind myself to eat. I made myself a ham and cheese sandwich, and brought it back to the den. Sitting in front of the television, I watched Jack Ruby shoot Lee Harvey Oswald on live television, right there with the sandwich in my mouth. In today's world of twenty-four-hour live television news—in a world where we've watched a space shuttle explode and terrorists fly commercial airplanes into our nation's tallest buildings—this might not seem so extraordinary. But at the time, live news was wholly novel; so novel that it was hard to make sense of what I was seeing, to absorb the idea that untold millions of Americans were witnessing this bizarre, dreadful event at the exact same moment. It was enormously depressing. That day, watching the violence unfold, having grown up knowing only peace, I don't think I could ever have predicted the tumultuous decade about to follow.

The following summer, after graduating from U of L, I was intent on getting an internship on Capitol Hill. I wanted to further understand the workings of the Senate beyond my studies, to learn as much as I could in the most direct way possible. By being there. I wrote a letter to Senator John Sherman Cooper asking if I might come work for him before starting law school that fall at the University of Kentucky. Cooper, a sixty-two-year-old World War II veteran, was considered a very independent Republican, and was not known for making quick decisions, especially about personnel. I'd heard the popular legend that the post office in Ashland, Kentucky, had stayed empty for the entire eight years of the Eisenhower administration because Senator Cooper could never decide who he wanted to make postmaster. I was a young man in a hurry, so when I didn't receive a response to my letter, I decided to spend my spring break in Washington, DC, where I stopped by Cooper's office at the Russell building on more than one occasion, reminding whoever happened to be sitting at the front desk of my name and my interest in working for Senator Cooper that summer. Whoever held the authority on hiring decisions eventually relented, and I was offered a job in the mailroom, an offer that may have been born only from a desire to make me go away.

Less than a week after graduating from U of L, I was on my way back to Washington, where I rented a room near American University and began my internship with Senator Cooper. I spent at least eight hours a day in the mailroom, reading letters and sorting the mail by subject area. I couldn't have been happier. Unlike Snyder, who was a freshman congressman, Cooper was a major player in the Senate, a consummate statesman, and my relationship with him would change the course of my life.

John Sherman Cooper was the first truly great man I'd ever met, and the greatest influence he had on me was what he taught me about statesmanship and governing. He was a practitioner of what I think is the finest form of democracy, the type first laid out by Edmund Burke. A British parliamentarian at the time of the American Revolution, Burke envisioned that people would elect representatives who would follow their own best judgment. This was, of course, well before the day of public-opinion polls, but many elected officials still felt compelled to pander to the popular view. That's not what Burke had in mind. In a speech delivered to the electors at Bristol, England, in 1774, Burke said, "Your representative owes you not his industry only, but his judgment; and he betrays, instead of serving you, if he sacrifices it to your opinion." This was how Senator Cooper approached being a senator.

While he was sensitive to his constituents' interests, those interests did not control him. Nothing proved this more to me than his opinion on the Civil Rights Act of 1964. The Senate had been mostly a graveyard for civil rights bills since Reconstruction. By mid-June of 1964, one month into my internship with Cooper, the civil rights bill had been debated in the Senate for fifty-seven days. One senator filibustered against it by speaking for over fourteen hours. But not John Sherman Cooper.

Senator Cooper had advanced racial equality for every American citizen for his entire public life. In the 1930s, as county judge of Pulaski County in south-central Kentucky during the Great Depression, he was known to take money out of his own pocket to buy a meal for a starving family of any color. In the 1940s, he was one of the first Kentucky circuit-court judges to seat blacks on juries. In 1963, he had tried to pass a bill barring discrimination in public accommodations. It was filibustered, just like the others. And he was determined that the 1964 civil rights bill would not meet the same fate.

From my job in the mailroom, I saw how besieged Cooper's office was with letters from thousands of people who opposed the bill. While I'm proud that attitudes have come a long way since then, at the time, some Kentuckians weren't ready for this bill. But despite the considerable opposition from back home, Senator Cooper never wavered. He worked to get the votes to break the filibuster.

It was powerful to witness him stand his ground. But I also wondered how he could hold fast against such forceful opposition. One day I got the chance to ask him about his thoughts on the mail he was receiving, and how it was impacting his thinking on the matter.

"How do you take such a tough stand, and square it with the fact that a considerable number of people who elected you have the opposite view?" I asked.

He didn't hesitate a moment. "I not only represent Kentucky," he told me. "I represent the nation, and there are times you follow, and times when you lead."

It was a statement I'd never forget, and it helped me to see that the best kind of representative—and a true leader—is one who doesn't take a poll on every issue, or weigh the mail to determine how to vote. There are some matters of concern where constituents are right and others where the best representative does what he or she thinks ought to be done. If a constituent doesn't agree with you, you can hope they at least like that you have conviction. If not, they can always vote you out.

✬ ✬ ✬

I would put that thought into practice a few months later, when I cast my own vote on Election Day of 1964. I had enrolled at the University of Kentucky College of Law that fall, and after living at home with my parents, I was ready to get out of the house and be on my own. I rented an off-campus apartment in Lexington with a few other guys and set about pursuing my political goals.

On my application to law school at the University of Kentucky, I wasn't shy about admitting that I had very little interest in a career in the law, and a whole lot of interest in a career in politics. Law school was just my way of getting there. It would end up being a great relief that I had no designs on a future as a successful lawyer because it dawned on me pretty quickly that I was not going to be a great law student. Knowing this, I looked for other ways to excel, mainly by participating in moot court, where I won the award for the best oral advocate, and becoming the president of the Student Bar Association, thereby reaching the goal I had set to be elected leader in high school, college, and law school.

Even as I advanced toward my own goals, I was horrified by the failure of one of my political heroes. When LBJ signed the civil rights bill into law on July 2, 1964, it had the support of most members of Congress, but there were a few exceptions, Barry Goldwater among them. To say that I was extremely disappointed that Goldwater voted against the civil rights bill doesn't nearly capture how upset I was. Not only did his vote undermine the vast majority of Republicans who supported the bill, but when Goldwater received the Republican nomination for president that year, his position came to inaccurately define the party's strong position on civil rights—which would continue to hurt our party for decades. The party of Lincoln had remained the party of Lincoln, but at the time, all anyone could say about Republicans on this issue was that we had nominated a candidate who opposed the civil rights bill.

Goldwater's choice to put our party on the wrong side of such an important issue—if not the most important issue of my generation—led me to seriously question if my sympathies truly lay with the more radical elements of the Republican Party. So great was my anger, in fact, that on November 3, 1964, I cast my vote for LBJ. It was a vote I would soon regret. Johnson's second term was marked by a bloody, divisive, and unsuccessful escalation of the Vietnam War and a massive and largely ineffective expansion of government here at home. As others have noted, Johnson waged a war on poverty and poverty won.

This was an important early lesson about Washington's overconfidence in its own ability to systematically solve complex social problems through government programs, which not only bloat government bureaucracies and centralize decision making among administrative elites, but also frequently carry significant and unexpected human costs, to say nothing of the opportunity costs associated with the economic stagnation they foster. Given what unfolded, I would come to regret this vote more than any I'd ever cast.

But my Election Day turn against Goldwater was an early marker for me nonetheless. On many issues I had found myself in agreement and sympathy with the gritty Arizonan. He spoke for many of us who believed something important was at stake in the battle against world communism. His willingness to take on labor union corruption and the reflexive embrace of big government was also refreshing. Yet Goldwater's rigid attachment to ideology blinded him at a crucial moment, and the consequences of that decision were not insignificant. Some argue that Reagan's presidency wouldn't have been possible without Goldwater. Perhaps. But we also got the Great Society in the bargain. And a stigma for our party that we did not in any way deserve. A century of principled advocacy for civil rights was forgotten the moment we nominated Barry Goldwater as our party's candidate for president. Sacrificing that proud heritage, not to mention our chances at the White House, was tragic any way you cut it.

☆☆☆

The most memorable experience from this time was one I had in the summer of 1965, at the end of my first year of law school, when I paid witness to a significant moment in history that came as the result of courageous, admirable leaders. I had decided to go to Washington to visit friends. While there, I stopped by Senator Cooper's office to say hello. In a stroke of blind luck, Cooper himself appeared, and motioned for me to follow him. I wondered where we were going. He'd done this one other time. On the last day of my internship a few years earlier, he'd arrived at my desk toward the end of the day.

"Come with me," he'd said, leading me outside, to where his car was waiting. Cooper and his wife, Lorraine, were known for the parties they hosted and the crowd they hung around with; they were the Kennedys' first dinner guests after JFK was elected president. Cooper looked the part. He wore well-tailored suits and Brooks Brothers shoes. We arrived at his home, and in the very parlor where people like Jackie Kennedy and Katharine Graham were accustomed to gather, Cooper, Lorraine, and I drank champagne and toasted the end of my internship.

But this time, we were on our way to someplace far more extraordinary. We walked together to the Capitol Rotunda, which was teeming with security. Then Senator Cooper told me what was happening.

"President Johnson is about to sign the Voting Rights Act of 1965."

Sure enough, the president of the United States emerged. Every good biography of President Johnson describes him as a larger-than-life man, with an imposing physical presence. They are correct. President Johnson towered over everyone else and had such a commanding presence, he seemed to fill the Rotunda. I was overwhelmed to witness such a moment in history, knowing that majorities in both parties voted for the bill.

For two more years, I gritted it out at law school, and at the time of my graduation, the Vietnam War was in full swing. Two days after taking the bar exam, I arrived at Fort Knox to begin basic training for my service in the army reserves. Since beating polio, I'd never been able to run for prolonged distances, and I struggled through the exercises. When I was sent to the doctor to be examined, he discovered that I had a condition called optic neuritis, and a few weeks into my military service, I was honorably discharged for this medical condition.

I moved back to Louisville, and took a job at a law firm, handling tax returns, divorces, and workers' comp cases. It was a time of highs and lows. On the one hand, I'd just gotten married to Sherrill Redmon, my college girlfriend of many years. But I was very unhappy professionally, sitting at a desk, shuffling papers.

Having seen in John Sherman Cooper what a life lived in pursuit of greatness could yield, I knew I had a very specific and far greater ambition: to follow in his footsteps, to become a US senator. I was not afraid to admit this ambition. My parents had taught me it's not what you acquire in life that's important, but what you contribute. I could see no better, more significant way to contribute than serving in the US Senate, where the biggest issues—war and peace, the economy—are considered and resolved. Knowing that was the job I wanted, I also knew I would have to work like hell to get there. Having a goal is a good way of achieving it, and for me, the best chance I had at achieving it was to play a smart and well-planned long game.

CHAPTER FOUR

"You Can Start Too Late, but Never Too Soon"

Legendary former Kentucky governor Happy Chandler always said, "You can start too late, but never too soon." Once I had set my goal of trying to become a senator, I knew it was time to start. It would be several years before I actually launched a Senate campaign—years spent preparing and planning in every possible way.

My first step was to find a way out of practicing law and into a job in politics. I had been at the law firm just a few months when that opportunity came. In 1968, Marlow Cook, the county judge of Jefferson County—the chief administrator, much like the mayor of Kentucky's largest county—declared his campaign for the Senate seat left vacant by the retirement of Thruston B. Morton. I didn't know Cook at all, but I sat down, wrote him a letter expressing my desire to work on his campaign, and hand-delivered it to his office at the courthouse. To my surprise, Cook invited me in to talk.

"What do you want to do?" he asked me.

I'd given it a lot of thought. "I'd like to be the state youth chairman," I said. Three years before the passage of the Twenty-Sixth Amendment, the voting age in Kentucky was eighteen. Gaining the youth vote could make a big difference for Cook, and at twenty-six, I was confident I could make a connection with younger voters. "And I'd like to do it on a full-time basis."

"You mean, get paid for it?"

"Yes, sir, that's what I'd like."

"Okay," he said. "Why not?"

I was overjoyed and went into it knowing full well what I had signed on to: long days, little sleep, and hard work. But on my first day on the job, I was surprised to find that come five-thirty, the people around me at campaign headquarters cleaned off their desks, pulled on their coats, and went home. The same thing happened the next day. This was nothing like what I had expected. And, in my quest to achieve as much as I could in my first political job, I saw an opportunity.

The next day, and most days after, I was the first to arrive in the office and the last to leave. If anybody called in over the weekend with a question, I was the one answering the phone. I organized the Young Kentuckians for Cook, which we later expanded to become Young Kentuckians for Nixon-Cook. Before long, Cook noticed my work, and after he was elected, he offered me $17,000 a year to come with him to Washington as his chief legislative assistant. As soon as I got home that night, I called my parents. "It's incredible," I said. "We're going to DC. And I'm actually going to get paid to do something this much fun."

Sherrill and I packed our things in our 1966 Mustang, and headed to Washington in search of an apartment we could afford on my salary. The nation's sense of security, first shaken by JFK's assassination in 1963, had been all but shattered after the assassinations of Robert F. Kennedy and Martin Luther King Jr. a few months earlier and with the growing resentment of the Vietnam War. We saw evidence of this as we drove into Washington, through neighborhoods dotted with burned-out buildings destroyed in the riots after King's assassination. It made our new city feel much farther away from Louisville than the nine hours we'd driven. We ended up finding an affordable apartment on Dumbarton Street in Georgetown, and as I arrived in Cook's office in the Old Senate Office Building on my first day, despite the national anxiety of the time, I couldn't believe my own good fortune. An apartment in DC. A job on the Hill as a legislative assistant, having a hand—no matter how minor it may have seemed—in the direction of our country. My dreams were actually coming true.

I managed a five-person legislative department, while also helping with speechwriting and constituent services. What I felt was exactly the opposite of my experience practicing law—everything was interesting to me. From my perch as a young man with dreams of being elected senator from Kentucky one day, I absorbed everything happening around me. Mike Mansfield, a Democrat from Montana, was Senate majority leader at the time. He'd go on to be the longest-serving majority leader in history, holding the position for sixteen years. His evenhandedness and clear respect for every senator, regardless of political affiliation, made him very popular not only among his Democratic colleagues, but among most members of the Republican minority as well. This was in far contrast to his predecessor, LBJ. The popular account of LBJ's life and legacy often leaves out this important detail, but by the time he left the Senate, LBJ's colleagues had had enough. They may have bent to his will while he was there, but the moment they had a chance to be delivered from his iron-fisted rule, they took it. With their support, Mike Mansfield would spend the next sixteen years restoring the Senate to a place of greater cooperation and freedom. And as I looked at what the Senate could be, his example offered a clue. There are many well-known stories about Mansfield's fairness and equanimity as leader. But they all seem to come down to one thing, and that was his unbending belief that every senator should be treated as an equal.

What I learned most from observing Marlow Cook was that when it came to being a freshman senator, he could have worked much harder. It's unrealistic to think that a first-term senator is going to have a significant impact. Freshman senators rank lowest on committees, and it takes time to understand the workings of the Senate and the complicated procedures that govern how the institution operates. But given these limitations of entering the Senate, it is still important to stand firm in one's beliefs. To do that, one has to have them, which Cook did not.

With political views that were a bit of an amalgam, born of no particular political philosophy, he tended to lumber from one issue to another. He also preferred the social aspects of politics: the conversational side of things. I became frustrated by the fact that he didn't work harder and, as time passed, how seldom he returned to Kentucky to stay in touch with constituents. One difference between me and a lot of the legislative assistants was that I was very much interested in what was going on back in Kentucky, and I became the contact in the office keeping abreast of the issues on people's minds back home.

✫✫✫

I worked with Cook for about two years before I began to feel the restless pull of wanting to get back home and figure out a way to get started on my own political career. In 1971, I accepted a position working on Tom Emberton's campaign for governor and returned to Kentucky, where I promptly made what I now consider to be my first big political mistake. The census of 1970 had brought about the creation of new state legislative districts in Jefferson County, where Louisville is located. Sherrill and I decided to find a town house to rent in a neighborhood that fell within one of the new districts that, obviously, had no incumbent, so that I could, while working for Emberton's campaign, also try a run for the state legislature. But soon after filing, I received notice that one of my opponents had filed a suit against me, claiming I didn't fulfill the residency requirement. It was only then that I looked carefully at what I should have noticed in the beginning: the constitutional residency requirement clearly stated that a candidate had to be living in the district at least a year prior to the election. This kind of hasty mistake was highly unusual given my meticulous nature. In the suit against me, I chose to represent myself, appearing in court to argue that *nobody* lived in the district the previous year because the district hadn't existed. The case went to the Kentucky Supreme Court, and in the end, while one of the justices said my argument was ingenious, it simply wasn't persuasive, and I was disqualified from running.

Failing to check the districting carefully was not my only mistake. My plan was to take a position working for Tom Emberton's administration after he won. Foolishly, it hadn't dawned on me that he might lose, but he did. When the results came in, it was difficult to accept the reality, but I knew I'd taken a risk, and when you take a great risk, there can be great rewards, or great disappointments. For me, I was facing the latter. I was without an income. I had very little savings. And Sherrill was pregnant with our first child. I had no choice but to get a job, and the only job I could get was as a lawyer.

The experiences of my mistake and Emberton's failure were both disappointing and embarrassing, but I also knew that I could wallow, or I could recognize the lessons that would serve me in the long term. First, I couldn't afford to be so careless, and I have tried never to make such a mistake again. And second, I had simply overreached. I wasn't ready to hold an elected office of my own, and my decision to run before I was ready was opportunistic. I had let my ambition get in the way of my judgment. From experience and observation, I knew that the most effective leaders were not ones who got where they were quickly, but were those who took their time, understanding the issues, learning the system, paying attention to what voters were asking for, and making sure they were superbly prepared. I vowed that this would be my approach going forward because if I wanted to be a strong, effective leader, and not just a short-term one, this was what was required.

But in the meantime, I was once again back at a law firm, not knowing much about practicing law, interested only in pursuing a political career, but confronting the very real necessity of having to eat. Which, given how ambitious and eager I was to get started on my road to becoming a senator, was a real inconvenience.

☆☆☆

After slogging through being a lawyer for a few years, providing for my family and building valuable life experience, I finally reached a point where I had had enough. One night, I had to travel to Springhill, Louisiana, for a case I was working on. I couldn't sleep, and at four-thirty in the morning, I went to find some coffee. Sitting alone in the dead of night, drinking bad coffee, I couldn't deny it any longer. I was dying on the vine. Not only did I not enjoy practicing law, but I wasn't very good at it. I knew I couldn't keep doing this. The good news was that I had begun to set my sights on a clear goal. In three years, the current county judge of Jefferson County would be up for reelection. Marlow Cook had held this position before he was elected to the US Senate. I hoped I might follow the path that had worked for him. Holding this office would give me the chance to have an impact on the issues facing my county while also helping to prepare me for a Senate run one day. By the time I left the coffee shop, I'd made a decision. Over the next three years, I would continue to make connections and get myself ready to run for the position, but in the meantime, I had to find a different way of making a living.

At exactly nine o'clock the next morning, I called my friend Vince Rakestraw. He was head of the Office of Legislative Affairs in the Justice Department in Washington, and was one of the better-connected people I knew.

"Have you got any jobs?" I said as soon as he answered the phone, explaining that I had the support of the deputy attorney general, Laurence Silberman, whose sister Jan was a friend of mine in Louisville. "I've got to get out of here."

Luckily, he did, and in October of 1974, four years after I'd left

Washington, I returned. Sherrill and I decided it would be easier for her to remain in Kentucky rather than uproot our lives once again, and I commuted home to Louisville every weekend. With Ford in the White House, I went to work as the deputy assistant attorney general in the Office of Legislative Affairs at the Justice Department, where I'd stay for fifteen months.

Nothing—and I mean nothing—confirmed my Republican skepticism about big government more than my confrontation with the unmovable federal bureaucracy I saw at work there. I came into contact with incredible laziness and inefficiency every day in the Office of Legislative Affairs. People shuffling paper, doing the bare minimum, spending their days in an endless cycle of bureaucracy that had no impact, no meaning, and no point. This was nothing like the idea of government that I espoused, and I would have found my job wholly unsatisfying if it weren't for the chance to encounter, above the stacks of paper, some of the nation's best conservative minds—Robert Bork, Laurence Silberman, Antonin Scalia—legal luminaries who were all serving in the department at the time. We'd hold nearly daily staff meetings, where I'd get a chance to hear them speak. As a young guy who felt as if I knew nothing about the law, I never opened my mouth. At the time, knowing squat about most legal matters, feeling as if I'd escaped the purgatory of practicing law, I was lucky to be in their presence.

Even though I was in Washington during the week, I continued my efforts to build my reputation in Kentucky in preparation for a run for county judge. I participated in a story about commuting back and forth to Louisville. I even called the *Courier-Journal* and offered to write book reviews for them—which they agreed to—just to get my name out there. A little over a year later, I decided that my wait was over. I had served as a staffer to a congressman, an intern to a senator, and a deputy assistant attorney general. It was time to return home, and to start campaigning, not yet for a Senate seat, but at least this time for myself.

✩✩✩

The first check I ever received for a political campaign was written by a guy named Marshall Royce as a contribution to my run for county judge. It was for $500, and it was thrilling that somebody was willing to bet some of his own money on my political future. I announced my campaign at the house Sherrill and I owned on Fleming Road. Beside us were our two daughters, Elly and Claire, then four and one. Our third, Porter, would be born two years later.

My old friend Joe Schiff volunteered to help manage my campaign, and we slogged through the summer, spending our weekends eating fish sandwiches and shaking hands at the Catholic picnics popular throughout the county. During the week, on the warm summer evenings, I'd travel up and down Dixie and Preston Highways as the sun went down, going in and out of stores by myself, introducing myself to the employees and customers at local diners and small businesses, and explaining why I was running for county judge. County government was a mess. People were escaping from the jail. Taxes were going up. I compiled a list of complaints from every neighborhood in the county—from broken streetlights to potholes—and vowed to address them if I was elected.

Approaching strangers, speaking in front of crowds—it was all extremely hard for me at the time. I've had time to work through it, but at my core, I'm quite shy. Often, on the way to these picnics or as I'd hear the jingle of the bell while opening the glass door on the next shop, I'd get actual pains in my stomach.

It took me an entire week, but I worked every one of the six buildings of the GE Appliance Park, an industrial complex that covers more than a thousand acres, and employed around twenty thousand people at the time. I spent my first day there studying how to make the best use of my time. I observed people's habits, like where they parked their cars, and which doors they typically went in and out of every day. I would therefore work one door of a building early in the morning and another door in the afternoon, to avoid meeting the same person more than once. The morning shift would arrive around 6:00 a.m. and the late shift around two in the afternoon. I was there for each of them, telling people my name and my plans to clean up county government and end the cronyism that defined government under the Democrats. Meanwhile, I was running ads on radio and TV. In one of my favorite commercials, I emphasized how dysfunctional the current administration was by using the very real example of a prisoner at the county jail who had escaped after popping the broken lock on his cell with his toothbrush. I was working my butt off, literally; I lost several pounds just during the time I spent at the Appliance Park. But this is what I had been working toward for years. I had to give it everything I had.

And I had to win this race. The thought of being unemployed if I lost kept me awake many nights. I was the father of two young girls, soon to be three, and nothing was more important to me than providing for my family. I could, if necessary, return to practicing law, but I desperately wanted to avoid that. And then my dad called.

"Look, Mitch," he said. "Your mom and I have been talking a lot about this. We both know what this means to you. And we know what's at stake, with Sherrill and the girls. You just go and give it your best. If things don't work out, we'll be there for you after the election if you need help."

I can hardly express what my parents' offer meant to me. Without it, I'm quite sure that on Tuesday, November 8, 1977, there may very likely have been an entirely different outcome. But that night, after a long campaign during which I was, due mostly to my dad's offer, laser focused, I was announced the winner over the incumbent Todd Hollenbach, and was elected Jefferson County judge.

☆☆☆

After being sworn in as county judge, there were two things I did immediately: buy my first pair of Brooks Brothers shoes, just like the kind

Senator Cooper had worn, and, with no intention of hiding my state-wide ambitions, begin to look for ways to become better known throughout Kentucky. I accepted just about every invitation I received outside the county and spent a lot of time over the next few years, in between taking care of matters in Jefferson County—where my role was to address everything from broken-down infrastructure to managing all of the county agencies—to find excuses to crisscross the state, meeting families and hearing people's concerns, from the coal miners of eastern Kentucky to the farmers out west.

In 1980, three years into my administration, I was a delegate to the Republican National Convention in Detroit that saw Ronald Reagan win the presidential nomination. It was a very exciting time for the Republican Party. Reagan ultimately outshone his conservative forebears because he articulated conservative principles with optimism, and he would lead the party of Goldwater to victory—winning forty-four of the fifty states that election—with that same openness and optimism. Reagan was a good example of the Edmund Burke style of governing that drew me to John Sherman Cooper. He enjoyed overwhelming electoral success because voters saw him as a person of conviction. They had confidence that he was doing what he thought was right, and they were willing to cut him slack even when they disagreed with him.

I spoke to a few Kentucky reporters at the convention, and one would go on to write that he found me rather quiet and subdued. He wasn't wrong—there was a reason I was a bit deflated. Shortly after returning home from the convention, Sherrill and I announced that we had chosen to divorce. The divorce was mutual and amicable, and we would share custody of our three daughters, but a change like that is never easy, especially when you are in the public eye. Throughout my career, I've been asked about my daughters, with whom I'm very close. However, I'm the one who has chosen a career in the public spotlight, not them. I've always protected their privacy, and I will continue to do so throughout this book.

In 1981, I was elected to my second term as county judge, and soon after, once again applying Happy Chandler's maxim, I immediately began to lay the groundwork for a run for the Senate. I was more convinced than ever that the Senate was the place where I could have the most impact, serving the people of my state, working to solve problems facing Kentucky, while also tackling national issues.

In three years, the Democratic incumbent senator Walter "Dee" Huddleston would be up for reelection for his third term. A former radio station manager who was first elected to John Sherman Cooper's seat after Cooper's retirement in 1972, Huddleston's liberal ways were hurting not just Kentuckians, but all Americans. In his twelve years in the Senate, Huddleston had voted to create 116 new federal bureaucracies. He'd voted twenty-one times to increase the national debt. The National Taxpayers Union—a bipartisan, independent watchdog organization that rates members of Congress on how wisely they spend taxpayers' money—had rated Huddleston an all-time big spender. This organization thought Huddleston was a terrible money manager, and I agreed. I formed a committee to begin to raise money to challenge him for his seat in three years.

When I told people close to me about my decision, almost everyone told me I didn't have a chance. But to me, the choice was easy. It was now or never to try to realize my dream to become a senator, to try to make the kind of difference I hoped to make, to have the type of impact made by people like John Sherman Cooper. After a decade of preparation and planning, and years spent gaining an understanding of the needs of Kentucky residents, it was time to put it all on the line.

"Mitch Who?"

When I announced my candidacy for the US Senate against Dee Huddleston on January 17, 1984, I knew that to win a statewide election in Kentucky, it helped to be three things: rich, well connected, and a Democrat. Because there was nothing I could do about that last one, I had to assemble the best team I could to help with the others.

Even though I'd essentially been campaigning for this position for many years, I entered the race a fairly unknown candidate running against a two-term incumbent in a heavily Democratic state. This meant that very few people were knocking down my door with offers to help, with one exception. Soon after my announcement, a twenty-one-year-old named Terry Carmack showed up at my courthouse office. Terry was a student at Murray State University in western Kentucky. He'd grown up on a farm outside Benton, in the western part of the state, and had just two jobs to boast of: working at a gas station and, from a wooden table set up in his family's carport, selling tomatoes to tourists driving past his house on their way to Kentucky Lake. He had no political experience, had not yet earned a college degree, and was, like everyone else in western Kentucky, a registered Democrat. But he was smart, ambitious, and for some reason, really wanted a job with me. I wasn't in a position to turn away help, but I was curious as to why he seemed so eager to join a contest nobody expected I could win.

"My dad's an electrician and my mom's a homemaker," he told me. "But every night, we sit around the dinner table and we talk politics. I've watched every convention I can remember. I'm an average student at a small college twenty miles from my home, and I want to know what might be out there for me beyond Marshall County. Everyone thinks I'm crazy for doing this, sir, but I know it might be my one chance to make something bigger happen for myself."

That was certainly good enough for me. I offered him a job, paying him $9,800 to be my advance man, arriving first at events to manage the crowd and prepare the press. (It wouldn't take long to learn there would be few crowds and even fewer members of the press at our events, prompting Terry to joke that being my advance man meant getting out of the car before I did.) Terry would go on to be one of my most trusted aides over the next thirty years.

I opened my campaign headquarters, a small suite of offices I'd rented on the fourth floor of an office tower near the Watterson Expressway. Joe Schiff, who'd been instrumental in my two previous campaigns for county judge, was a family man whose wife liked to see him home in time for dinner. Knowing the long hours this race would require, I needed a new campaign manager. While Joe would remain very involved, I turned my attention to a Kentuckian named Janet Mullins. Although she had no experience managing a campaign, Janet, a young, smart single mom, had worked for three years for Oregon senator Bob Packwood, the last year as his chief of staff. She'd recently moved back to Louisville from Washington, and as soon as I met her in person—by chance one evening at a parent-teacher conference at our children's school—I wanted her to run my campaign. Years later, Janet would be referred to in the *Courier-Journal* as having "a salty tongue." That's one way to put it. Another is to say she could hardly utter a few sentences without using a profanity. While it may have put others off, I found it amusing, and very much enjoyed being around Janet. She had a sharp political mind and the exact type of energy my campaign needed. When I called to offer her the position as my campaign manager, I was delighted to hear she was interested. But there was one caveat.

"I have a teenage daughter who begged me to leave Washington," she told me. "I moved to Louisville for her, and have promised her we'll never go back to DC. If you win, I won't be coming with you."

"I can live with that," I told her.

"Then count me in," she said.

While I didn't know this at the time, Janet was able to accept the job in light of her promise to her daughter because she was absolutely sure I didn't stand a chance.

She was hardly the only one. From the day I announced, I was firmly aware of where I stood against Huddleston in the polls. I was doing best in Jefferson County, but even there, I was getting creamed. The rest of the state was much tougher sledding. My main priority was to get out, meet people, and help them learn my name. In the first two days of my candidacy, I visited nine cities.

The campaign would quickly become characterized by Murphy's Law. Whatever could go wrong, did. In late February, I opened my morning newspaper to read that my former boss, Marlow Cook, who'd become a Washington lobbyist since losing his Senate seat, was endorsing Huddleston. Even though Cook was quoted as saying he was out to lend aid and support to Dee, not to hurt me, I still considered this an act of betrayal.

Things got more interesting two months into the campaign when, to everyone's surprise, John Y. Brown Jr., the former Kentucky governor, announced he was mounting a primary challenge to Huddleston, filing six hours before the deadline. It was reminiscent of Brown's last-minute entry into the Democratic gubernatorial primary race five years earlier, which he won after a two-month campaign among a crowded field of candidates.

It's a popular idea that divisive Democratic primaries are good for Republicans, but there's little evidence to support that. In fact, I was concerned about the opposite: that with Brown's decision, I'd be left out of the whole thing, seen as nothing more than a bystander to the Democratic contest that pitted a sitting senator against a former governor who was not only one of the (extremely wealthy) cofounders of Kentucky Fried Chicken but also married to a former Miss America, Phyllis George.

But, of course, I didn't voice these concerns publicly. Instead, I expressed my pleasure over Brown's candidacy, saying that when the Democrats finished beating the hell out of each other, I'd be around to pick up the pieces. I urged the people of Kentucky to understand that there were three candidates in the race, not two, and I reminded the press it was their obligation not to turn this into a two-man race. I released a television ad and posters, describing myself as Kentucky's next great senator.

Brown, who would drop out of the primary six weeks later, probably summed it up best with his response to my comments: "Mitch who?"

☆☆☆

Four months into it, I needed to get more aggressive. Some ideas to accomplish this were better than others. My dad volunteered his time to help. I'm pretty sure he was the only person alive who thought I was going to win this thing, and I gave him the job of calling representatives of political action committees in Washington, trying to convince them to support me. If anyone could do this job well, it was my dad. He was not someone accustomed to being told no. As family legend has it, my mom was visiting her sister Edrie Mae in Five Points when my father first called to propose. My mom hung up, thinking he'd had too much to drink. He called back, eight more times. He'd propose every time, and every time, she'd hang up. While my mom was eventually persuaded by my father's persistence, the PACs, unfortunately, were not.

Despite his best efforts, he only got bad news—PACs are incredibly risk-averse and there was no way they were going to give money to a challenger trailing far behind in every poll.

What we needed was a new campaign angle that would capture the attention of the voters and break the race open. Janet had the idea to host a press conference every Monday called "Dope on Dee," in which we pointed out Huddleston's problems and his lackluster performance during his two Senate terms. But these accomplished very little. Organizing them took too much of Janet's time—looking for new places to hold the press conference, trying to find new things to say—and before long, we announced we were going to discontinue "Dope on Dee."

Yet I continued to believe if I could only show the voters how their senator had let them down, they would turn to me as the brighter, hardworking alternative. There was no disputing that Huddleston had been a mediocre representative of the state's interests, not least because of his record of repeatedly missing important votes. I thought this was something to look into, and was especially curious if one reason for his having missed votes was the number of lucrative speeches he was giving. Janet told me this was a waste of our time. "I've worked on the Hill," she said. "There are ways to hide this. If you miss a vote to give a speech, you wait a few days to cash your honorarium check. That way, it's impossible to make a link between a missed vote and a paid speech. Everyone does it."

I trusted her experience, but still, I had to keep searching for the silver bullet—the thing that would bring us out of obscurity and into the race, because by midsummer, after six months of campaigning each and every day, my numbers had barely moved. Huddleston released the results of a poll that showed him up sixty-seven points to my twenty-three. I knew that when it came down to it, there were just two types of voters: those who didn't support me, and those who did but were sure I was going to lose.

On the first Saturday in August, it was time for the Fancy Farm

Picnic, Kentucky's most important political tradition. Begun in 1880, this gathering takes place at a Catholic church in Fancy Farm, a rural country town of about five hundred residents in western Kentucky. Against the backdrop of rolling hills, cornfields, and wide Kentucky skies, candidates vie for audiences and airtime. Thousands of people attend. While the children try out the carnival-like games, and blue-grass bands perform for the crowds, politicians prepare to give a stump-style speech the way we did in Kentucky decades ago, long before the advent of political ads and teleprompters. It's where you get to broadcast your message in your own voice, and hope it connects with the people. Driving into Fancy Farm, along a street lined with Dee Huddleston signs, I was nervous but exhilarated.

The morning I was slated to speak, I woke up before the sun rose in the budget motel room I'd rented, unsure of what I was going to say. Someone had prepared a perfectly awful speech for me, which I had no intention to use. I took a seat at the desk and began to write notes on the only paper I could find—the backs of envelopes. I took the stage later that day, feeling the prickly heat from the August sun, as well as from the crowd who welcomed me with a cacophony of boos and jeers. Steeling myself, I came out swinging, the same way I had thirty years earlier on Dicky McGrew's front lawn. With everything I had, I made my most compelling case for why I was the best candidate. Not only because my opponent was no longer the right choice for our state, but because I would advance the ideas of limited government, fiscal restraint, and free enterprise. I would ensure a strong military, traditional values, and American exceptionalism. I would stand firmly on the side of constitutional principles and the rule of law. And I'd never tire of fighting for the safety and prosperity of our country.

The next day I woke up expecting that, finally, my effort would have paid off and people would stop asking "Mitch who?" and begin to notice I was worth taking seriously. First thing, I went to get a copy of the *Courier-Journal*, and sure enough, there was a big story on Fancy Farm:

the entirety of it about Wendell Ford, the junior senator from Kentucky who'd spent his time engaging in a shouting match with a constituent. It was utterly exasperating. He'd captured the headlines and he wasn't even running for office that year.

If there was one experience that summed up my campaign the best, it was a day not too long after this, in late September. I had been single for four years, and living alone in a small condo in Louisville, off Gardiner Lane. I was dating a woman who was getting increasingly aggravated by the fact I was never around. On this particular evening, I came home from another long day to find that the one tree in front of my condo had been struck by lightning, and had split down the middle. Inside the house, the goldfish I'd somehow managed to keep alive while on the trail was floating belly-up in the fishbowl. I went upstairs to check my answering machine, only to hear a message from my girlfriend saying she'd finally had enough. We were over. I am not a man who wavers from his mission, but I'll admit that I went to bed that night questioning if this was all worth it when it seemed so clear that I didn't have a chance. I knew that I needed to ask for some strength.

As I lay there, my desperation reminded me of an experience I'd had as a child in Augusta, Georgia. During the many afternoons I spent playing in someone's backyard, the other boys and I abided by one enduring rule: whoever called out "general" first got to be in charge. The self-declared general would choose the game we'd play, decide on the rules, and create the teams. I was very good at being the first one to think of doing this, and much to the irritation of my playmates, it was a rare occasion that I wasn't the general.

Until one afternoon, when another young boy named Stanley Martin responded to my call of general by looking me square in the eye.

"God," he said.

I was dumbfounded. Standing there, I thought about protesting, but what could I say? I could hardly argue that a general should take the lead over God. After all, I did know my limitations.

That night, alone in my darkened house, I considered if it was time to recognize that God was on the other side and perhaps I'd gone as far as I would go. I turned these doubts over in my mind and considered them fully, but by the time I fell asleep, I'd abandoned them. I'd spent my whole life preparing for this race. While it was getting increasingly difficult to walk out the door each day, having to pretend I had a chance at this, I simply didn't know how to quit. Kentuckians, like most Americans, were commonsense conservatives. Most of them may have registered as Democrats, but when it came to the important issues facing our county, I believed they agreed with me. So even if I might eventually regret the outcome of this election, I didn't want to ever regret my effort. I couldn't leave anything behind.

And if I couldn't remain positive, at least I could maintain my patience and perseverance and do the one thing I had learned a long time ago, in the halls of Manual High School, on the advice of my dad: to win the election, I had to run a better campaign.

CHAPTER SIX

Giving It All I've Got

As Election Day neared, I continued to travel the state. Sometimes I'd rent a small single-engine plane to cover as much territory as I could in a day. The pilot I found was Pat Datillo. She was a little old lady whose husband owned a local vegetable stand near the airfield, and even when she wore her thick, Coke-bottle glasses, she couldn't see very well. One afternoon, she flew Terry and me from Louisville to Hazard, a small town located between two mountain ranges. As we approached, we dipped below the clouds. Suddenly the mountains of eastern Kentucky spread out in front us, as far as I could see. It was spectacular.

After we were safe on the ground, I jumped out of the plane. Pat yelled after me from her pilot's seat. "Hey, Judge, see the top of those mountains?"

"Yes, sure do."

"If it gets too dark that I can't see them, we ain't taking off."

I rushed to the campaign event, and a little while later, I looked up to see that it was quickly getting dark. "We gotta go," I said to Terry.

We raced back to the plane, jumped in, and barely cleared the mountain before the sun went down.

The moment felt undoubtedly risky, but I didn't have much of a choice. Everything about my decision to run had been risky, and I had to work harder than I ever had. This meant getting to every event I could: the tobacco festival in Logan County, the Catholic picnics in eastern Jefferson County, the Sorghum Festival in Morgan County, the Hillbilly Days festival in Pikeville. At each, weaving my way through vendors selling barbecue and funnel cakes, and booths set up for bingo for the kids, I'd shake hands and introduce myself while Terry handed out postcards printed with my name on one side and the University of Kentucky's upcoming football schedules on the other. He did his best to meet my request of adhering a "Switch to Mitch" sticker on the lapel of every passerby in his path. As dismal as my chances felt, I allowed myself to accept the fact that I really enjoyed campaigning. In fact, I was even beginning to have some fun.

During the week, I was on the phone. We'd gotten the names and phone numbers of people who had previously donated to a Republican candidate. I'd call and ask for a contribution while Terry sat beside me on another phone, asking if we might stop by for a visit. I'd drive for hours to spend forty-five minutes at someone's home, sharing my vision for the state. On the ride to the next house, to the next conversation and plea for money, I'd handwrite a note to the person I'd just left, reminding them of the financial pledge they'd made. Sometimes people would gather friends at their home and invite me to speak. Standing in those living rooms, a plastic cup of iced tea in my hand, I'd reiterate the words I truly believed: it was time they elected a senator with the guts to deal with the problems facing our country—like the budget deficit, which had been mounting for decades as a result of the inability of some elected officials to stem government spending.

"Who is standing up for Kentuckians and their interests in this instance?" I'd ask the crowd. "Not the senior senator from Kentucky. In the twelve years he's been in office, he's voted in favor of budget deficits or for increasing the national debt on no fewer than twenty different occasions." I paid to have bumper stickers made, but knowing those things mostly ended up forgotten in a kitchen drawer, I devised a strategy to make sure that didn't happen.

"Okay, raise your hand if you want one of these bumper stickers," I'd say when I was done speaking. Most people were too polite not to raise their hand in my presence. "Now it's not that I don't trust you to put it on your car, but keep those hands raised. We want to make this as easy as possible for you." Terry would then dash around the room with a notebook, jotting down people's license plate numbers, before heading outside with a bottle of Windex and a roll of paper towels. He'd carefully affix the bumper sticker to the back window, right behind the driver's seat, so it would be easily visible by every driver following.

Money was so tight we had to take desperate measures to conserve it. Janet and I devised a gimmick to save money on phone calls. While on the road, I'd place a collect call to the office. When the receptionist answered, the operator would announce a collect call for a code name we'd created to let her know it was me calling. The receptionist would tell the operator that person wasn't available, which, under the rules of collect calls at the time, allowed me to leave a brief message with a callback number. I'd hang up, retrieve the dime from the pay-phone slot, and wait for Janet's call.

We had to do this because a statewide election is, in essence, a television event, and producing it costs money. The only way voters are going to vote for you is if they know who you are, and the only way they're going to know who you are is if they see you on TV. This is even more crucial if, like me, you were running against an entrenched incumbent whose name people already knew. So I needed airtime, but more important, I needed the right airtime, and the right message.

This is why one of the smartest moves I made during this campaign was to hire Roger Ailes, later the founder and CEO of Fox News Channel. Roger had been one of the first television consultants in politics, starting with Nixon's 1968 presidential campaign. I was happy he agreed to do it, because I sure needed help.

"I think we should do some positive TV ads," I suggested at a meeting in the summer of 1984. "Let voters get to know me."

"Sure, we could do that," Ailes said. "I'll do positive ads that make you look nice so that people like you. You'll lose, but you can always run again next time."

"Well, what do you suggest?" I asked.

"Do you want to look nice, or do you want to take out your opponent and win this thing?"

"I want to do what it takes," I said. "I want to win this thing."

"Then leave the ads to me."

"Okay," I said. "But look. You need to tell me the truth. Do you think it's over?"

Ailes is not one to turn serious that often. But he looked very serious when he answered me. "No," he said. "But I have to be honest, Mitch. I've never seen any candidate come from this far behind this late and win."

☆☆☆

A few days later, Janet stopped me the moment I got to headquarters. I could tell by the serious look on her face that something big had happened, and given the experience of this campaign, I assumed it was bad.

"Okay, you were right," she said.

"I was? About what?"

"I finally looked into Huddleston's financial disclosure statements. He definitely missed votes because he was giving paid speeches." She told me that most senators paid a lawyer to prepare their statements, but Huddleston had prepared his himself. And lo and behold, there it was: the silver bullet. By comparing his personal financial disclosure with missed votes in the Senate, she found twenty-four instances in which he had been off earning personal money while the Senate was in session, voting.

The news ignited everyone on our team. I called Roger Ailes to fill him in, and luckily, I caught him on the right day.

"Someone I work with just ran into Huddleston's media guy at a party in Philly," Ailes said. "He was laughing that you're forty points behind, and he said he was going to kick your ass—and mine—all over Kentucky. I've been plotting his murder ever since. Let me think about this."

That night, Ailes was watching television, when a commercial for dog food aired, showing a group of puppies scrambling after a bag of kibble. This gave him an idea—one that, a few days later, at a strategy meeting at headquarters, in a cloud of pipe smoke, he outlined for me: a commercial depicting Kentucky hunting dogs on the scent for Huddleston, the lost member of Congress.

"I've looked into it," Ailes said. "We're gonna get bloodhounds, because they're big in Kentucky. And I've called Snarfy."

"Snarfy?"

"Yeah, Snarfy. He's this guy I know. An actor. He looks like he could be from Kentucky. He snarfs. I don't know, it's something he does before he starts a scene. Clears his throat or something. So we call him Snarfy."

"Okay."

"He's going to be led by this pack of dogs, hunting for Huddleston, who has clearly been busy giving paid speeches instead of voting. I love it. What do you think?"

I had no idea what to think. It was insane. "I think it's probably better than anything else we got. What do I have to do?"

"Absolutely nothing. I've written the script already. I'll do it and see what happens. If it fails, you can blame me."

"Okay," I said. "That's a good plan."

"Look at it this way," Ailes said. "You got nothing to lose."

He was right, and I was willing to try anything. Roger and his assistant Larry McCarthy, who would work on many of my later campaigns, went to work on tasks I'd bet had never before been assigned in a political campaign: finding dogs to film, preparing a man named Snarfy to act like he was a Kentucky farmer. They shot the commercial over a few days, and in September the ad that would eventually become widely known among political science junkies as "Bloodhounds" was released. In it, a man (Snarfy) is holding the straining leashes of a pack of dogs. He leaves Capitol Hill in search of Huddleston, traveling to the same places Huddleston had traveled for paid speeches, like the beaches of Puerto Rico and downtown Los Angeles. Ailes was particularly nervous about the scene he had to film at the US Capitol. His plan was to unleash the pack of dogs, and turn them loose on the steps of the Capitol.

"We may get arrested for this one," Ailes told his small crew. "So we gotta do this in one shot." He placed a pile of hamburger meat at the top of the steps and some in Snarfy's pant cuff so the dogs would stay close to him until they were unleashed. "I can see the security guards watching," Ailes said. "Do this quick or we're on the way to the big house. One . . . two . . . action!"

By the time the dogs had reached the top of the steps, Ailes and his crew were surrounded by guards.

"What are you doing?" one demanded.

"Why, does this look odd to you?" Ailes looked at his cameraman. "You get the shot?" He nodded. "Okay," Ailes said to the guards. "We're done here. Thank you."

When the ad aired, I immediately saw the effect. On the trail, people began to approach me, to shake my hand and comment on how funny they'd found the ad. This momentum was just what I needed. Elated, I also knew I had to continue to work tirelessly to keep it going, which meant remaining on the air every day until Election Day.

But with each small victory there seemed to be another disappointment. Ronald Reagan was up for reelection and I'd hoped to be helped along, at least a little, by riding his coattails. As the Kentucky Senate candidate, I was allowed to attend the presidential debate between Reagan and Walter Mondale, held on October 7 at the Kentucky Center for the Performing Arts in Louisville. Reagan had a poor showing, appearing old and distracted. Afterward, I joined a sour-looking Nancy

Reagan, who was clearly upset with her husband's performance, at a post-debate rally at the Louisville Hyatt, where I expected Reagan to mention my race and give his endorsement. I had a camera crew ready to film the moment, which we'd planned to immediately turn into our next TV spot. My stomach was in knots as Reagan appeared on the ballroom's balcony to address the crowd. And sure enough, he did mention me, calling me his "good friend Mitch O'Donnell."

I thought this would be one of the most embarrassing political moments I'd ever have to suffer, but then a few weeks later, at an event in northern Kentucky, Vice President George H. W. Bush referred to me as Mayor McConnell, the mayor of Louisville.

☆☆☆

Eleven days before Election Day, I got a break. The National Republican Senatorial Committee, headed at the time by Senator Dick Lugar from Indiana and Executive Director Mitch Daniels (who'd go on to become the very successful two-term governor of Indiana), had started to pay attention to my race. I was the only Republican Senate challenger in the country running against a Democratic incumbent having any positive movement, and the committee decided I might be their guy. They began to send out fund-raising letters on my behalf, and before long, checks from across the country began arriving at headquarters.

This gave us the resources we needed for one more assault in the media—this time to show voters that I was catching up to Huddleston in the polls. We made a quick decision to release a new "Bloodhounds" ad. For this one, we found an out-of-work Shakespearean actor from New York to play the part of Huddleston. Chased by Snarfy and those same bloodhounds, our actor ran through cornfields, the sidewalks of a small town, and the aisles of a local diner, until he could run no farther and was shown hiding up a tree. The announcer proclaimed: "We got you now, Dee Huddleston. Switch to Mitch."

The Friday before the election, I spent the day in the Fifth District and decided to unwind over a late dinner at Café Metro, a little bistro in the Highlands neighborhood of Louisville, with a new female friend. As my glass of wine arrived, her eyes lit up.

"Oh, I forgot to mention this," she said. "But on the way over I heard a commercial about you on the radio. It was quite nasty."

The radio. While we knew Huddleston was going to be attacking me on TV over the weekend, we hadn't thought to check to see if he was running on the radio. It was a careless mistake at a crucial moment, but I knew I couldn't allow him to run negative radio ads without a response. I had to fight back. "Thank you," I said, trying to keep my composure. "Can you excuse me for a minute?"

I went to the bar and asked to use their phone. Janet was at headquarters. "There's an attack ad on the radio. Get it as quickly as possible. I'll call you back in a half hour." I returned to the table and explained as graciously as I could to my date that I couldn't stay. After helping her to her car, I was on my way to headquarters. Janet had found the ad, and we immediately called Roger Ailes.

"You have to hit back," he said. "Let's tape a response and get it on the radio right away."

I called the studio we'd worked with and asked the manager if he'd be willing to open at 5:00 a.m. He agreed, and by two o'clock in the morning, we'd written our response. I was waiting in the parking lot of the studio in Jeffersontown by the time the manager arrived before dawn.

Our volunteers were ready too. By 6:00 a.m. I handed a tape of our ad and a blank check to each of ten people waiting in ten cars, who immediately left for every major radio station in the state—in Madisonville, Hopkinsville, Bowling Green. They'd arrive at the station, knock on the door, and ask if Huddleston's ad was running. If it was, we'd tell them that however many radio spots Dee had bought, we wanted to match him.

I finally arrived back at my condo in Louisville at 8:00 a.m., exhausted. I'd gotten very little sleep in the last thirty hours, but I was full of anticipation and hope. I pressed through the weekend—a parade on Sunday, a fly-around to seven media markets the day before the election. On November 5, as I walked toward Atherton High School among the other voters, prepared to cast my vote for the next senator from Kentucky, I knew that whatever happened now, I'd given it my all.

☆☆☆

The night of the election, NBC projected me the victor very early. By 9:30 p.m. Huddleston had conceded defeat, but while I joined the others in the ballroom at the old Henry Clay Hotel, where the music blared and the crowd roared in celebration, I was concerned. The win was announced so early. Could I really trust the results? I took the stage around eleven o'clock that night to claim victory. Because I hadn't expected to win, I hadn't prepared any remarks. But all day, I'd been thinking back to that November night in 1956, when I watched John Sherman Cooper and Thruston Ballard Morton win their own Senate races. Feeling quite emotional, I dedicated my win to them.

Leaving the stage, I walked over to Terry.

"I haven't seen Janet or Joe," I said. "Where are they?" Terry said he'd seen them head downstairs, and when I found them sitting together in a quiet room, my heart sank.

"Do we have a problem?"

The look on Janet's face was grim. "Our margin of victory is narrowing," she said. "We're down to a couple thousand votes."

That night, I went to bed feeling queasy and woke the next morning to learn that Huddleston had called for a re-canvass, in which election officials look at the back of the voting machines and re-add the numbers. We were nervous about them stealing the election, but everyone I consulted with told me that if there was stealing going on, it had already occurred. As those around me continued to celebrate, and I was asked to appear on national morning shows the next morning to talk about my victory, I had a nagging feeling that it wasn't over; that somehow, this was all going to slip away. In a matter of months, I'd gone from that night of having to tend to my destroyed tree and my dead fish to this morning, appearing on the national morning shows, all while a re-canvass was going on. It was a true out-of-body experience.

It would be two weeks before the re-canvass was complete and I was officially confirmed the winner. When it was over, I'd won by an eye-lash: just 5,100 votes. "That's four-tenths of one percent," Roger Ailes said when I called him with the final results. "One vote per precinct."

It may have been the slimmest of margins, but I was exhilarated. A win is a win—especially when you consider how far behind I had been at the start of the race. It felt even better when I considered the context of the election. Despite Reagan's landslide victory, the Republicans lost two seats in the Senate, and out of the entire Senate, only one Democratic incumbent lost: Dee Huddleston.

I received word that I'd be attending an orientation in Washington, DC, for all incoming senators and I convinced Janet to come with me, as my first chief of staff. She had to buy her daughter a puppy for breaking the promise she'd made, but she agreed. As I packed for life in DC, feel-ing exhilarated, I received a letter from my father. He was never com-fortable expressing his feelings, and I was extremely touched by what he wrote.

"There is something I have wanted to say to you, but somehow when we have been together, I haven't found the right words . . . You have dem-onstrated a great humanity and a lot of class. I believe very strongly that you will be a truly great leader and senator. You may be assured that you will continue to have my strong support as your father, and as a citizen."

Reading that letter, I felt a lump form in my throat. I had so much to thank my parents for. My dad, for bestowing me with the grit and determination I'd needed to stay in the fight, as he had done him-self four decades earlier in World War II. My mother, without whose patience and resolve in helping me to overcome polio, I would never be where I was at that moment—having accomplished the thing I'd always wanted.

I thought of writing them back to say this, but I didn't. Instead, I vowed to myself that I would do everything I could to make them proud, and to do in the Senate what I'd done in my efforts leading up to this moment: give it everything I had.

CHAPTER SEVEN

Slow and Steady

In the Senate, most things revolve around seniority, and my seniority—or total lack thereof—was immediately apparent. In 1985, I was one of five freshman senators: Phil Gramm and myself on the Republican side, and Al Gore, Tom Harkin, and Jay Rockefeller on the other. Of one hundred senators, I ranked ninety-ninth, second only to Rockefeller simply because he'd been sworn in a few weeks after me, and I was dead last among Republicans.

If you've ever watched Senate proceedings on C-SPAN 2, you know senators spend most of their time milling about the chamber, but sometimes, on particularly important or solemn occasions, we sit in the seat we've been assigned. Soon after I arrived in Washington, a member of the Senate floor staff came to me with the seating chart of the Senate Chamber. Seats are chosen based on seniority, and when your number is up, you are given a choice of the seats that remain. Well, when I was shown the floor chart, there was just one spot left: the very last seat, in the corner, where even the light is not very good. The first time I took this seat, I looked around the room and thought to myself, None of these people are ever going to die, retire, or be defeated. I would always be last among my colleagues. But the experience also reminded me of walking into the auditorium at Manual High School my first day, feeling like the odd man out in the back. As I had that day, I set a goal on this one: despite my standing as the lowest ranked of my colleagues, I would work to be the most effective senator I could and to eventually gain the respect of my peers.

I'd been a student of the Senate for a long time, and I knew what this meant. I was not a singular savior who had arrived with the ability to immediately make a difference or prove a point. At its best, the Senate is a place where consensus is necessary and my main job was to practice patience, make decisions on principle, as I'd learned from John Sherman Cooper, and try to ensure I got a second term. To do all of those things, I first had to get to know the institution, and understand its rhythm and workings—something that would take me an entire term in office.

I liked Phil Gramm immediately, but he was also the colleague I found most intimidating. A fellow freshman, he'd been elected to the Senate from Texas after serving three terms in the House, and I soon found out it was going to be pretty hard to feel good about myself if I constantly had to be compared to Phil. A former college economics professor, he was extremely bright and, perhaps due to his experience on the House side (a distinct advantage shared by many senators, and one I'd often envy that first term), he seemed to find his footing from day one. Just two years into it, he introduced the Gramm-Rudman-Hollings Balanced Budget Act, designed to cut the federal deficit, which, at the time, was the largest in history. It bewildered me that he had been able to help enact a major piece of legislation while I was still trying to figure out how to get from my office in the Russell building to the Capitol.

As green as I felt, at least I was a member of the majority party, and Ronald Reagan was in the White House. It was an honor to serve at the same time as Reagan. He made conservatism appealing because he was appealing. Unlike the eat-your-spinach types like Barry Goldwater, he delivered the right message with cheery humor and everyman common sense. And when he put his philosophy into action, we soon found out that having conservative views was more than just okay. The economy took off like a rocket after the across-the-board tax cuts he championed.

Of course, that's not to say that I always agreed with him. In fact, the only time people took notice of me my first uneasy years in the Senate was for something most freshman senators try to avoid—voting against the president of my own party. Less than two years into my first term, when people still didn't know my name, President Reagan vetoed a measure that would have imposed stiff economic sanctions against the apartheid regime of South Africa. Going against party lines, I voted to override Reagan's veto.

My vote wasn't going to make me popular with my president, many in my party, or even some of the voters back home. Larry Cox, one of my closest aides in Kentucky, had become my state director, and it was his job to keep me informed of the opinions of the people in Kentucky. Their concerns were about jobs, the collapse of the tobacco market, and the farm credit crisis that had left many Kentucky farmers in a desperate financial position. "People think we have enough to worry about here without getting involved with what's going on in South Africa," Larry told me.

In weighing my position, I thought again of John Sherman Cooper and his choice twenty years earlier to go against some in his party, including the GOP nominee for president, Barry Goldwater, to support the Civil Rights Act of 1964. I felt we needed to do everything we could to change the apartheid regime, and my vote on this would be the first time I'd show my colleagues, and myself, that while I was a great admirer of Reagan, I wasn't afraid to go against the prevailing party view if I thought it was wrong. Remaining true to my conviction was, as Cooper taught me and Edmund Burke had argued two centuries earlier, the essential element of being a good senator.

Another critical requisite for becoming an effective senator is to remain one, and I therefore knew that one of my most important jobs during my first term was to make sure I got a second one. I also knew something else. I'd been paying careful attention to Bob Dole, the majority leader at the time. He sat at a desk at the front of the chamber, and I studied the way he conducted the business of the Senate, the influence he held from that chair. While I would venture a guess that the ultimate goal of many of my colleagues was to one day sit at the desk in the Oval Office, that wasn't my goal. When it came to what I most desired, and the place from which I thought I could make the greatest difference, I knew deep down it was the majority leader's desk I hoped to occupy one day. And I planned to do everything I could to prove myself capable of doing so.

☆☆☆

By the time my first term was complete and I faced a reelection campaign in 1990, I was feeling more confident. But I had a long fight ahead of me. To get to the Senate, I had succeeded in convincing the voters to fire Huddleston, but most Kentuckians still didn't have a good idea of who they'd hired to replace him. Hoping to change that, I invested a considerable amount of resources into building a state staff as talented and hardworking as my staff in DC. I opened six state offices and made the somewhat overambitious pledge to visit every one of Kentucky's 120 counties during the first two years of my term. Nearly every weekend, and during all of my recesses, I went home to Kentucky to attend town hall meetings everywhere from Paducah to Pikeville. Some days I'd begin with a meeting as early as 7:30 a.m., followed by a lunch meeting at noon, and end with a 6:00 p.m. meeting that would go into the night.

Meanwhile, I supported Vice President George H. W. Bush as the Republican presidential candidate over Majority Leader Bob Dole. I decided to tell Dole, in person, that I'd be supporting Bush. He was not pleased. When colleagues asked me how he'd reacted, I jokingly told them he was fine, and that I didn't have too much trouble getting used to my new office in the basement next to the boiler. (Of course, Dole and I later became fast friends and frequent allies.)

I prepared for a tough campaign against former Louisville mayor Harvey Sloane. It was a terrible political environment: Bush was unpopular, there was a fear of impending war in the Persian Gulf, and gas prices were spiking. All of this made it a tough setting for a run for reelection, and I turned to the incredibly talented Steven Law to run my race. But it became tough for me in a way I couldn't have imagined as personal matters overshadowed the difficulties of the campaign.

My dad became very sick during the course of it. Two years earlier, he'd been diagnosed with colon cancer, and as my campaign began, it was becoming clear to my mom and me that my dad's condition was worsening. By this time, they were living in Shelbyville, Kentucky, about thirty miles outside Louisville. My mom had never gotten over the idea that Louisville was too big for her small-town tendencies, and they were both much happier in Shelbyville, which reminded them of Athens, Alabama. My dad had retired from DuPont, but the quiet life did not suit him. He took a job with the Roll Forming Corporation in Shelbyville, as well as getting into politics himself. He became the Republican Party chairman of Shelby County, where he was a beloved and respected figure. Knowing how hard he worked in this position, and how much he cared about seeing his home county embrace conservative ideas, he'd be pleased to know that Shelby County now votes overwhelmingly Republican.

His illness, and what was clearly becoming the prospect of his death, was extremely hard on me. There are people we can't ever imagine dying because they're so alive, and this was my dad. I was with him every chance I had, and when I couldn't be, my state director and good friend Larry Cox was—making sure my dad got to the hospital for his treatments, and after he was hospitalized, checking in on my mom. In August, my dad's condition further worsened, and we were told there were no other protocols to help him. He died on September 28.

These few weeks were among the hardest in my life. I deeply missed my dad and was worried about what his death would mean for my mom—how she'd get along without him. At the same time, I had just seen my oldest daughter off to college in Massachusetts, and I missed her terribly. On top of all of this, the campaign was taking a lot out of me. In fact, a week before election night, it looked as if I might lose the race. Looking back, I'm not quite sure how I got through it all, but I do know that I'm grateful to a local minister who spent many long hours on the phone with me during this time.

I'm also grateful that the people of Kentucky voted to keep me in office for a second term. Come election night, delivering my victory speech, I was exhausted, spent, and very emotional as I dedicated my win to the person I'd most wished could have been there to see it: my dad.

☆☆☆

When I first set the goal of becoming a senator, a large reason was the chance to weigh in not only on matters of importance to Kentucky, but also on national ones. Few decisions are more important than those surrounding war and peace, and the weight of my job—and the steadiness it required—became clear to me in a very concrete way at the beginning of my second term, when I was forced to face the prospect of our nation at war. A few weeks after the election, in January of 1991, I had just left for a short vacation when I got word that President Bush was calling a special session of Congress to debate the Persian Gulf War resolution, giving him the authority to do any and all things necessary to extricate Saddam Hussein from Kuwait. Five months earlier, on August 2, 1990, Hussein's forces committed an egregious act of aggression on Kuwait, a sovereign ally of ours, taking control of the country and, with it, 20 percent of the world's oil reserves.

The resolution passed the House rather overwhelmingly, 250–183, but it was to be an altogether different story in the Senate. As the subject was seriously debated—there were few senators who didn't speak on the issue—I was well aware of the gravity of it all. Our mission was clear—to get Iraq out of Kuwait—but of course, it wasn't possible to know if we'd be successful.

That said, I felt confident in my vote to support the resolution. This was a clear case of a very bad guy whose actions were wreaking havoc on the citizens of Kuwait and the world oil supply. Unfortunately, not everyone was able to put politics aside. Senator Al Gore had been keeping his own counsel, appearing undecided for as long as possible to create a lot of drama around his vote. As Bob Dole would later tell me, a few hours before the vote Gore found Dole in the Republican cloakroom. Gore told Dole—who was controlling the floor time given to those voting in support of the resolution—that if he was allowed to speak toward the end of the debate, he would vote in favor of the resolution. It was clear to me what he was doing. At the time, much as a result of George McGovern's overwhelming loss to Richard Nixon in 1972, Democrats believed that to win the White House, they could not be seen as dovish. By getting the time to speak in favor of this resolution—and what he was really after, the extra attention—Gore's main objective was, opportunistically, to show himself to be on the right side of an important national security issue. It was vintage Al Gore.

The resolution passed the Senate fifty-two votes to forty-seven, and the war that followed was extraordinarily successful. In daily Senate briefings from military brass up in S-407, the secure room on the fourth floor of the Capitol, I saw how the impressive accuracy of our precision bombing technology was enabling us to keep civilian casualties to a minimum. On February 24, 1991, ground forces went into Kuwait, and in less than a week, they'd mopped up the Iraqi army and forced them out of the country.

The American public seemed overwhelmingly pleased with the quick success of this mission in Kuwait, and afterward, Bush enjoyed a nearly 90 percent approval rating. With the 1992 presidential campaign just around the corner, we thought he had earned an easy reelection. We couldn't have been more wrong. The tide quickly began to turn. The Berlin Wall had come down in late 1989; the Soviet Union was breaking up. The Russians sided with us in the Persian Gulf War, and now, in the wake of the end of the Cold War, a petulant mood settled over the nation.

☆☆☆

Bush had already broken his infamous "Read my lips: no new taxes" promise, and people were especially angry about Congress's vote, two years earlier, to give itself a 40 percent pay raise. These two issues became war drums for the Democrats, and coupled with an economy that was growing fast but not fast enough, an anti-incumbent mood began to settle over the country. Nobody represented this more than Ross Perot, the Texas billionaire. If my approach to politics and life has been the long game, his might be described as the few-minutes game. Appearing on *Larry King Live* on February 20, 1992, he announced his intention to run as an independent if his supporters could get his name on the ballot in all fifty states. They did, and he spent tens of millions of dollars to self-finance a new party called the Reform Party, which may just as well have been called the Perot Party, as it was little more than an exercise in ego.

I was the Kentucky campaign chairman for Bush in 1992, and as I traveled the state, attending campaign events, I felt how dispirited and down people were. And the more dispirited they felt, the more the young, articulate, and charismatic governor from Arkansas captured their imagination.

Bill Clinton's path to the nomination—which included accusations from Gennifer Flowers that she and Clinton had had a twelve-year affair, a Bill and Hillary appearance on *60 Minutes* denying it, and then

Clinton's admitting it was true—was shaky, to say the least. People obviously seemed willing to overlook this, evidenced by Clinton's strong showing in the primaries.

It was a terrible election night. Perot received 19 percent of the vote, Bush 37, and Clinton 43. The conventional wisdom afterward was that Perot had cost Bush the election, but in reviewing the election, many pollsters concluded that Clinton would have won with or without Perot in the race. The results made me think of British prime minister Winston Churchill being defeated in July of 1945. After successfully guiding his country through World War II, it was as if the British decided to give Churchill a gold watch and say, "Thank you very much, but you're retired."

Luckily, as discouraged as I felt about the election results and the idea of having to face life in the Senate with a Democrat in the White House, I had a few personal reasons to celebrate. Under Howard Schnellenberger, my beloved University of Louisville football team began the season 7–0, just as the McConnell Center at the University of Louisville was getting under way. Second to my work in the Senate, this center is the thing about which I'm most passionate and proud, and, just like my work in the Senate, creating it had required slow and steady work. The center provides a scholarship to forty of the best and brightest undergraduate students—ten in every incoming freshman class—all Kentucky natives. My hope, which has certainly come to fruition, is that by studying in Kentucky, these bright young men and women will then choose to remain in Kentucky after graduation, using their talent and leadership skills to advance our state. In addition to the scholarships, the center also provides students the opportunity to meet and interact with the long list of incredibly talented speakers we would bring—Colin Powell, Hillary Clinton, George W. Bush, Chief Justice John Roberts, Vice President Joe Biden—exposing them to excellence and encouraging them to set their horizons higher. After I had worked for many years to get the center off the ground, in 1991 it was gratifying to welcome the first ten scholars to the program that fall.

But I must say, even as pleased as I was with these developments, they greatly paled in comparison to the major highlight of 1993: my marriage to Elaine Chao. As great as my political ambitions were, so was my ambition to find the perfect partner. And in Elaine, I did.

CHAPTER EIGHT

Love

I t was my friend Julia Chang Bloch who had first suggested that I meet Elaine. I'd known Julia and her husband, Stuart, since I was a staffer for Senator Marlow Cook in 1969, and we had become close friends. Julia would soon be appointed the ambassador to Nepal, becoming the first Asian American US ambassador in history. I'd been divorced for nearly ten years and was growing increasingly tired of the single life.

"Okay," I said to Julia one evening. "I'm looking to meet someone new."

Elaine Chao was, at the time, serving as the chair of the Federal Maritime Commission. I know this doesn't sound very romantic, but after Julia mentioned to Elaine that I might be calling, I asked my assistant to call Elaine's assistant to arrange a meeting.

I had a particular event in mind for our first date: a party in honor of Vice President George H. W. Bush, hosted by Prince Bandar bin Sultan, Saudi Arabia's ambassador to the United States, at his lavish home in McLean, just outside Washington. Elaine and I joined about fifty others for a formal sit-down dinner, followed by a private, and moving, performance by Roberta Flack. When I picked Elaine up at her apartment at the Watergate, I was taken by her beauty, and proud to have her on my arm that evening.

We began to spend time together, choosing to largely forgo the typical DC social events for late, quiet dinners at one of our favorite casual restaurants in Georgetown or on Capitol Hill. I was impressed by her intelligence and confidence, and how close she was to her parents and five sisters, whom she spoke of fondly. During our courtship, over chicken enchiladas at La Loma or shared platters of hummus and Greek salad at Taverna, I learned the story of her upbringing.

Elaine's parents, James and Ruth Chao, were born in China and married in Taiwan, where they'd both relocated amid the political turmoil of the Chinese civil war. James had been born in a small farming village in Jiading District outside Shanghai. He studied maritime navigation and quickly rose through the ranks. In an effort to advance his schooling, James took a national examination, and not only did he score number one in the nation, he scored higher than any other student had ever scored. He was written up in the newspapers, which helped him gain a visa to go abroad. Given the choice to go anywhere in the world, he and Ruth chose the United States, knowing the great opportunity that exists here.

In 1958, with two children under five and a wife seven months pregnant, James left for New York, uncertain of when he'd next see his family. He worked his way across the ocean, piloting a ship from Taiwan to Portland, Oregon. He then flew to New York City, arriving in the middle of the night with two suitcases carrying everything he owned. He rented a small room from an elderly woman who offered space in her Upper West Side apartment to Chinese exchange students. But things did not pan out as he'd expected.

"All the universities he applied to required his transcript," Elaine told me. "But it was locked away in China, which had been closed to the Western world since 1949." James was despondent and worried that nothing would come of this opportunity. His supervisor at the shipping company where he worked referred him to the dean of the Asian Center at St. John's University, who would lead him to Dr. John Clark, dean of the business school at St. John's University. Clark saw a lot of promise in James, and offered him admittance to St. John's.

"But in order to stay," Dr. Clark told him, "you have to maintain an A average."

For the next three years, James worked part-time toward his MBA while working various jobs, including one at the shipping company. In 1961, he sent word to Ruth back in Taiwan that he'd finally saved enough to bring them to America. Right before leaving, Elaine—whose Chinese name was Xiao Lan—was given her American name by a missionary couple, Gardner and Ruth Tewksbury, who had taught her father English.

After thirty-seven long days crossing the Pacific and traveling through the Panama Canal aboard the *Hai Ming* ocean cargo carrier, my wife, then eight years old, arrived with her mother and two sisters in New York harbor on July 17, 1961. James was there waiting. After three years of separation, her family was finally reunited.

Elaine described to me the first American home she had—a one-bedroom rental apartment in Jamaica, Queens. Just as my mother had been to me, Ruth was her children's cornerstone. Elaine related how her mother transformed their drab apartment, which overlooked the entrance to the local elementary school, into a home, arranging the living room furniture to create a small, private space behind a sofa for Elaine, equipped with her very own desk.

When Elaine's father brought her to her first day of third grade at PS 117, she didn't know one word of English. She was the only non-English speaker. Walking into her classroom and seeing her teacher, Elaine bowed deeply from the waist, as is Chinese tradition when meeting a revered elder. Her classmates erupted in laughter. Later they laughed at her again when, during roll call, she stood to be marked for attendance when the teacher called another student, named Eli. Elaine had trouble telling the difference between her name and his. For weeks she would stand to be counted when his name was called. Her classmates mocked her every time.

From the beginning, Elaine worked hard to learn American ways and to fit in. At school, she carefully copied every word as it was written on the blackboard. Then later at home, after returning from work and before he'd begin his own studies, her father would sit with Elaine, in her small quiet nook behind the sofa, and patiently teach her the pronunciation and meaning of each word.

Within a year she was fluent, but it takes more than language to feel fully assimilated. Elaine wore hand-me-down clothes, donated by a family at the local church, and loved the Barbie doll her mom had bought, as much as she loved Barbie's house, made of cardboard, her bed an upside-down tissue box. And Elaine, like her mom and sisters, struggled to understand American culture.

One thing I love about Elaine is the way she helps me understand how certain American customs look from the outside. I'll never forget one early experience she conveyed to me. Not long after arriving in New York, as the weather turned chilly, Elaine and her sisters were doing their schoolwork when they heard a knock on their apartment door. Not expecting anyone, and not knowing any of their neighbors, Elaine's mother ignored it, thinking someone had made a mistake. But then there was another knock, followed by loud chants. Frightened, Elaine and her sisters followed their mother to the door. Opening it slowly, they found a crowd of people; the children were dressed in strange hats, some with paint marks on their faces, others with masks covering their eyes. The children thrust large sacks toward Elaine's mother. Terrified, and sure they were being robbed, Ruth went to the cupboard to find something to give them and grabbed the first thing on hand: a loaf of bread. She offered a slice to each person holding a bag, but they were not interested. Eventually they left. Ruth locked the door, turned off the lights, and she and her daughters spent the remainder of the evening—their first Halloween in America—uneasily ignoring the knocks and chants.

In 1964, Elaine's father received the MBA from St. John's that he'd been working toward for so long. In him, I saw the result of a principle I've always held dear: we work hard so our kids can have better lives and more opportunities than we do. Four years later, as Elaine was starting junior high school, the family moved into a four-bedroom split-level house in Syosset, New York, on Long Island. Over time, Elaine would overcome the challenges of understanding the American educational system: She went on to graduate from Mount Holyoke College and then earned an MBA from Harvard University. She went on to work in the banking industry and be selected as a White House Fellow. During the four years we dated, Elaine would serve as US deputy secretary of transportation and then the director of the Peace Corps. Her father's success was equally impressive: James eventually became highly successful as the founder of his own shipping and finance company.

From the beginning, even though we grew up in different worlds, I could relate to her experience. I moved twice at the same ages she had—eight and fourteen. My moves were nothing compared with hers. I did not have to negotiate a new country, culture, or language. But when I told her the stories of my own moves at these young ages, of leaving Big Dad and Mamie and having to start over again in a place where people made fun of my strange southern accent, I knew she understood in a way that few others had before. We both knew the feeling of not fitting in and had worked long and hard in order to prove ourselves, sharing the conviction that the only way to fail in America is to give up or die. In that way, we were kindred spirits.

I've come to understand that there is a part of being raised in a traditional Chinese culture that has remained with Elaine: She is not always forthcoming with her emotions. She's more comfortable keeping things to herself and leaving others to guess at what she is thinking. But in 1992, after we'd been dating for three years, Elaine broke with this tradition and made her feelings very clearly known: it was time to get married or move on.

We were married on February 6, 1993, which, fittingly enough given our political leanings, also happens to be Reagan's birthday. It was a small ceremony in the historic chapel in the US Capitol, attended by Elaine's family, my daughters, and Stuart and Julia Bloch. Afterward, we celebrated with our wedding guests over dinner in the Grant Room at the Willard Hotel. It was an exceedingly joyful day. After fifty years on this planet, and thirteen years as a bachelor, I felt as if I had finally gotten something very, very right.

☆☆☆

Newlywed life was exactly as we wanted it: happy, easy, and unglamorous. While many in Washington like to spend their weekends attending Georgetown cocktail parties or an event at the Kennedy Center, Elaine and I spent most of ours at home in Kentucky. In our town house in the Highlands section of Louisville, I did most of the cooking, grilling steaks on the back patio or making Elaine one of my favorite southern dishes, like scalloped oysters. Then as now, Saturday afternoons in the fall were reserved exclusively for University of Louisville football games and tailgating. In the last twenty years, I've missed few home games and there's absolutely nothing about the college football experience I don't enjoy. I gather with my football buddies around an RV in the parking lot of Papa John's Cardinal Stadium, and we make a day of it. We meet before the game to talk about what might happen and then again after the game to talk about what had. Our biggest concerns are how the Cardinals will do that season, and what we'll eat each week; such are the serious considerations of the tailgaters of America.

While I'd never argue that my wife is the world's most zealous football fan, she put up with this tradition, and even joined us on occasion, her schedule permitting. At this time, Elaine was the CEO of United

Way, America's biggest charitable organization. She had been tapped for this position, chosen out of a nationwide search of well over six hundred candidates, at a difficult time in United Way's hundred-year history. Its previous CEO, William Aramony, was accused of using the organization's money to fund his extramarital affairs, among other immoral and illegal practices. In 1995, he was convicted of twenty-three felony charges and would spend the next six years in prison. Naturally, news of the scandal had shaken public trust in the organization, and Elaine had her job cut out for her. A few days into it, we planned to have a quiet, late dinner. When she arrived at the restaurant, she looked a little weary. The waiter sat us at a back table, and after ordering our drinks, Elaine rested her forehead in her hand. "The situation is really challenging," she said.

I didn't doubt it. I took her hand in mine. "Well, look at it this way," I offered. "There's nothing tougher than following somebody who did a great job, and nothing that makes it possible for success better than following somebody who made a mess of things."

"You think I'll be able to restore public trust to the institution?"

"I do. If anybody can do it, you can."

Well, Elaine certainly did a great job. Over four years, she led the organization to once again become solvent, steady, and respected.

She had the same effect on me. Elaine never tires, and she certainly never tires of speaking to people. When she accompanied me to political events across the state, I could see how taken people were with her warmth and ability to connect in a way that is sometimes more difficult for me. Where I'm reserved, she's only too willing to sit and chat forever. Of course, as an Asian American, Elaine was at first considered a bit unusual in Kentucky. As I like to say, my wonderful state is many things, but diverse is not one of them. We're 92 percent white, 7 percent African American, and, on the weekends Elaine is home, 1 percent other.

Another tradition of our weekends in Kentucky was Sunday lunch with my mom in Shelbyville. I had been quite concerned about how my mother would fare after my father's death three years earlier, but she handled his absence with quiet grace, the same way she had handled the one other time they were ever apart: fifty years earlier, during his time serving in World War II. Elaine and I would pick her up at her house and take her out for a good southern meal at the Science Hill Inn or to Claudia Sanders Dinner House, a restaurant owned by the wife of Colonel Sanders. Over biscuits and gravy, fried chicken, and fried okra, she'd tell me of the events of her week. Her days were spent tending to her yard and reading, and painting, a hobby she'd developed years earlier, creating still lifes and landscapes, some of which now hang in our home. Friends from the Baptist church my parents attended, or old political acquaintances of my dad's, would stop by to make sure she had everything she needed, and each week, a woman from the local hair salon arrived to take my mother to her standing appointment.

Since my dad's death, I had been calling my mom every day at 5:30 p.m. to check in. It didn't matter if I was in the middle of a meeting or at an event; everyone on my staff knew that promptly at five-thirty I would break away to make this call, even if it lasted no longer than a few minutes. I could usually tell from her hello how my mom was feeling that day. Her health had been failing for some time—she'd fallen while at home a few months before our wedding, and had since been under the care of a home-based nurse—but even so, I was wholly unprepared for the call I received from a Shelbyville hospital room in late October 1993. When the nurse arrived at my mother's house that day, she'd found that my mom had suffered a massive stroke, and had fallen into a coma. Hearing this news, I immediately left for the airport, where I took the next direct flight to Louisville. When I arrived in Shelbyville, I found my mom in a hospital bed, hooked up to life support. Her doctor explained that my mother had suffered serious brain damage, and there was no hope she'd recover.

I asked the doctor and nurses to leave the room, and I climbed onto the bed, sitting close beside her. I stayed with her until night fell, thinking of all the days five decades earlier that she and I lay together on a different bed, this one in Five Points, Alabama. Then, as she fought for my future, helping me to recover from polio, she had transformed that small bed into a nearly limitless world, helping me to erect towns made of toys on my blankets, and reminding me of my own unlimited possibility, despite the odds that were fairly stacked against me. Those days, and all of the days that had followed—in the way she made me feel as if I belonged when I clearly didn't, in her belief in me when my own faltered, in her deep devotion to me—she taught me that if nothing else, I was very deeply loved. Now, as she prepared to die, sitting in bed beside her, holding her hand, I told her again and again that the same was true for her.

She died the next day.

CHAPTER NINE

Standing My Ground

I n between these highs and lows of my personal life, I also faced many challenges in the Senate as I finished up my second term. And I knew that what I needed most when it came to confronting them was something that I had learned many years earlier from Bernie Ward, the principal of my elementary school in Augusta, Georgia, who had a big impact on my success at baseball. When it came to settling fights between boys at school, Bernie had what in today's world might be considered an old-fashioned (if not also illegal) tactic. Inside his principal's office at Wheeless Road Elementary School, he kept two sets of soft, oversize boxing gloves. When boys got into a dispute, as often happened in those days, he'd call them to his office, give them each a pair of gloves, and send them outside.

Though I didn't get into many of these fights myself, I did observe more than a few of them. And what I saw was that the kid who typically won these fights was not the one who swung the most or hit the hardest, but rather, the one who stood the firmest. With legs securely planted, and arms raised to ward off the punches, the victor would stand his ground as long as it took for the other boy to wear himself out from the work it took to swing those heavy gloves, throwing fruitless punches.

The same approach was helpful in the Senate, where being effective, and staying around for a while, requires a penchant for standing firm. And as I had learned during my first term, sitting in that back-row seat, ranking last among my colleagues, in order to stand firm in the Senate one must understand how Senate procedure works, have a solid understanding of the principles of the Constitution, and be willing to make tough decisions that your friends don't like.

☆☆☆

It was an understanding of the importance of procedure that led to some of my proudest early legislative accomplishments, especially my efforts to raise the alarm on assaults against the First Amendment. In my view, it is absolutely essential for the integrity of our politics and the health of our democracy that we not grow complacent in the face of attacks on free speech. Our Founding Fathers wrote the First Amendment because they believed that even with all the excesses and offenses that freedom of speech would undoubtedly allow, truth and reason would triumph in the end. I therefore felt it was my job to recognize them when I saw them, which I did in September 1994, during the 103rd Congress, with the final stages of the Democrats' campaign finance reform bill debate.

While I might rank this as being right up there with static cling as an issue that most Americans care about, campaign finance reform is one about which I've become very passionate. It's also one on which my thinking has evolved quite significantly.

Early in my career, before I ever ran for elected office, I argued in favor of campaign finance reform measures such as creating a ceiling on campaign spending. But in 1974, I taught a course called American Political Parties and Elections at the University of Louisville. I had a two-year-old daughter and a pregnant wife, and we were struggling to get by on the salary I earned practicing law, and I took this position to help supplement our income. It was in the course of this work, and my deeper study of the issue of campaign finance, that I began to understand the issue for what it truly is: one of First Amendment rights, particularly the right to free speech.

The Founders had a lively fear that with the passage of time, the Constitution they labored to create would be distorted by the enemies of freedom or the ambitions of the powerful, which is exactly what I came to realize was at play in campaign finance reform initiatives. I was particularly influenced by the seminal 1976 Supreme Court case *Buckley v. Valeo*. In this decision, which struck down limits on campaign spending, the court wrote that the "concept that government may restrict the speech of some elements of our society in order to enhance the relative voice of others is wholly foreign to the First Amendment," which, the court wrote, was designed "to secure the widest possible dissemination of information from diverse and antagonistic sources," and "to ensure unfettered interchange of ideas for the bringing about of political and social changes desired by the people."

For those who, at first blush, might not see the link between the First Amendment and campaign spending, the court elaborated: "A restriction on the amount of money a person or group can spend on political communication during a campaign necessarily reduces the quantity of expression by restricting the number of issues discussed, the depth of their exploration, and the size of the audience reached. This is because virtually every means of communicating ideas in today's mass society requires the expenditure of money."

To put it simply, enacting limits on what people can spend in an election ultimately limits the very discourse the First Amendment was designed to protect. For the framers of the Constitution, the highest form of speech—the one most needful of absolute protection—is political speech, particularly at those moments of national decision we call elections. Underneath my liberal colleagues' efforts to regulate political speech through campaign finance reform measures was the great, untested premise that the collision of private interests with politics is somehow inherently corrupting. But what they weren't (and still aren't) able to understand is that the opposite is true. A government that spends multi-trillions of dollars a year is big enough to take away everything we've got. In the face of something so powerful, of course the public would want to elect somebody they agree with, to influence the course of legislation. To the maximum extent possible, the government needs to stay out of the way of that process, allowing everyone who wants to speak—politicians included—to do so as loudly as possible. Despite the argument offered by the Left, limiting a candidate's speech does not level the playing field, it does the opposite. Like trying to place a rock on Jell-O, pushing down on one type of speech just raises that speech elsewhere, allowing someone else to control the discourse—the press, the billionaire, the special interests, the incumbent.

On a more personal level, my first run for the Senate brought these issues to light in a concrete way. I never would have been able to win my race if there had been a limit on the amount of money I could raise and spend. The only way a guy like me had a chance—a guy with no real political connections and no money, no strong political party apparatus to rely on, holding views opposed by the mainstream media and organized political groups like the labor unions—was to get around the inherent advantages of the liberal majority party by raising enough money to take my message directly to voters.

During my first term, I'd fought to kill a major campaign finance reform bill, and the experience had given me a little more self-confidence in those otherwise uncertain years. Now, in my second, up for debate was Boren-Mitchell, and it was awful. It included spending limits and public subsidies for congressional campaigns, essentially creating a tax-funded entitlement program to pay for political races. The Democrats had a lot riding on this measure. Campaign finance reform had been a significant feature of Bill Clinton's presidential campaign, but here we were, two months before the 1994 election, and he hadn't managed to enact one piece of legislation on it. The bill passed both the House and Senate, and before heading to the president's desk, it needed to be referred to a conference where members of both houses would come together to iron out differences. At that time, the appointment of members of those conferences required three motions put to the Senate by the majority leader in a process that was typically a formality. But I had been spending a good bit of time with Bob Dove, a former parliamentarian whose job was to help advise Republican senators on procedure. The thing about guys in Dove's position is that while they have an almost inexhaustible knowledge of parliamentary rules, they typically only answer the specific question they're asked. However, one afternoon, Bob, Steven Law, my chief of staff at the time, and I were having a conversation about where things stood with the Boren-Mitchell bill when Bob said something that astonished us:

"Why does nobody think to debate the appointment of conferees? It's never been done before in the Senate's history, but it's clearly a debatable motion."

This was a stunning piece of news. These appointments were debatable motions that could be filibustered. And because the legislation had come up so late in the Senate's session, the Democrats were running out of time. They needed to send the bill to conference, come up with a final bill, and send it to Clinton to sign all before the session ended and we left for recess. I sensed an opportunity.

Filibustering is sometimes presented as an obstructionist tactic by its opponents, but in my view, if legislation as awful as this bill is brought up for consideration, there is a duty to obstruct its passage. So when the first committee nomination was made, I announced my intention to filibuster the nomination, knowing the Democrats would invoke cloture. Under cloture, if three-fifths of the senators present vote to end a filibuster, it must end. But after cloture, you are allowed thirty hours of debate, with no single senator allowed to speak for more than one hour.

I conceived of the idea of using those thirty hours of debate post-cloture to stall the appointment of conferees. This would require a tremendous amount of organization. We couldn't afford to lose control of the floor at any point, and because of the one-hour time limit, I couldn't accomplish that myself. I went to work, organizing my colleagues, convincing people to take part in my plan, and lining up senators around the clock to show up and use their full hour. The other side was completely caught off guard, and they were furious. But on our side, as the members of my conference began to realize we'd figured out a novel way to beat this bill, a real esprit de corps developed. My staff helped prepare people's speeches, and I set up cots in an anteroom off the Senate Chamber for anyone who'd committed to speak in the middle of the night—much like the idea of "going to the mattresses" in *The Godfather*. And we did it. We burned the clock for the full thirty hours and killed the motion.

When the second motion was up for approval, I thought we had a chance of defeating cloture this time because, unbeknownst to anyone but me, I had secured votes from a number of Democratic senators. But Bob Dole, the minority leader at the time, and Alan Simpson, the whip, thought I was wasting my time.

"We can't win this," Dole said. "Why are you spending so much effort on it?" But in the end, five Democrats voted against cloture, and we defeated the bill by filibustering the motion.

The experience was exhilarating, and I was extremely proud to have used the rules of the Senate to protect the First Amendment, and to keep congressional elections from being taken over by the government. I was, however, royally skewered in the media. Majority Leader George Mitchell blamed the Republicans, and me personally, for using obstructionist tactics to kill the bill—and he predicted that come the election in the fall, my actions would turn voters toward the Democrats.

He couldn't have been more off the mark—the 1994 midterm elections would be the Republicans' best elections in decades. Not only would we pick up eight seats in the Senate, and regain the majority, but much to everyone's surprise, with a net gain of fifty-four seats in the House of Representatives, we also took the House for the first time since 1952. Meanwhile, the American people, and my colleagues in the Senate, were finally beginning to know who I was.

☆☆☆

These efforts to stand my ground against campaign finance reform measures were the first of many that would come to earn me a moniker of which I'm quite proud: First Amendment Hawk. But a few months after Boren-Mitchell was defeated, a constitutional amendment was proposed to ban flag burning and I was faced with another First Amendment fight that would prove to be far more difficult.

When my father died in 1990, we held a service for him at the First Baptist Church in Shelbyville. Several hundred people came, and it was a very emotional day. I sat beside my mother as the pastor spoke. Before my father's coffin was lowered into the ground, the American flag that had been draped over it was removed, folded, and presented to my mother and me. That flag is now one of my most prized possessions. It honors my father's military service in World War II, when he fought to protect the freedoms that flag represents, and it rests proudly on the mantel in my Senate office.

The same year my father died, my feelings about the flag in general, and that flag in particular, were so strong that I stood on the floor of the Senate and spoke in support of a constitutional amendment to ban the desecration of the flag. But when the 104th Congress came into session in 1995, and we were asked to consider just such an amendment, I strongly argued against it.

It's never easy for a politician to change his mind, and when it comes to an issue such as the flag, which is all but guaranteed to stir people's deepest patriotic sentiments, it's even trickier.

I revere the American flag as a symbol of freedom, and I don't share the slightest shred of sympathy with anyone who would dare desecrate it. To do so demeans the service of millions of Americans, including my father, and it's an action that deserves rebuke and condemnation. But behind the flag is something much larger—the Constitution. When my father fought in Europe, he fought not for the flag itself, but for what it represents, including the freedom to express ourselves fully and to live our lives as free Americans. Our Founding Fathers believed the answer to offensive speech was not to regulate it, but to counter it with more speech, because no act of speech is so obnoxious that it merits tampering with our First Amendment. Our Constitution, and our country, is stronger than that. So altering our First Amendment, even for the worthy purpose of protecting the flag, was not—and is still not—something I could support.

When the amendment was proposed, I knew that as politically unpopular as it would be, especially in my own state, I had to oppose it. I was not willing to cherry-pick on the issue, arguing that political speech should be protected while offensive speech should be limited. Speech is speech, and it's certainly not the role of government to decide what is offensive and what is not. To do so would not only weaken the First Amendment, it could also set a dangerous precedent for the entire Bill of Rights. If we successfully carve out an exception to one basic freedom, those who seek to curtail our Second Amendment rights—the right to bear arms—might carve out another. Or the right to own private property, as expressed in the Fifth Amendment, could come under assault.

My staff was concerned that I was going to vote in opposition to the amendment as reelection was looming, but this was too important to me, upcoming election or not. After all, we've had a regularly scheduled election every two years since 1788, and at any point in American history one could have said, "Oh, we can't do this. The election's coming up." An election is always coming up and it should never dictate votes. So not only did I vote against the amendment, I became the lead proponent of defending flag burning as a constitutional right.

Not long after, I was invited to attend a campaign event at a VFW hall in south Louisville. Knowing how the audience of veterans was going to feel about my vote on this matter, it would have been a lot easier to turn down the invitation or to go and make excuses for how I had voted. Instead, I decided to confront the issue head-on. As I walked into the large, overly lit room crowded with about seventy-five veterans, I felt like Daniel heading into the lions' den. But I did exactly what I'd come to do: I took my place behind the podium and spent the evening hearing from people who'd come to speak their minds. It wasn't easy. The stories I heard were raw and emotional—stories about the battles that had taken people's brothers and friends, about months and years spent away from wives and children, all in service to our country. I listened to every one of them, and when they were done, I spoke. I explained my position to them the same way I had to my colleagues in the Senate. What I was ultimately fighting for on this issue was not just our flag but what it represented: our freedom. You could not guarantee other freedoms by limiting one. It was a rough evening, but as I prepared to leave, a man approached me.

"I think you're dead wrong and I don't agree with you one bit," he said. "But I admire you for coming here and defending your position." I walked into the night, the warmth of his handshake on my palm. I knew I'd done the right thing, and though it wasn't an easy or politically expedient decision to make, I felt sure of my decision. And quite sure my father would have been proud of me for making it.

✰✰✰

As challenging—and politically risky—as my decision to stand firm in this instance was, I'd face my most challenging task not long after. In the summer of 1995, Kyle Simmons, my new press secretary, walked into my office, looking a little drained. "We just got a call from Schief-fer," Kyle said, referring to Bob Schieffer, who was then the moderator of *Face the Nation*.

"What's his question?"

"He didn't call with a question," Kyle said. "But with a comment."

"Okay, what's that?"

"He says I'm making you look like shit."

"Great work," I said. "Keep it up."

Whereas a few years earlier I would have been happy if even one reporter showed interest in my efforts, at this time, the phone calls wouldn't stop. Journalists from across the country were calling to ask about the work that was monopolizing a fair amount of my time: inves-tigating one of my Republican colleagues in my position as chairman of the Ethics Committee.

When I was interning with Senator Cooper in 1964, he was working to establish the Ethics Committee. Before 1964, ethics was not of great concern to the Senate and, in fact, things operated far differently than they do today. Virtually every senator had a source of outside income, and it wasn't considered improper to give paid speeches or be affiliated with, and paid by, a law firm. But that would all change in 1964 in the wake of the Bobby Baker case.

Bobby Baker was Lyndon Johnson's secretary for the majority, and a rather unsavory character. He was accused of bribery and arrang-ing sexual favors in exchange for congressional votes and government contracts. His investigation fell to the Rules Committee, which was neither a particularly important nor interesting committee assignment. Either way, it wasn't equipped to take on the task of investigating Baker, but as Cooper realized, that was the least of its problems. The makeup of the Rules Committee, like every committee in the Senate, is predi-cated on which party holds the majority. Its membership is based on a ratio that's roughly in proportion to the two parties in the Senate, and the majority party controls all committees. Given this, Cooper foresaw the possibility of the majority going after members of the minority with no fear of reprisal, or, if a majority member was in trouble, simply using the force of the majority to thwart any investigation that might arise. Understanding the implications of this, Cooper went to work helping to establish the Ethics Committee. It would have six members, three Democrats and three Republicans, and four votes would be required to move forward. That would, of course, immediately provide protection for the minority against the tyranny of the majority in a misconduct case.

Back in 1993, I'd been asked by Bob Dole to serve as vice chairman of the committee, and after we won the majority in the Senate after the 1994 elections, I became committee chair. At the time, there was a very difficult case in progress. Bob Packwood—a Republican from Oregon who was first elected to the Senate in 1968, at age thirty-six—had come before the Ethics Committee in December of 1992, after the *Washington Post* published allegations of sexual misconduct. Packwood issued a general apology and sought treatment for alcoholism afterward, but it was still up to us to look into the details and decide if any action needed to be taken.

Investigating Packwood was not, to put it lightly, an enviable task. He was a smart and capable guy, as well as the chairman of the Finance Committee, arguably the most influential committee in the Senate. I also knew Bob personally, having first gotten to know him when I worked in Marlow Cook's office. Since becoming a senator myself, Packwood and I had been allied on a number of issues, like campaign finance reform.

Kyle came on board in the midst of this, and from day one he had a clear mandate from me: do not speak to the press about it. He'd later tell me he felt as if he'd been hired as the press secretary for the CIA, that's how silent we were on the matter. This was important not only as a matter of honoring the privacy of my friend, but also as a matter of Senate procedure. It's a tradition to this day that the deliberations of the Ethics Committee are entirely confidential. We had to remember at all times that this was not a trial, but a private process.

Unfortunately, because of the number of charges against Bob, and the salacious nature of those charges, there was tremendous interest from the press. Journalists, as well as some of my colleagues, assumed I was keeping the details quiet in order to sweep the matter under the rug. Senators Barbara Boxer from California and Carol Moseley Braun from Illinois were particularly adamant that we hold public hearings. Senator Boxer even threatened the committee, saying that if we didn't vote to make our hearings public, she would offer an amendment on the floor of the Senate forcing the issue.

In the history of the committee, there wasn't one example of the full Senate trying to micromanage or control the committee's decision. In any important case, the Ethics Committee would finish its work and if Senate floor action was required, the chairman would bring the issue to the floor. Senator Boxer obviously wanted to ensure we followed the right path, and thought that flouting procedure was good politics in the service of justice. But I found it highly regrettable, especially since I had no intention of sweeping this matter under the rug. In fact, I was considering what to do very seriously. (Neither Senator Boxer nor I could have predicted that two decades later, we'd find ourselves reminiscing about this early intersection of our Senate careers over dinner and drinks, during our efforts to jointly pass a multi-year highway bill.)

Over the course of the investigation, the committee interviewed 264 witnesses, took 111 sworn depositions, issued forty-four subpoenas, read 16,000 pages of documents, and spent 1,100 hours in meetings. And as the details emerged, the darker the situation appeared. It became clear that Packwood had systematically abused his power and privilege. Rather than expressing regret and remorse, he made things worse by adopting a bunker mentality and becoming aggressive and antagonistic. In the course of interviewing witnesses during the investigation, it came to the committee's attention that Packwood kept a diary. The Ethics Committee subpoenaed the diaries, but Packwood refused to honor the subpoena and we had to go to the floor of the Senate to enforce it.

Packwood litigated and took the fight all the way to the US Supreme Court. It delayed the investigation by several months, but eventually we got access to his diaries, at which point it was clear that Packwood had altered them after the investigation had begun in order to thwart our efforts. This matter was the most egregious one. After a tremendous amount of deliberating, and a fair amount of soul-searching, I knew that given the alteration of evidence, there was only one remedy I called a meeting of the members of the committee and suggested that Bob be expelled from the Senate. Both political sides agreed this was the proper course. On September 7, 1995, after our committee, on my motion, unanimously recommended that Bob Packwood be expelled from the Senate for ethical misconduct, he resigned.

To recommend expelling from the US Senate a colleague, a member of my own party, and a friend with whom I had served in the Senate for over a decade was one of the most difficult things I've ever had to do in my career in public service. The decision was made more painful by the fact that expelling Packwood meant our party would lose his seat. This did not sit well with many in my party, and I was painfully aware that this decision might dash my hopes of one day holding a leadership position. But I felt it was important to stand firm and send a clear message to the nation that no man is so important to the well-being of our nation that we have to compromise our fundamental principles.

☆☆☆

As I had learned from Senator John Sherman Cooper, it was my job to stand firm in what I believed, even when it meant making tough decisions like these, and it was the voters' job to decide if these decisions should allow me to stay in office. Their chance came soon enough when, on January 15, 1996, I announced my campaign for my third Senate term.

The day of my announcement, I prepared to embark on a fly-around of the state. The plan was to begin in Frankfort, where I'd officially announce at the state capitol, in front of the bust of John Sherman Cooper, who had died five years earlier, and then on to eight different media markets to reintroduce myself. Early that morning, Larry Cox drove me to Bowman Field, a private airstrip in Louisville, where the prop plane we'd rented for the day was waiting. I had asked Kyle Simmons to run my campaign, and he was waiting for us in Frankfort.

Once we were aboard the plane, one of the engines had trouble starting. It would sputter, but not fully turn over. Well, it's a darn good thing this happened. As we subsequently found out, the plane had been used the night before and a young guy who worked at the airfield had topped off the gas. But rather than using aviation fuel that prop engines require, he'd mistakenly added jet fuel. I got off the plane and Larry was waiting.

"I could smell it was the wrong fuel as soon as the pilot engaged the engine," he said, looking a little stunned. "We're lucky. If there'd been enough aviation fuel in the tank to get those engines started, you would have been able to lift off. But as soon as that aviation fuel was burned through and the jet fuel got into the injection system, both engines would have cut off immediately."

It was a true near miss, and Larry was visibly shaken. About five years earlier, Senator John Heinz was killed when his chartered plane crashed outside Philadelphia, and since then, Larry had gone to great lengths to make sure our travel was always as safe as possible—no more single-engine planes flown by Pat Datillo. I was shaken as well, but we didn't have time to dwell on it. "I have an appointment to announce my reelection in Frankfort in about an hour," I said. "Let's find a car to get us there."

Later that day, Larry was able to secure another plane so that we could stay mostly on schedule, and I made it to every one of the planned events. I was running against Steve Beshear, Kentucky's former lieutenant governor, who had attended University of Kentucky law school at the same time as I did. Right from the beginning, I decided not to run as a so-called revolutionary. This was the term assigned to members of Congress who had, in the run-up to the congressional elections two years earlier, signed on to the so-called Contract with America, a document that acted as a policy platform, detailing ten items Republicans promised to take action on if we took control of the House. Many of these issues were commonsense things, such as encouraging small business, streamlining procedure in the House, and welfare reform.

I agreed with the Contract with America, except for one thing: term limits, which—fortunately—was the one item that didn't pass the House. To put it bluntly, term limits is one of the worst ideas that's ever come on the American scene. It's born of the shortsighted notion that learning and experience is bad, when just the opposite is true. This is the case in any industry—why would you want to retire people who have the most experience in their field? From my study of the history of the Senate, and my own experience, I knew that the more senior members of Congress are typically those who have a greater perspective, and with it, a greater insight and sense of courage. From what I saw in the most experienced of my colleagues—people like Ted Kennedy, George Mitchell, Bob Dole, and Pete Domenici—they'd been convinced of things as a result of their experience and were less inclined to react to whatever whim happened to be speeding across the nation at the moment. If you're going to read every poll and knuckle under every hiccup, you're going to be a pretty lousy representative.

And as someone who'd run twice for the Senate, and was currently in the midst of another reelection campaign, I knew we didn't need to legislate term limits, because we already had them. They're called elections.

Very happily, I won mine that November. Not only did I beat Beshear, but in a year that Bill Clinton carried Kentucky for the second time, I was reelected by twelve points. It was a landslide, a truly remarkable result, and I have to admit, after all the years of rough campaigns, of barely getting by, after two terms of standing my ground, this one felt awfully good.

CHAPTER TEN

The Value of the Team

If you were to stop by my office in Washington, DC, today, you'd have the pleasure of meeting a woman named Stefanie Muchow. Stef started as an intern in my office in 2003 and is now the person you have to see if you want to see me. For the last several years, she has steadfastly guarded my door and managed my schedule, made me far more efficient than I'd otherwise be, and is the first person I look to speak with when it comes to any sports-related event. Like me, she's a die-hard Washington Nationals baseball fan, and unlike me, she tended to believe the Cincinnati Bearcats had a chance of beating the University of Louisville Cardinals each season. I know the press likes to portray me in a certain way (I've been called everything from humorless to evil), but to actually know me is to know that when it comes to people like Stef and the rest of my staff, I'm a bit of a softy. Because no matter how unpleasant politics can sometimes get, even in this world of forced smiles and canceled plans, of bland buffets and late-night calls, it's hard not to feel optimistic when you are surrounded by a team as talented as mine.

Many of the hiring decisions I've made were based on an instinct I had during a short, often chance, encounter with people, and I've very rarely been wrong. I'm often reminded of something Senator Daniel Patrick Moynihan said to one of his staffers who was more than a little intimidated by the idea of working for him. "You already have all of these Ivy League grads on your staff," this staffer said to Senator Moynihan. "What do I have to offer?"

"Let me tell you something," the senator answered. "What they know, you can learn. But what you know, they will never learn." The man the senator was speaking to was Tim Russert.

I've long believed in this sentiment—if you give talented people the chance to do something they've never tried, you're likely going to be surprised at how well they do it. Terry Carmack, that young man who showed up at my campaign office back in 1984 with no political experience and no connections, is now my state director, and one of my closest aides. I was so impressed with Kyle Simmons when I met him in an elevator at a hotel in Louisville that I hired him as my press secretary after a conversation that lasted no longer than the time it took us to get from the tenth floor to the lobby. He went on to be my campaign manager and chief of staff. When Billy Piper came to inquire about the job as my driver in 1991, it didn't take long to know I had just met a young man with a lot of promise. This, despite our somewhat awkward interview, during which he told me he wasn't even a Republican.

"And why is that?" I'd asked him.

With beads of sweat forming above his eyebrows, he told me that when he'd first registered to vote in his hometown of Louisville, he'd registered as a Republican. "But the clerk handed the paper back and told me I needed to check the Democrat box," Billy explained. "I asked her why and she said that was the only way I'd ever get to vote for the governor. She said, 'In Kentucky, the governor is always a Democrat, and the race is always decided in the primary. So if you want to help choose our governor, honey, you gotta be a Democrat.' I really wanted to be able to vote for the governor, and so I did what she said."

"Well, I think you'll make a fine addition to our staff," I said. "But

God, I sure hope all Kentuckians aren't as gullible as you." Billy put a lot of effort into proving just how astute he is, and over the next twelve years he'd work his way up from driver to become my chief of staff.

As my third Senate term began, I was well aware of how much the success I had enjoyed was due not just to Elaine and my parents but also to the support of my staff and friends, and I decided to throw a party to honor and thank them all. I rented the Kentucky Derby Museum at the Churchill Downs racetrack, sent out more than two hundred invitations, and hired a band. The best date I found to do this was very fortuitous. It was November 8, 1997, exactly twenty years to the day I was elected county judge in Jefferson County.

I was glad to celebrate with my colleagues and friends that wonderful evening. The party was also a great way to underscore how long I'd lasted in politics and, remarkably, the fact I still enjoyed the privilege of doing the work I'd set the seemingly unreachable goal of doing so many years earlier. Someone made me the name tag I wore throughout the evening: "Mitch O'Donnell, Mayor of Louisville"—the names I'd been called by Ronald Reagan and George H. W. Bush during my first Senate campaign, when they were hardly the only two people who had trouble remembering who I was.

In the remarks I made after dinner, I made it clear I had no intention of working any less hard than I had been working for the last decade. This wasn't a retirement party, but more, I hoped, a halftime celebration, and I certainly had reason to celebrate. With my third term under way, I was a far cry from that back-row seat in the Senate Chamber. Now I was chairman of the Rules Committee, chairman of the Foreign Operations Subcommittee within the Appropriations Committee, and, most significantly, a year prior, my colleagues had elected me chairman of the National Republican Senatorial Committee (NRSC), one of five leadership positions in my party.

As the head of the NRSC, I was now building not just my own talented staff but also a slate of senators who could most effectively advance a conservative agenda. I'd known for many years (if not, truth be told, from my first day in the Senate) that I wanted to one day hold a leadership position in my party, helping to call the plays and not just run them. And this particular job was a good fit for me. Unlike many members of Congress who view their efforts to get elected as a burden, I've always greatly enjoyed campaigning. I relish the contest—the excitement of it, the matching of wits, the debates—for the same reason I like sports. There's a certain amount of time you have to battle it out, and when the clock runs out, there's a clear winner and a clear loser. As we headed toward the 1998 midterm elections and the 2000 presidential election, I was thrilled to be helping to call the Republicans' plays.

✩✩✩

I liken the beginning of an election cycle to the Kentucky Derby. Some of our candidates are not going to make it around the first turn, while others seem on their way to victory from the first shot. It is the job of the NRSC chairman to help the party avoid jousting with windmills or buying landslides, and to focus our efforts and money on the candidates we might help win.

I had been eyeing the chairmanship of the NRSC—a job overseeing fund-raising and strategy to help Republicans get elected to the Senate—for some time, and had, in fact, run for it twice unsuccessfully. In 1990, I was beaten by my good friend Phil Gramm, and two years later, I foolishly decided to take him on again. (I nearly beat him that second time, losing the race by just one vote.) It was Phil himself who nominated me for the position in 1996.

By the time that Phil nominated me, I had learned the most important lesson when it comes to running for a leadership office: the best way to avoid a contest is to have no opponent. In the months leading up to the December vote for the NRSC chairmanship, I'd gotten on the phone with every one of my Republican colleagues to tell them of my interest in the job, and to ask for their support. Come the day of the vote, I'd secured enough votes that I had already wrapped up the position, and I ran unopposed.

In my first Senate race against Dee Huddleston, gaining the attention and support of the NRSC had been a real game changer, allowing me the funds to stay on the air the last eight weeks of the campaign, giving us the push we needed in the end. It was gratifying to now be on the other side, to help usher into office promising candidates committed to advancing the conservative agenda. As I like to remind people: winners make policy and losers go home.

I named Steven Law, who'd been my chief of staff, as executive director of the committee. Going into the 1998 elections, we were all still feeling confident from our astounding 1994 wins. That, coupled with Clinton's falling approval ratings and ongoing problems with the Monica Lewinsky scandal, raised Republican expectations higher than I was comfortable with. Expectations were so high, in fact, that my good friend Majority Leader Trent Lott suggested to the members of our conference, on more than one occasion, that he expected us to get to sixty Republicans, the number required for complete control of the Senate.

"Quit running around telling people we're gonna get to sixty," I told him one morning after yet another one of his pronouncements. As much as I hoped we might, and as hard as I was working several races across the nation to get us there, I still tend to view each election cycle with a lot more equanimity, having never forgotten the lesson I'd learned back at thirteen years of age, on the pitcher's mound of the all-star game. As soon as you think you're good enough to pitch a no-hitter, up walks an opponent prepared to knock your first pitch straight over that fence.

Sure enough, our expectations were too high. If we were to continue the baseball analogy, the elections of 1998 felt like our team had entered the World Series with the expectation we'd sweep, only to lose it all in four games. We were still in the majority in both houses, but the high expectations bred great disappointment. In the House of Representatives our party lost six seats, the worst midterm results in sixty-four years by a party not holding the White House. This led to a lot of internal unrest and, on the House side, a leadership revolt. Newt Gingrich, who just two weeks before the election had predicted a gain of ten seats, resigned as Speaker; John Boehner was replaced as conference chairman by J. C. Watts; and there was a very spirited contest for Dick Armey's job for House majority leader. He was challenged by both Jennifer Dunn from the state of Washington and Steve Largent from Oklahoma. Armey managed to hang on, but not without a fair amount of acrimony.

The unrest in the Senate was minor league in comparison, but there was some frustration because when the smoke cleared, we had stayed even with fifty-five Republicans. The chairmanship of the NRSC is a two-year term, and just a few weeks after the results were tallied, I was up for reelection. It was a little off-putting when my colleague Chuck Hagel from Nebraska announced he was mounting a challenge to my reelection, holding press conferences to say that due to our lackluster performance in the 1998 elections, new leadership was needed. But come December 1, when my Republican colleagues met to elect the leaders of our party, I beat Hagel 39–13. Afterward, a reporter for Hagel's hometown paper, the *Omaha World-Herald*, called the Senate historian's office to ask about the margin. It turned out mine was the second-biggest victory in a leadership election in the Senate since World War II.

While that was gratifying, I still took the results of the 1998 election cycle pretty hard. I felt like the captain of a team that had come up short, all while I'd begun to earn the reputation as a skilled political operative. Much to my surprise, I'd been included on the *National Journal*'s list of the hundred most important people in Washington,

DC, among people like Bill and Hillary Clinton, Secretary of State Madeleine Albright, and Federal Reserve chairman Alan Greenspan. After years of semi-obscurity, working among some of the sharpest political minds in the nation, it felt good to gain some respect, but now, after my first election cycle as chair of the NRSC, the results were disappointing.

What made these election results all the more incensing was that Democrats enjoyed these gains, and a surge in popularity, at the same time their president was about to become the second in the history of our nation to be impeached by Congress. In the end, I believe that the reason Clinton was not removed from office was that Democrats were able to keep public opinion on their side, framing the impeachment trial as a partisan exercise and arguing the popular view that political investigations are nothing more than politics.

We Republicans had also clearly overplayed our hand. Over Democrats' objections, the House Judiciary Committee had released Clinton's videotaped grand jury testimony and more than three thousand pages of the so-called Starr Report, including sexually explicit details revealed in Monica Lewinsky's testimony and photos of the infamously stained blue dress. Clinton's testimony was broadcast on television, and rather than turn against him, the public—seeing him sweating through long questioning sessions, looking boxed in—began to feel sorry for the guy.

While some of my Democratic colleagues, like Senator Robert Byrd, later said that removing Clinton wouldn't have been good for the country, I disagree. I think what's not good for the country is the message that the president of the United States can subvert the justice system by lying under oath. But he would, subsequently, pay a price: in 2001, his Arkansas law license was suspended and he was disbarred from practicing law before the US Supreme Court. At the time, however, American public opinion seemed to be that people everywhere lie about sex. Viewing it this way, the exuberance Republicans displayed about the matter conveyed the impression that the issue was only politics, and after admitting to the affair, lying under oath, and being impeached, Clinton's approval went up while ours went down. My team was going to have to do better.

☆☆☆

As the impeachment trial was wrapping up, Kyle Simmons came into my office with a copy of that day's *Courier-Journal*, Louisville's daily newspaper, which has never, shall we say, had much fondness for its senior senator. "Listen to this," Kyle said. "'Never mind all Monica all the time. It's been preempted by all Mitch all the time. He's been on CBS, NBC, ABC, PBS, Fox News Channel, CNN, MSNBC, CNBC, even Court TV. If you haven't seen Kentucky's senior senator on television lately, your set either is unplugged or broken. McConnell's face and voice have been on national TV networks forty-two times since December 20, the day after the House of Representatives passed two articles of impeachment.'"

I had to laugh. Fifteen years earlier, I spent many mornings praying even one local reporter would show up for my "Dope on Dee" press conferences, and here I was now, fielding calls from people like Cokie Roberts and Larry King. Given my understanding of the rules of the Senate, which I had gone to great lengths to study, I'd become the go-to guy for reporters looking for insight on the impeachment process. "Tim Russert is quoted here saying you're smart, focused, and prepared," Kyle said.

"Well, that's a nice compliment, and it was fun while it lasted," I said. "And we can now prepare to return to obscurity."

That, however, wouldn't turn out to be true at all, because on its way to the Senate floor once again was that old, nagging issue of campaign finance reform, an issue that would divide the conservative coalition I sought to build and would also raise questions about the way we raised money to support our team.

When the McCain-Feingold bill was first introduced on September 16, 1999, I knew it was going to get even more press attention than the issue typically does because John McCain, the principal Republican sponsor on the issue, was in a tight race for the Republican presidential nomination, against George W. Bush, and every campaign dollar counted. At the center of this bill was what is called soft money. At the time, federal election law allowed political parties to raise and spend as much money as they wanted as long as this soft money was not spent on the direct advocacy of a candidate's election. Unlike hard money, with its firm limits on contributions, soft money was largely unregulated, meaning there was no limit on the amount donors could give to a party. S. 1593—the so-called McCain-Feingold bill—was out to change that by banning soft money given to political parties.

Having made campaign finance reform a principal issue in his campaign, John McCain was prepared to do everything he could to get this bill to pass. But I was equally prepared to try to stop it.

This, of course, was not going to make me many friends in the mainstream media. During my appearance on CNN's *Inside Politics* to discuss the bill, Margaret Carlson of *Time* magazine called me a thug. The *New York Times*'s Maureen Dowd likened Congress to a bordello, calling me the "hard-boiled madam." Liberal columnist Mark Shields compared me to Dracula. In a book about campaign finance reform by left-wing writer Elizabeth Drew, I was roundly demonized from one cover to the other. Fortunately, I'd learned not to be bothered by namecalling and could laugh about it.

In October, I was asked to discuss McCain-Feingold on CNN's *Capital Gang*, alongside Margaret Carlson, Al Hunt, Mark Shields, and Bob Novak. "Let me just say one thing about how wonderful it is to be here tonight with so many friend and admirers," I said at the beginning of the broadcast. "Margaret's called me a thug and Al's called me a legislative lightweight. Mark has equated me with Dracula, and Bob has called me a backbencher. I feel like a lamb at a convention of lions. I can't wait for the group hug at the end of the program."

I was comfortable making light of the situation because not only did the barbs not bother me, they were helpful in demonstrating why I was prepared to do whatever it took to kill this bill. Soft money is what allows conversations on issues to take place. For example, as I pointed out during an appearance on *Meet the Press* at the time, the *New York Times* had printed 114 editorials on campaign finance reform in the prior thirty-four months. Under the existing law, as a candidate or member of the Republican Party, I could use soft money to buy issue ads to respond to the *New York Times*, presenting the other side of the issue. To buy the amount of space the *New York Times* had used in its 114 editorials on the subject would have cost me $3.5 million. By limiting the soft money, you limit my ability to buy those ads, thus limiting the conversation and allowing the press—the biggest and best-financed special interest in America—to control it. This is particularly perilous to conservatives because the large national corporations that own most of the newspapers in America share views that are remarkably similar—meaning overwhelmingly on the political left. To the extent that conservatives are unable to market their message through the expenditure of money, whether it's hard money or soft money, the agenda will be set and controlled by an institution like the *New York Times*, which is free to sermonize 114 times on any issue it wants, whether by what it writes on the editorial page or the front page. And, as I was learning, the media will do whatever they can to continue to control the conversation by using aggressive tactics to shut others up—like calling me a thug.

They are, of course, free to have their say, but when I once again led the filibuster to kill the 1999 McCain-Feingold bill, it was becoming increasingly clear, to the press and to my colleagues, that I wasn't going to allow them to shut us up either. It felt pretty good. As Winston Churchill said, "There's nothing more exhilarating than being shot at without result." I'd been shot at on this for many years, and they'd missed every time.

But, I have to admit, I was beginning to wonder how long I could remain unscathed.

✩ ✩ ✩

As the elections of 2000 approached I was, of course, hoping that the Republican Party would fare far better than it had two years earlier. When it came to who was going to be sitting in the Oval Office, the stakes were enormous. The next president would likely pick at least two Supreme Court justices, and with the number of seats in play, Republicans had the chance to take control of the entire government for the first time since Eisenhower was president in 1954. I encouraged my Republican colleagues to continue to do the best we could, and the lesson I learned from this period was crucial: don't misbehave, by which I mean, engage in good sportsmanship and be good team players. You can have policy disputes, but don't smear, backstab, or manipulate. Tell the truth and try not to bicker. The test of how long any party is going to be able to stay on top often depends on the strength of the team as a whole, on whether they get along, with everyone making a conscious effort to minimize jealousies and differences.

To make an example of this, I organized monthly breakfast meetings with our Republican congressional delegation from Kentucky and strongly recommended that none of us ever criticize one another publicly. History has taught us that no one party will hold political dominance for very long, but I think to the extent that you can provide good government, tell the truth, and avoid bickering, you can prolong your period of power. The work that I put into my position as chairman of the National Republican Senatorial Committee was all about making sure that our moments in the sun were long and radiant, and as 2000 approached I was determined to help Republicans work together not only to win a majority in the Senate but also to give America a whole new type of leader.

☆☆☆

When I watched the 1956 conventions in the basement of the house my parents owned at 5509 Westhall Avenue in Louisville, I never could have pictured, no matter how vivid the imagination of my fourteen-year-old self, that on July 31, 2000, I would speak at the Republican National Convention, which nominated the forty-third president of the United States.

As an enthusiastic supporter of Governor George W. Bush, I was happy to be involved at such an exciting moment, although I'm sure I didn't make even half the impression on the convention audience as did my wife. Prior to my 1996 reelection campaign, Elaine had resigned from United Way. She wanted to be with me on the campaign trail and was worried her role as CEO of a charitable organization that was prohibited from political campaigning could pose an issue. She'd since become a Distinguished Fellow at the Heritage Foundation, joined a number of boards, and had an active speaking schedule. She was invited to speak at the convention about her own story of immigration to the United States, and Bush's belief that immigration is not a problem to be solved, but a sign of the continuing appeal of the American dream.

There were many things I liked about Bush as our candidate, foremost among them his leadership abilities. During his first four years as governor of Texas, he was faced with a Democratic legislature. Unlike what we'd seen from the Democrats in the last eight years of the Clinton-Gore administration, he didn't point fingers. Rather, he brought people together and got things done, like signing into law the two most consumer-friendly tax cuts in Texas history, giving nearly $3 billion back to the people of his state, and reforming welfare more than a year before Washington decided to do the same. As a result, he was overwhelmingly reelected for a second term as governor of Texas, garnering nearly 70 percent of the vote. And, not unimportantly, Bush is a very likable guy, unlike Al Gore, who I've always thought has the personality of a cardboard box.

As election night loomed, there was a clear sense the presidential race would be razor thin—the contest between Bush and Gore was tight from the moment Gore earned the nomination—and neither party could count on any coattails, which was bad news for the Senate races I was overseeing as chair of the NRSC. The class of 1994 was up for reelection, and to be perfectly candid, many in this class had been elected more in response to the fanatically liberal first two years of Clinton's presidency than on their own merit. Even many incumbents who'd had a good four years were running in tough states.

The offices of the NRSC were abuzz with worry and a tremendous sense of pressure. In Michigan, where Spence Abraham was running, we threw everything we had at Debbie Stabenow but still couldn't get Abraham over 40 percent in our polling, which, if you're an incumbent, means you're going to lose. In Minnesota, we gave up on Rod Grams as soon as it looked as if he, too, wasn't going to keep his seat.

The oddest contest by far was in Missouri, between Republican incumbent John Ashcroft and Democratic governor Mel Carnahan. Carnahan mounted a campaign against Ashcroft, who'd held the seat for one term. Just three weeks before election night, Carnahan's plane crashed outside St. Louis, killing him, one of his advisers, and his son, who'd been piloting the plane. Under Missouri law, it was too close to the election to change the ballot, and Carnahan remained the candidate. In the days following, the local networks aired several tributes to him, and with the prevailing anti-incumbent mood, and a desire among voters to do something good, they began to turn their support to Carnahan. The day before he died, he had a 45 percent disapproval rating. Three days later, it had gone down to 15 percent. The acting governor, Roger Wilson, announced that if Carnahan was elected, he would name Jean Carnahan, Mel's widow, to fill his seat.

Come November 7, 2000, I arrived at my offices at the NRSC early in the morning, prepared for a long night. To me, election night shares the air of excitement that surrounds the kickoff of a University of Louisville Cardinals game, or the first pitch of the World Series. And that night, when I stood beside some of my most trusted team members and heard Tom Brokaw open NBC's election night coverage by saying, "We're about to take you on an exciting and bumpy ride," I felt the familiar surge of anticipation.

Well, nothing could have prepared me for just how bumpy that night would be—a night that began what just may have been among the most miserable thirty-five days of my life.

CHAPTER ELEVEN

Resilience

S pencer Abraham in Michigan. John Ashcroft in Missouri. Bill Roth in Delaware. Washington State doesn't look good." I was sitting in silence on a black office chair in our war room on the second floor of the NRSC, while a rowdy crowd of at least a hundred supporters, friends, and colleagues enjoyed an open bar and unlimited hors d'oeuvres in the large conference room downstairs. Elaine sat next to me as Steven Law, the executive director of the NRSC, read out these names—the seats that we were on our way to lose. As the numbers rolled in, the results were grimmer than I'd expected, but all of us were distracted by what was appearing to be an utterly bizarre and worrisome presidential election.

☆☆☆

I was sitting in that chair at 7:50 p.m. when NBC declared Florida for Gore, and the rest of the major networks soon followed suit. I was still sitting in that chair just before 10:00 p.m. when the networks reversed their decision and announced that Florida was too close to call. I could hear the party downstairs breaking up. Typically, Steven and I would have gone down to join the crowd, to enjoy a drink and make a few statements of where things stood, but we couldn't pull ourselves away. Elaine gave up around midnight and headed home, but there I was, still sitting in that chair at around 2:00 a.m. when Fox News called Florida for Bush. Like lemmings over a cliff, the other networks followed. I could hardly watch. By 4:00 a.m. all the networks had flipped again, and most retracted Bush's win.

Just before dawn, with the election bogged down near the swamps of Florida, I finally gave up, got out of that chair, and decided to go home. It was clear we were not going to learn the final results that night and what we did know for sure was terrible. In the Senate, we lost in Florida, Delaware, and Michigan, and there was likely going to be a lengthy recount in Washington. I felt very unsettled when I went to bed, and I slept like a baby—meaning I woke up every two hours and cried.

That weekend, looking as if we were nowhere near a resolution, I flew home to Louisville feeling miserable. To add to the upheaval, Elaine and I were in the middle of moving. After getting married seven years earlier, we'd remained in the small town house I'd owned since 1980, stuffed in together like sardines in a can, and we'd finally decided we needed more room. So that weekend, between distractedly unpacking boxes and trying to remember where Elaine wanted me to put things, I was completely glued to the television, too afraid to go out in fear I'd miss something.

On November 10, three days after Election Day, the machine recount, automatic under Florida law, was complete, announcing Bush the winner, but Gore kept fighting, arguing that elderly people in Palm Beach County couldn't figure out how to use punch cards. The weakness of that argument, however, is that more people in America voted on punch cards than any other way. I don't recall anybody else filing lawsuits or having difficulties explaining to their constituents how to vote. On November 26, Florida secretary of state Katherine Harris certified the election results, giving Bush a 537-vote victory over Gore, but there were legal challenges on both sides. As the battle played out in the courts, my staff and I were consumed by it, trying to process every latest bit of news, watching Gore try to become the Tonya Harding of American politics.

When the Florida Supreme Court ignored the law and decided to let the counting continue, it looked bleak and I was beginning to doubt Bush's victory. I had an extra reason to be concerned. Since 1901, the Joint Congressional Committee on Inaugural Ceremonies (JCCIC) has been responsible for the planning and execution of the swearing-in ceremonies and inauguration of the president. As the chairman of the Rules Committee, I was named chairman of the JCCIC, which meant I would be presiding over the inauguration. I had been receiving phone calls asking me to review schedules, to approve the invitations, to comment on planned remarks. I did what was asked of me, but the thought of having to introduce Al Gore as the next president of the United States was enough to make me want to call in sick.

Politically speaking, I don't think I have ever felt better, including after my own election victories, than when George W. Bush was finally declared our president on December 12, 2000, in *Bush v. Gore*. People who were unhappy with the result continued to question the legitimacy of the election, but Bush was vindicated in the end. In the months to follow, various news organizations would conduct the recounts the Gore campaign had tried to insist on, and in all the various ways they'd requested. And every time, Bush won.

I was, I have to say, expecting a hue and cry for election reform especially with regard to the Electoral College. This election was the first time since 1888 that a candidate won the popular vote but not the presidency, and at least one poll afterward showed that more than 60 percent of the American people supported a constitutional amendment to replace the Electoral College with a direct national election for president. This was hardly surprising. Since the earliest days of the republic, opponents have raised their scorn against the Electoral College. President Andrew

Jackson famously called for its abolition as early as the 1820s, and its opponents have only grown more strident as we have drifted in time and memory from the Founding generation. But thankfully, cooler heads have prevailed. As someone who takes the long view on important matters like this, I support America's election procedure for two important reasons.

First, it is an organized and reasonable system for tallying a massive amount of votes. What the Electoral College does is create fifty separate elections in which you can achieve finality. With the exception of Maine and Nebraska, it's winner take all. You carry a state that has twenty-five electoral votes, you get all twenty-five. If we eliminated the Electoral College, we'd frequently be faced with Florida-type recounts on a national level, because it is not uncommon for elections to be very close. Having to conduct a recount of every close election in every precinct in America would create the potential for enormous instability.

Second, the Electoral College ensures that all Americans get fair and equal representation from their presidential candidates, because presidential elections are state-by-state battles to accumulate a majority in the Electoral College. To say that one candidate won the popular vote and another won the vote of the Electoral College misses the point. Neither in 2000 nor at any other time in American history has the goal of a presidential race been to win the national popular vote. If that were the goal, the electoral strategies of both candidates would have been very different. In efforts to maximize their raw vote totals, you would have seen George W. Bush spending much of his time in his own state of Texas, while Al Gore would have camped out in California. Their campaigns would have been different and the result would have been different.

Is the Electoral College method of presidential selection the easiest to understand or the most efficient in its execution? No. But our system is not designed to be simple and efficient. It is designed to provide a final result and promote national unity in a large and diverse nation. For two centuries, it has done a pretty good job at that. And I expect it will continue to do so for many centuries to come.

But in the meantime, as the Electoral College did its job, the future of the Senate was in flux too. We lost five seats—even John Ashcroft lost to Mel Carnahan. He'd later take this difficult loss in good stride, jokingly boasting that no man alive had ever beaten him. Going from a fifty-five-person Republican majority to fifty-fifty, the Senate was dead even for the first time since the 1880s. The situation created a tricky question—who held the majority? After extensive negotiations between Republican leader Trent Lott and Democratic leader Tom Daschle, it was decided that the money allocated to operate the Senate would be divided equally among the two parties, but because Dick Cheney, the vice president (and official president of the Senate), was a Republican, Republicans would be considered the majority.

☆ ☆ ☆

The morning of January 20, 2001, dawned with gray skies and the promise of rain, but I woke up feeling giddy. It was Inauguration Day in Washington, and Republicans were about to take control of the White House and both houses of Congress for the first time since 1954. Since then, Democrats had enjoyed a period of dominance; we'd held control of the House and Senate in the 1990s but, unfortunately, had a Democrat in the White House at the time. Now, finally, it was our turn and I was eager for our chance to move our country in the right direction by pursuing a more conservative agenda under George Bush and our congressional leaders.

Elaine was awake, already at work in her office upstairs. I fixed the coffee and delivered her a cup before going to my closet to grapple with the important decision about which tie to wear. Standing there, I thought back to my first day at Manual High School, when I watched the president of the student council speak so confidently in front of a few hundred students, in awe of the courage it must have taken to do that. When my mother told me that day, after I voiced my wish to someday speak as the leader of the student body, "You could do that too, if you want to," I had deeply doubted her, and after becoming the student body president, I took every opportunity that presented itself to get up and speak, to push myself through the discomfort of it. And now here I was, headed to the White House to meet the president-elect, who I would introduce before a crowd of millions. How much I wished my parents were there to join me.

I arrived at the White House midmorning to meet the other members of the committee, and in the Blue Room, which is typically used to receive a president's guests, and where the official White House Christmas tree stands, we waited for Clinton, Gore, Bush, and Cheney to arrive. Once they did, there was a fair amount of awkward, silent coffee sipping, but given the close and bitter election, it was better than I had expected. At about 10:45 a.m. we were told the car had arrived to take us to the Capitol. I crowded into one side with my good friend Democrat Chris Dodd, the vice chair of the inauguration committee, while Clinton and Bush sat on the other. It won't surprise anyone to hear that on the way to the ceremony, Clinton did most of the talking. He was quite animated, telling stories about his experience with protesters, many of whom lined our route to the Capitol.

Bush listened quietly and watched out the window. When there was finally a pause in the chatter, he said with his trademark smile, "You know, I didn't realize until recently that there are protesters who have all five fingers, and not just the middle one." Even Clinton had to laugh at that one.

Arriving at the Capitol, we were led inside, where we waited to be escorted to the platform. Outside, the choirs of both Manual High School and the University of Louisville performed (there are some advantages to being the chair). I noticed Clinton yawning. He'd been doing the same thing in the car. I leaned toward Bush. "Mr. President, do you notice that Clinton's yawning a lot?"

Bush had. "The guy likes to party," he said. "Maybe he was up all night."

Well, we subsequently found out he had been up all night, but he wasn't partying. He was pardoning. The Constitution grants the sitting president the power to commute the sentences of criminals, and in his last moments in the White House, on his way out the door, Clinton had gone on a pardon binge, issuing 140 of them. Many were highly controversial, but none more so than that of Marc Rich, a wealthy friend of the Clintons who had been indicted on sixty-five federal charges, including tax evasion, racketeering, and illegally making oil deals with Iran during the Iran hostage crisis. Rich had fled to Switzerland to avoid the charges, and during Clinton's presidency, Rich's wife gave more than $1 million to the Democrats, including $100,000 to Hillary Clinton's Senate race in New York and $450,000 to the Clinton library foundation. Even Jimmy Carter called his pardon disgraceful.

When I followed Bush onto the platform, a bitter wind was whipping around the Capitol. Some of the staff of the JCCIC had floated the idea to host the ceremony indoors, in the Capitol Rotunda, which is where Reagan was inaugurated in 1985 because of bad weather. But Bush made the call to conduct the ceremony outside so that the thousands of people who'd traveled to Washington from all corners of America could be part of the event. It was a breathtaking sight—2,000 people sat on the platform, 300,000 others lined the mall. I took my seat next to Bush, feeling exceedingly proud and, I have to admit, more distinguished than I'd ever felt. Until I realized I'd just sat in a puddle. Apparently, someone had forgotten to wipe the rain from the chairs, and as I greeted the people around me, a look of practiced composure on my face, I wondered if they, too, were experiencing the feeling of very cold water seeping through their clothes and onto their skin.

"Mitch," Bush said. "Where's my podium?"

"I'm sorry, sir?"

He nodded to the spot a few feet away—the spot from which he would deliver his inaugural address in about thirty more minutes. "Where's my podium?"

He was right. There was definitely no podium. "Don't worry about it, Mr. President." This was the only thing I could think to say, because I had no idea where his podium was. Surely my job as the committee chair did not mean I was the one who was supposed to rent a podium? It was a ludicrous idea and one that my staff later found very funny because, in fact, a dedicated team of people had been working on the inaugural ceremonies for more than a year, long before anyone knew who'd be sworn in that day. Blueprints for the platform had been finalized the summer before, invitations were designed months in advance, and security plans were developed over twelve months. When the music stopped playing, a door built into the floor opened, and the podium rose from underneath. I looked at Bush and nodded, as if I'd known all along this was planned.

At 11:30 a.m., I called the fifty-fourth inauguration, the first of the millennium, to order. Witnessing Bush being sworn in just after noon by Chief Justice William Rehnquist, his hand on the same Bible his father had used twelve years earlier, was truly a remarkable sight. There was the incoming president's father, who was defeated by the outgoing president. And the outgoing president's vice president, who received a greater number of votes, but yet was defeated by the incoming president. All of them standing nearly side-by-side, each one having had an enormous impact on the lives of the others. It was further evidence, if we needed any, that there's always an orderly transfer of power in the United States and the losers sooner or later take their medicine and honor the results of the election and move on. And that's, of course, what happened again, as it has every four years since the beginning of the republic.

After the swearing-in, I took the podium and looked up, through eyeglasses dotted with raindrops. It was my high honor to be the first to introduce George W. Bush to millions of Americans, and citizens around the globe, in this way: "Ladies and gentlemen, the president of the United States."

When the ceremony was complete, I accompanied Bush and others to the President's Room inside the Capitol, located near the Senate floor, to sign the nomination papers designating the members of his cabinet. I couldn't have been prouder that one of those members was my wife, Elaine Chao, the new secretary of labor and the first Asian Pacific American woman appointed to a US president's cabinet.

When the celebrations finished, and we prepared to head into the 107th Congress, I was ready to move on. The election process had been heart-wrenching, and it had tested the bonds of our union. But it did not break us. Soon political life returned to normal with a new president and the peaceful transference of power, proving, yet again, that the United States is truly a resilient nation.

An idea that would be tested, in the most unfathomable way, just months later.

☆☆☆

In September, there's a back-to-school feeling in Washington, and when I returned from an August recess spent in Kentucky meeting with constituents and catching up with friends, the halls of the Capitol were infused with renewed energy and optimism. Bush's first months in office had been tremendously successful. In June, just before breaking for the recess, he had signed into law the first of what would be two sweeping tax cuts. It felt good to deliver such a key policy so early in his presidency, and I was equally hopeful about what we would accomplish his second year. As I settled back into work, my calendar got booked with working breakfasts, policy lunches, and committee meetings. I'm certainly nowhere near the most social politician in Washington, but every year there are a few get-togethers I actually look forward to. So it was this fall, when Elaine and I received an invitation from President George W. and Laura Bush to the Congressional Picnic, a Texas-style cookout on the South Lawn of the White House. It was scheduled for the evening of September 11.

That morning, I was preparing to head out for my day when I watched, on television, the second plane hit the South Tower of the World Trade Center. I spent the remaining hours of that terrible day as most Americans did: at home, watching TV, reeling from the enormity of the tragedy and fearful about what this horrific attack would mean for my nation, my government, and my children. Like everyone else who witnessed those terrible images, I knew our world had forever changed. I immediately called my office. Hunter Bates, my chief of staff at the time, told me the Capitol was being evacuated. Elaine was already at work at the US Department of Labor Building, just across from the Capitol, and she soon arrived home, accompanied by thirty-five members of her staff who, due to traffic and the shutdown of public transportation, couldn't make it home themselves. Someone went out later to pick up pizzas, but other than that, we all stayed together, watching the news.

In the late afternoon, I joined most other members of Congress for a briefing at the Capitol Police Headquarters. Democrat Tom Daschle, who had become majority leader the previous June as a result of Jim Jeffords's switch from Republican to Independent, announced that the Senate would convene the next day. We all bowed our heads in a moment of silence for those who had lost their lives. Standing on the Capitol steps, knowing that had it not been for the heroic actions of the passengers of United Flight 93, who had brought their plane down rather than let it be flown into the very building behind us, I felt a complex mix of emotions. Grief, yes, but also anger at the evilness behind these terrible acts, and pride in our strength in the face of them. Afterward, as people began to disperse, someone started singing "God Bless America." Everyone stopped and joined in, our voices echoing off the stone of the Capitol. That moment made it perfectly clear that despite what the terrorists may have desired, they weren't going to change the American way. Our resilience was needed now more than ever, and it was found in abundance. The shocking events of that day did not weaken or undermine the foundations of our democracy, foundations that were forged more than two hundred years ago and have been continuously strengthened throughout our history. We fought for our freedoms then, and we would continue to defend them now.

The unity felt the evening before informed all our dealings the next day. In some ways, it seemed fitting that the Senate was so closely divided at 51–49, because in the face of the terrorist attacks, we were not Democrats or Republicans. We were Americans, elected to represent and defend our country. The American people rallied in support of the new war against terrorism, and in the wake of the attacks, the horror and grief of these events pressing on us, Congress rushed to strengthen security.

On September 14, I attended a memorial service at the National Cathedral for those killed in the attacks, and sat behind Bob Mueller, the new head of the FBI, who'd been on the job just one week. Before the service began, I patted Mueller on the shoulder.

"You're going to get these bastards, aren't you?"

"You bet," he said.

Within three days, the Senate passed a $40 billion emergency supplemental bill to aid in recovery and reconstruction efforts; October 7 saw the launching of Operation Enduring Freedom, in the form of strategic air strikes in Afghanistan; and then on October 26, 2001, President Bush signed the Patriot Act into law. The bill passed 98–1, as most of us knew how critical it was that our law enforcement officials have the tools necessary to fight the war on terrorism. By allowing us to more effectively pursue and prosecute those involved in terrorist activities, the Patriot Act helped to keep America safe.

✧✧✧

Just one year after the anniversary of the September 11 attacks, the Senate voted 77–23 to give President Bush the authority to use military force against Iraq. While this war would become highly controversial over the next several years, Saddam Hussein presented the rare situation where a regime change clearly needed to occur before another tragic attack was perpetrated on innocent lives. That was the lesson of 9/11: you don't react, you act. You deal with our enemies before they hit us, and in doing so, prevent the type of massive destruction we suffered on September 11.

When the resolution authorizing the use of force against Iraq came before the Senate, we were being asked to decide some fundamental questions about the world in which we live. But more significantly, we were being asked to decide what kind of world we would choose for our children. Essentially, the question was this: Were we going to be safer if the United States led the effort to rid the world of Saddam Hussein? At the time, there was international agreement that he was amassing weapons of mass destruction. Nine days after al-Qaeda attacked us on our soil, Bush had promised Congress and the world that America would bring the war on terrorism to the terrorists wherever they may hide.

I was frustrated when others, such as Russ Feingold, argued that diplomatic initiatives and weapons inspections must be given a chance to succeed, or that Iraq posed no immediate threat to the American people or our allies in Saddam's backyard. All we had to do was look at recent history. Hussein had violated each and every one of the sixteen UN Security Council resolutions pertaining to Iraq. His armed forces continued to fire on American and coalition aircraft in the no-fly zone. Al-Qaeda terrorists continued to leave footprints on Iraqi soil and Hussein and his henchmen continued to make billions of dollars by exploiting the UN's oil-for-food program. Iraq had answered a decade of UN demands with a decade of defiance. And Bush had given the UN and the international community a final chance to disarm Saddam Hussein through diplomatic means. But Bush also made it clear that if reason failed, force would prevail.

The resolution passed with only twenty-three no votes, sending our nation into war. Of course, this war would become a matter of great controversy over the next several years, and there are a lot of questions surrounding the wisdom of the decision to invade Iraq. But at the time, everyone made the best decisions based on what we knew then, and what we knew—what the intelligence was saying—was that Saddam Hussein had weapons of mass destruction. Given Saddam Hussein's use of chemical and biological weapons against his own people and his neighbors, it would have been reckless to dismiss that intelligence and the immediacy of the threats posed by his regime to the United States. We already knew he was a mass murderer and that he was armed and dangerous—to treat him otherwise would have been very dangerous indeed.

CHAPTER TWELVE

Practicing Patience

G iven the state of the world, it was not easy to focus on reelection in my race for a fourth term against Lois Combs Weinberg in 2002. I carried 113 of the state's 120 counties and was reelected with 64.7 percent of the vote, the largest majority by a Republican in Kentucky in history—beating the margin by which John Sherman Cooper beat John Y. Brown in 1966. Going back to my days of following baseball as a kid, I've never given up an interest in statistics, and since my first campaign, I had a clear—though, it seemed at the time, highly unlikely—goal that I would one day surpass that margin. This was, therefore, quite an exhilarating moment for an old intern of Senator Cooper's and even earned me one of the nicknames President Bush was famous for bestowing: Landslide McConnell.

On the night of my swearing-in, Elaine arranged a private dinner for me in the Presidential Room at the Occidental. Nearly fifty people attended, including Elaine's parents and members of my senior staff. It was a very special evening because it celebrated not only my reelection but also something else, something that I had been hoping for and working toward for many years: my election as whip, the second-ranking leadership position in the new Republican Senate majority. It had taken much patient work for me to reach that position. Little did I know how much patience I would have to exercise in it—or how much patience I would need as I considered my next goal.

☆☆☆

In early 2002, several months before my reelection, Senator Larry Craig from Idaho, then policy chairman, had come to my office in the Russell building to tell me he was thinking about running for whip. But what he didn't know was that I had already secured the votes myself.

In 1996, our conference had voted to impose term limits on every leadership position other than majority leader. With a six-year term limit for whip, Don Nickles's term would expire in 2002, leaving the position open. Once again applying the maxim that you can start too late but never too soon, I had begun, as early as May of 2001, one and a half years prior to the leadership vote, to roll up enough support to get me elected. Larry never saw it coming.

I was not coy about my desire to work my way up the leadership ladder in the party. I had been around long enough to know that the members helping to call the plays were the ones who had the most significant influence over setting the agenda and, thus, enacting policy. I had approached my goal of becoming whip with a great deal of planning and preparation, using the same strategy I had used four decades earlier to become the president of the Manual High School student council—quietly whipping votes and wrapping up early support. Meeting with my Senate colleagues one by one, and urging confidentiality around each meeting, I expressed my intention to run for the position when it opened in 2002, and asked for their vote. Inside my suit jacket pocket was the whip card I carried with everybody's name on it. I'd been carrying it every day over that nearly two-year period, and on it, I had meticulously recorded a "yes" with each promise of support. Just as I'd learned that the best contests are those with no opponent, I'd also learned that when asking for someone's vote, a yes was the only thing that meant yes. Everything else—"You'd make a great whip," or "I'm confident you would handle the job well"—was not a vote I could count on. If that was the response I heard, I'd thank my colleague for the compliment, and then ask again: "Do I have your vote?" It's a binary question that has just one of two responses: yes or no, and in many ways, this was good practice for the job. Party whips can whip up scores of votes each session, and the same rule would apply then; after all, when it comes to votes on the Senate floor, there are no votes for "This would make a fine bill." By the time that Larry sat across from me a few months before the leadership vote, expressing his intention to run, the card in my pocket was filled with enough "yes" marks to know I already had it.

Leadership votes always hold a special air about them, none more so than the vote held in the Mansfield Room on November 13, 2002. After being nominated for the position of whip by my friend Senator Bob Bennett, I spoke, pledging my support to the Republican conference and Trent Lott, elected that day for his third term as majority leader. By this time Larry Craig had figured out he couldn't beat me. He'd withdrawn from the race, and I was chosen unanimously.

I felt a quiet elation in my election. It was a vote of confidence from my driven, ambitious, and incredibly smart fellow senators. I consider every vote I get, in any election, a gift and a victory, and these votes were particularly rewarding. It was also the culmination of a long campaign, one that took me an important step closer to what had, by this time, become my ultimate goal: to assume the number one spot in my party, and in the Senate, majority leader.

After the dinner Elaine hosted for me at the Occidental, we were both looking forward to returning home to Kentucky for a quiet holiday. When we arrived at the airport to fly home, my bag was laden with my holiday reading: *The Junction Boys* by Jim Dent, the story of Bear Bryant's implausible efforts to turn around the Texas A&M football program, and biographies of James Madison and Benjamin Franklin. I was also eager to spend time at the McConnell Center at the University of Louisville. With Gary Gregg, the center's director, we'd been hard at work lining up a roster of great speakers for the following spring, like Senators Patrick Leahy and Elizabeth Dole. But as soon as I walked into my house, my phone started ringing, and it wouldn't stop for several days, as I became embroiled in my first job as whip: to secure the votes of support needed to keep Trent Lott from being ousted as majority leader.

✩✩✩

On December 5, 2002, just a few weeks after Lott had been reelected majority leader, a large crowd gathered in the Dirksen Senate Office Building to pay tribute to Senator Strom Thurmond on his hundredth birthday. Thurmond, who was first elected to the Senate from South Carolina in 1954, was set to retire in January, and friends and colleagues joined members of his family to wish him well. Lott was one of the afternoon's speakers, and just a few minutes after taking the podium, he spoke these words: "I want to say this about my state: When Strom Thurmond ran for president, we voted for him. We're proud of it. And if the rest of the country had followed our lead, we wouldn't have had all these problems over all these years, either."

His comments sparked a media firestorm, and the long knives came out. People claimed that Lott's statement was an implicit endorsement of segregation. He issued multiple apologies, calling his statement a poor choice of words made in the spirit of a lighthearted celebration. But nothing he did could alleviate the wrath. The longer the issue remained on the public's radar, the more nervousness there was in the conference. While I couldn't defend what Lott had said, I felt that what we clearly had here was a case of selective outrage. The year before, Democratic senator Robert Byrd, a former member of the Ku

Klux Klan, had used the N-word on national television and nobody clamored for his resignation; in 1995, Democratic senator Wendell Ford from Kentucky, then minority whip, used the same term during a radio interview, and the *Courier-Journal* had defended him. Why did they get away with saying these things, when Lott did not? Because as a Republican from Mississippi, Lott fit the stereotype often advanced by the media. His critics were unrelenting and unforgiving. And, surprisingly, it wasn't the liberal press leading the revolt, but the conservatives. George Will, Bill Kristol, Charles Krauthammer, and the editors of the *Wall Street Journal* lambasted Lott, essentially demanding he step down.

So much for my plans for a quiet holiday. Instead, I was back at my office, calling my colleagues, trying to get a feel for the dimensions of the damage. I urged people to remain loyal to Lott. It was my hope the situation would resolve itself quickly, but those hopes were dashed in mid-December, when I arrived at ABC's studio for an appearance on *This Week*, hosted by George Stephanopoulos. Right before I went on, to talk about the situation with Trent Lott, Stephanopoulos informed me that he'd received confirmation that Don Nickles, the Republican senator from Oklahoma and outgoing whip, had said Lott ought to step down. This was the first significant break in the dike. When I later heard Nickles's statement—"Lott has been weakened to the point that it may jeopardize his ability to enact our agenda and speak to all Americans"—I knew the tide had turned too far. It was not an easy call to make, but by the end of the week, I knew what I had to do. I picked up the phone and made the difficult call to my friend.

"I think it's been unfair," I said. "But I also think it's over. We can't fix the damage."

As far as my colleagues understood it, three people were thinking about putting their names in the ring to replace Lott as leader after he resigned: Don Nickles, Rick Santorum, and Bill Frist. But what they didn't know was that there was a fourth. Me. Though I wasn't public about it, I was strongly considering the possibility, knowing that this opportunity might very well be my last shot at becoming majority leader. After all, I was now sixty years old. Younger, ambitious guys were coming up all the time. I also knew this could not be a rash decision. Above all else, I did not want to try and fail.

When it came to summing up the competition, I was most concerned with Bill Frist. He's like the guy from that beer ad: the most interesting man in the world. A former lung and heart transplant surgeon, he flies his own planes, runs marathons, and travels to Africa to volunteer his time caring for people in medical need. He'd also done a superb job as chairman of the National Republican Senatorial Committee during the 2002 cycle. Under his chairmanship, the Senate went from 51–49 Democrat to 51–49 Republican. You'd have to go back to Teddy Roosevelt's presidency to find the last time the party of the president regained the majority two years into his first term.

I called Kyle Simmons into my office. Kyle was one of the people I trusted most in the world, and I knew I could trust him with this. When I told him what I was thinking, his face registered nothing but concern.

"The party is looking for a change right now," Kyle said. "I know you've wanted to be the leader of this party for a long time, but your path to this position will be a promotion you have earned. This election is about change. The conference wants to go in another direction. They want someone like Frist. I think you have to wait it out, practicing what got you elected whip and what you're best at. Patience. And if the opportunity comes again, you'll be ready. But that time is not today." That was easy for a guy in his thirties to say, but it was harder for me to accept.

But hard or not, Kyle was right. It was not my time and the best I could hope for was that my patience would eventually be rewarded. I threw my support behind Bill Frist, and on December 23, 2002, after we elected him majority leader, I pledged my support for his leadership the same way, just four weeks earlier, I'd pledged the same to Trent Lott. The experience was once again proof that careers in politics can rise and fall with great speed. I did not want that to be my fate. My climb had been slow and steady, and that climb would continue.

In the meantime, with the leadership elections behind us, it was time to get down to business. On January 25, a few weeks into the session, Elaine and I decided to stay in Washington for the weekend. I'd been invited to appear on *Meet the Press* on Sunday, and Elaine and I were also planning to attend the annual gathering of the Alfalfa Club. If you've never heard of the Alfalfa Club, you're certainly not alone. It's an odd organization that was started in 1913. Its origins were to celebrate the birthday of Robert E. Lee, if for no other reason than it offered an excuse to get together for an evening of frivolity during the dead of the winter. (I'm sure Lee himself would have been surprised to learn that ninety years later Vernon Jordan, once the president of the Urban League, would serve as the club's president.) It meets just once a year, on the last Saturday in January, and has no purpose whatsoever. And yet, in a town composed of exclusive clubs, it might just be the most exclusive yet. Its nearly two hundred members come from all sectors and include politicians from both sides of the aisle. The annual dinner is typically attended by the president, vice president, the entire cabinet, corporate CEOs, and assorted self-important people. I'd attended as a guest of Senator John Sherman Cooper early in my Senate career, and in 2000, I had been selected as a member myself. While I typically find these tuxedo and gown events to be a chore, this dinner is nothing if not a lot of fun. Each year there is a mock candidate for president of the United States, running on the Alfalfa ticket. These "candidates" make (or attempt to make) funny speeches, poking fun at ourselves and each other. I was asked to give one of these speeches years later, and I was so nervous about bombing, I nearly declined.

As I left the office on Friday evening, I was in a jovial mood. I stopped by the desk of my scheduler to wish her a good weekend. She handed me my schedule and on the way home, I skimmed it. It included information about who would be my security detail for the event—a new part of life now that I was whip. There was also a note, highlighted in a bold font, not to drink any caffeine or eat after midnight on Sunday, in preparation for my annual physical, and a stress test, that Monday. I paid little attention because I had no reason to believe this appointment would be anything other than completely uneventful.

☆☆☆

My doctor walked into the small examining room at the Bethesda National Naval Medical Center, a look of concern shadowing her face. "I don't have great news, Senator," she said. "You failed the stress test."

I was stunned into silence. I have always enjoyed good health. I've never smoked cigarettes, I exercise fairly often, and other than an occasional cheeseburger from Good Stuff on the Hill, I eat as best I can. Hell, I even bypassed the so-called candy desk most days. It's been a tradition since 1965, when Senator George Murphy of California began the practice of keeping a supply of candy in his desk for all senators to enjoy. Since then, the candy desk has been located in the back row of the Republican side, closest to the Senate Chamber's most heavily trafficked entrance.

"It could be a fluke and mean nothing," the doctor continued. "But we have to take precautions. I'm going to schedule you for a cardiac catheterization. That'll allow us to take pictures of your heart and see if there's any reason for concern."

"When will we do that?"

"Right now."

It's probably not a common excuse offered to put off a pressing medical procedure, but Bush's State of the Union address was the following day, and I wasn't going to miss it. The doctor agreed I could postpone the test until that Friday, and throughout the week I did my best, with limited success, to put it out of my mind. I was also careful not to worry my staff. Everyone was arriving back in the office with a new spring in their step, elated to finally be sitting in the whip's office. Kyle was the only one I told, and I instructed him to tell the others I was taking that Friday as a vacation day. Not one person bought it. I'd missed one day of work in the thirty-five years since I'd gotten out of law school and nobody thought that now, just a few weeks into my first term as whip, I had decided it was a good time to treat myself to a matinee and an afternoon nap.

The doctors at Bethesda National Naval Medical Center performed the catheterization on Friday morning. Afterward, I was sitting in a chilly recovery room, still in my hospital gown, waiting for the results. Kyle had sent me a few e-mails about the upcoming votes on judicial nominations, including the status of the Democrats' filibuster on Miguel Estrada's nomination to the DC circuit court. When the doctor walked back into the room, I put my BlackBerry down. I was feeling impatient to hear that everything was fine so I could return to the office and deal with these matters.

But he didn't tell me everything was fine. What he told me was that he had very bad news. I needed a triple bypass.

I took a moment to collect myself and then called Elaine and Kyle. In a gesture of kindness I'll never forget, Bill Frist came to the hospital that day after hearing the news from Kyle. This was his area of expertise—he'd performed plenty of these procedures himself as a successful heart surgeon at the Stanford University School of Medicine and Vanderbilt University Medical Center. Elaine had arrived by this time, and after reviewing the results of my test, Frist told us he agreed with the doctor: I had no choice but to undergo surgery. He recommended a surgeon named Alan Speir, who that very day was performing a double bypass on Florida senator Bob Graham. Dr. Speir came in the afternoon, to explain the procedure to Elaine and me.

"When do you want to do it?" Dr. Speir asked.

"How about Monday?"

Elaine looked at me, startled. "Are you sure? You want to do it that soon?"

"I want to get it over with," I said. In fact, if I had to make this choice again, I would have chosen to have the surgery the next morning, because it ended up being an extremely anxious weekend. My mind was filled with questions. Would I survive the surgery? Would I feel like myself again? Would I be able to do the job I'd just been elected to do? I wasn't used to having health problems, and I had no symptoms whatsoever. And yet here I was, wondering if the position I had worked so hard to attain was about to slip away.

Both Bill Frist and Dr. Speir were reassuring. Frist called over the weekend to check in. "You have a long career ahead of you, Mitch," he said. "It's a good thing this was found before you had a heart attack. Follow the recuperative protocols and you'll be just fine."

Elaine and I arrived at Bethesda hospital on Sunday night, and shortly after five o'clock the next morning, I was taken into surgery. It lasted a few hours, and went off without complications. After one night in intensive care, I was moved to a private room, and a few days later, I could feel my strength returning. Elaine went home for the afternoon to try to get some work done, and as soon as she left, I called Dr. Speir with a very pressing question.

"Am I able to eat whatever I want?"

"Do you mean right now?" he asked.

"Yes, tonight, for dinner."

"I don't see why not," he said. "Just take it easy."

"What about chicken enchiladas?"

"Chicken enchiladas?"

"Yes," I said. "Is there any problem with eating chicken enchiladas?"

In the ensuing silence, I thought he had likely begun to worry if he'd overprescribed my dosage of pain medication. "No," he said. "I think a chicken enchilada should be fine."

I hung up and immediately called BJ Stieglitz. BJ had been working as my body man since I'd become whip, helping me to stay on schedule and get where I needed to be.

"I have a favor to ask," I said. "Will you go to La Loma on the Hill and get two orders of chicken enchiladas and bring them here this evening? I need them before five o'clock."

BJ agreed, and when he arrived later that evening, the enchiladas still hot in their aluminum containers, I asked if he wouldn't mind pulling over the rolling cart, setting out napkins, and trying to find some proper flatware. Not long after, I heard Elaine in the hall, speaking to the nurses, asking how I was feeling. When she walked into the room, her worried expression turned to one of confusion as she took in the sight: the rolling cart set beside my bed was laden with fresh flowers (the get-well cards removed), two plastic cups of ice water, each with its own bendy straw, and our favorite meal—chicken enchiladas from La Loma.

"Happy anniversary, honey," I said. "It's been a truly wonderful ten years."

☆☆☆

While patience has been an integral part of why I'd been able to reach the goals I'd set throughout my life, one thing I have no patience for is sitting still. Whether it's a weakness or a virtue, I haven't really caught on to the value of a vacation. I enjoy my work too much to have ever felt the need to develop outside hobbies, and the busier I'm kept, the happier I feel. Which is why my recovery from this surgery was so difficult.

I was told I'd be out of work at least one month. The idea was painful, but I remembered what Bill Frist had told me: follow the recuperative protocols. So I resigned myself to the fact that the best thing I could do was to rest. A nurse came every morning to monitor my progress and make sure I was moving around to help rebuild my strength, and Elaine was sure to be home every day by six o'clock. We spent our evenings watching television—a far departure from our normal lives—and enjoying each other's company. I began to catch some of the night-time talk shows, which I rarely did, and turned on the set one night to hear Jay Leno speaking about me. "The number two Republican in the Senate, Mitch McConnell, underwent heart surgery last week," he said. "He's doing fine. Nothing was actually wrong with his heart; it's just whenever a Republican is elected to a leadership position, they have to have their heart bypassed." It hurt my entire body to do so, but I couldn't help but laugh.

The following week, Walter Isaacson's *Benjamin Franklin: An American Life* sat on the table unopened, as I was simply too tired to read. Instead, I watched U of L basketball, and more movies than I usually see in a year, turning to AMC and Turner Classic Movies, hoping for a good western. I must have seen *Red River* and *Stagecoach* a couple of times each. Though this might sound easy, if not enjoyable, for me it was not. I longed to be back at the Capitol, engaging in the important work of the Senate. Now the highlight of my week was picking up *TV Guide* to see if a John Wayne movie might be playing.

It was also hard on my staff. Kyle was working overtime to keep the office moving. He frequently stopped by the house to discuss what had happened that day Stef, who had just recently started working for me, came with newspaper clips and memos. Nan Mosher, who was my office manager in the Russell building and had come with me to the whip office, brought swatches of fabric for the drapes we were installing or the carpet we had to choose for the new office. I received regular calls from my good friend Lamar Alexander. I'd first met Lamar in 1969 when I worked for Marlow Cook and Lamar was serving in the Nixon White House. Lamar would go on to become one of my closest confidantes and a very good friend and I was happy to be working with him in the Senate. Alan Speir also frequently came over to check on me.

"Why do you have your pajamas on?" he asked one day, as soon as he walked in. "You ought to get those off, and put on some real clothes." He was right, and while I was loath to admit this to him, I had begun to feel a little depressed. My life had been reduced to the basics—when I'd sleep, what I would eat, how far I'd attempt to walk that day—and I worried I wasn't making progress. Dr. Speir told me this was common. The surgery is very invasive, and it's often followed by a feeling that you're not getting better fast enough. When he told me, about four weeks after the surgery, that I could return to the office for a few hours a day, I felt the depression lift. On my first day back, I was touched when Congressman John Shadegg from Arizona went out of his way to see me.

"I just thought you might need to talk to me," he said.

"Why is that?"

"I had the same operation you did last March," he said. He told me of his experience, including his own feelings of gloominess afterward. It was helpful to understand that, like everything else, recovery is a process. And it was reassuring to see how fit and healthy he was now.

I was happy to be back at work, but I quickly realized my limitations. My first day back, I stayed until about five-thirty in the afternoon, but that night, I knew I'd overdone it. I was almost too tired to sleep. The feeling was deeply unsettling.

I waited another week before trying it again, and at about five weeks out, I felt strong enough to spend a few hours at work each day. Nan had set up my hideaway office near the Senate Chamber with a comfortable couch. Elaine sent over large pillows and a blanket, and I'd often go down to the hideaway between meetings and votes to nap.

It would take several more weeks, but I finally felt able to put in full days. In mid-May, the Senate was tasked with dealing with the Medicare Part D proposal, which would add a prescription drug benefit for seniors. It turned into a very late night session, as happens from time to time. I had been on the floor since 9:00 a.m. At one point, I looked up at the clock to see it was one-thirty the next morning. I'd barely even noticed.

Finally, my life had returned to normal.

CHAPTER THIRTEEN

Frogs in a Wheelbarrow

There are a hundred senators serving at any one time in the US Senate, and of those hundred, ninety-six sit in offices in three buildings across Constitution Avenue, in offices of varying appeal. I once had an office in the Russell building at subterranean level. The only windows it had were near the ceiling. We all had to crane our neck to see outside, and there was very little reason to do that, because the only thing to see out those windows was a mound of dirt. I then had an office once used by both Nixon and Goldwater. The door to the hallway was pocked with holes, because Goldwater would shoot his BB gun at a bull's-eye he'd hung on the door.

The other four senators—the two leaders and whips from each party—have an additional office under the dome of the US Capitol for their leadership staffs. In January 2003, I had moved into this rarefied real estate, just steps away from the Senate Chamber: the suite of the majority whip. I'd worked in the Capitol for nearly twenty years, but I was reminded in a new way how extraordinary it is. The suite I was given was the John Fitzgerald Kennedy Room, which had been used by Kennedy beginning the summer of 1960 after he won the Democratic nomination for president, and his increased responsibilities required an office close to the Senate Chamber. He used the space until his inauguration in 1961. It was a room unlike any other I'd ever inhabited.

The term "whip" comes from the sport of foxhunting. In a foxhunt, the "whipper in" is the assistant to the huntsman and it's his job to keep the hounds from straying away from the pack. As party whip, I now had the same responsibility: to encourage party discipline while making sure we had the votes required to enact the party's agenda. I would always need to know how my colleagues planned to vote because Frist, as party leader, would not bring a bill to the floor if he didn't have the votes to get it passed.

But I also knew that my job was not only to count votes, but to grow them. I didn't want to go to Frist and say we're three votes short on a bill we wanted to pass. Instead, I saw my role as saying we are three votes short, and this is what I'm going to do to get those three votes—by figuring out what policy change that required, or convincing those three people to vote our way. Having to understand where senators fall in the political spectrum, where allegiances exist, where political vulnerabilities lie, whipping votes is politics at its most visceral.

One of my predecessors in the whip office, my friend Trent Lott, once said the job of trying to wrangle the support of colleagues, and keep everyone satisfied, is like trying to keep frogs in a wheelbarrow. There's not a lot you can do to force them to stay there—so you have to persuade them. While I didn't have a lot of carrots and sticks to offer, what I did have was an ability to listen, an acute sense of my members' needs based on decades of close observation and study, and an instinct for timing. In important moments, that was all part of the sale. The job, and the new challenges it presented, required a lot of equanimity on my part, which, as those around me know, I have in no small measure. My longtime friends, with whom I've been tailgating before University of Louisville football games for many years, like to joke that they know I'm thrilled by a play or big win because I use both my hands to high-five. Once, a staffer told President George W. Bush that I was particularly excited about our winning a certain vote. "Really?" Bush replied. "How can you tell?"

It's true. I'm not one to get riled up very often. But I think that my tendency to remain measured, even at times of extreme pressure, or when others show great emotion, has served me well in the Senate, and particularly during my tenure as whip. My goal was not to express my emotions, but to make sure we got the votes we needed, and to make things happen.

☆☆☆

Nothing proved this more than one particularly nerve-racking vote, which was coming to the Senate floor in 2005, just before Christmas. We were all eager for the holiday, but we were down to the wire on an important vote—the passage of $39.7 billion in deficit cuts.

The vote was very, very close. The bill was also quite significant. Not only was cutting the deficit a major goal of President Bush, it was also a difficult vote to get support for, as it was the first effort in eight years to restrain spending in programs like Medicaid, Medicare, and farm subsidies. While there was a lot of big talk about cutting the deficit in general, it's not an easy vote to cast, and we were losing five of our fifty-five-member Republican conference, who refused to support the bill.

Going into the vote, it was absolutely necessary that we got this vote count right. Howard Baker, the senator from Tennessee who served as Republican majority leader in the 1980s, and later as Reagan's chief of staff, once summed up the job of the whip like this: "Count carefully and often. The essential training of a Senate majority leader perhaps ends in the third grade, when he learns to count reliably. But, fifty-one today may be forty-nine tomorrow, so keep on counting."

Following this advice, I counted. And then I counted a few more times. With each count, I was feeling as sure as I could be that on the deficit reduction bill, we were split exactly at fifty-fifty. This was not news that I wanted to bring to Frist, or the president.

The only way to break a fifty-fifty tie is by using the vote of the vice president, who serves as president of the Senate. I asked Kyle to look into where Vice President Cheney was, should we need him to come to the Senate to vote. It wasn't good.

"He's in Afghanistan," Kyle said. "And before you think about asking him to come back, I have to remind you that that's nine and a half time zones away."

"Try to get a phone number for him."

Later that day, as I dialed the vice president's number, I felt the weight of this decision. I was as confident as I could be in my vote count. I had to be, because when you're about to ask the vice president of the United States to get on a plane from Afghanistan, where he was doing important work, and fly back to Washington to break a fifty-fifty tie, you better be sure your count is accurate.

Thankfully mine was, and with Cheney's vote, the bill passed 51–50. Although my staff likes to say that my heart rate never gets beyond eighty-five, I might allow that, during this experience, it got to at least eighty-six.

☆☆☆

In October of 2003, eight months after my surgery, I led a delegation of senators on a trip to Iraq and Afghanistan. It was important to show my support to the American troops who were putting their lives on the line for our freedom, and I knew there was no better way of getting a sense of what was really happening in the war on terror than by putting my own boots on the ground. The trip lasted eight days, and we covered a lot of ground: Baghdad, Mosul in northern Iraq, Islamabad in Pakistan, and Bagram Air Base and Kandahar Province in Afghanistan. I met with General David Petraeus, then the division commander of the

101st Airborne; Hamid Karzai, the president of Afghanistan; and, the high point for me, many of the brave men and women of the 101st Airborne Division of the US Army, who are headquartered at Fort Campbell in Kentucky. What I saw here was different from the almost exclusively negative press coverage offered by an awful lot of reporters who never liked this idea in the first place. Morale was very high— among both our troops and the citizens of Iraq. Our delegation was met by youngsters on the streets, who waved American flags and gave us the thumbs-up sign.

Not long after I returned from this trip, Saddam Hussein was captured, found hiding in a hole. This self-proclaimed great warrior and supposed descendant of Mohammed was shown on television with a doctor combing his hair for lice. Not quite the blaze of glory Hussein may have expected he'd go out in.

Saddam was no longer in power, and our policy of preemption was producing exactly what we wanted in the neighborhood. In December of 2003, Vice President Cheney called me at home.

"I want to give you a heads-up," he said. "The president's about to announce that Gaddafi has given up weapons of mass destruction." Talk about a vindication of Bush's policy of preemption. Plus, having gone on this trip with no health problems, I knew I was going to be all right. Which was good, because I was once again about to take on the issue of campaign finance reform, this time all the way to the US Supreme Court. And for this, I'd certainly need a strong heart.

☆☆☆

After nearly two decades in the Senate, and countless fights against campaign finance reform, I had earned not just the official title of whip but also the unofficial title of spear-catcher on the issue. But in March of 2002, the final spear had been thrown, and this time I was unable to catch it when the Senate passed, by a vote of 60–40, John McCain and

Russ Feingold's Bipartisan Campaign Reform Act. I simply didn't have the votes to stop it, and despite my best efforts to convince Bush to veto the bill, he signed it into law that same month. The outcome of this bill was clear. It was going to hurt both parties. What it wouldn't do was what its supporters said it would: reduce the amount of money spent in politics. In fact, a good deal more would be spent, just not by the parties. I was, and am, all for outside groups doing whatever they want. What I'm not for is a decision to shackle political parties, making it harder for them to compete with outside groups, which was just what this bill did. As I told my colleagues on the Senate floor, in the moments before our vote, the bill would be a stunningly stupid thing to support.

But my fight wasn't over. The day after McCain-Feingold passed the Senate, I announced that I had put together a powerful coalition—including groups as varied as the NRA and the ACLU—and a top-notch legal team, who'd be taking the case to court. My team included Ken Starr, the former solicitor general and member of the DC circuit court who'd become a household name as the independent counsel during the Clinton impeachment and an investigator in the Whitewater controversy. Ken is not only a very likable guy, he's also an extremely skilled litigator, and one of a few dozen DC-based lawyers whose specialty is to argue in front of the US Supreme Court. I also tapped Floyd Abrams, the most prominent—and probably the most liberal—First Amendment lawyer in America. He had represented the *New York Times* in the Pentagon Papers case, and wasn't exactly accustomed to representing conservatives. As I liked to say, the *New York Times* editorial page may be with McCain, but I've got their lawyer. (Floyd would later tell me how flummoxed his liberal friends were to learn he had joined my team. *Mitch McConnell? You like that guy?*)

We were prepared to take our case all the way to the Supreme Court, and in fact, I had been ready with a legal team since the early 1990s, when I faced the possibility that a bill might make it to Bill Clinton's desk. I became the lead plaintiff in *McConnell v. Federal Election*

Commission, challenging the constitutionality of McCain-Feingold in US district court in the District of Columbia. Some pundits called this the most significant political speech case in over a quarter of a century, while other pundits continued to slam me for it. Common Cause had called me the Darth Vader of Reform, a comparison I had a bit of fun with. One morning, walking up to dozens of reporters, their microphones ready to capture my words, which they'd likely twist the next day in papers across the country, I welcomed them by announcing: "Darth Vader has arrived."

While a lot of ink was spilled discussing my role as the dark knight of reform, there were scant articles about what was at the center of my case: the issues brought up by the McCain-Feingold bill are issues that go to the very heart of our democracy. What is permissible in terms of the raising and spending of money in political campaigns? How much freedom should individuals have when it comes to donating money to a political candidate? Who gets to say where the limits are on these issues? The McCain-Feingold bill was attempting to define those limits. Just as I had since entering this fight twenty years earlier, I deferred to the Constitution, which guarantees the broadest freedoms when it comes to speech of any kind, including political advertising.

When the three-judge panel in district court issued a mixed verdict on the constitutionality of the law, I appealed the decision, and on September 8, 2003, the US Supreme Court heard oral arguments in *McConnell v. FEC*. It took two months to issue a decision. At 272 pages long, and with an overall 5–4 majority, the court found that the McCain-Feingold bill did not violate the First Amendment. It was extremely disappointing, and though it wasn't easy for me, I had to accept the ruling. While I've always had an open-door policy with my staff, in the days after the decision, I was distraught enough to want to spend a fair amount of time with my office door closed. From my desk in the whip office, I had a clear view across First Street to the Supreme Court Building. In the shadow of this view, and after all my years working to block this awful legislation, I found it nothing short of depressing that when it was finally enacted, it was under a Republican House, a Republican Senate, and a Republican president.

But I'd taken the fight as far as I could, and it was time to move on. I called John McCain to congratulate him. "You won and I lost," I said. Although we were on different sides of this issue for many years, I like and admire John McCain. He and I would go on to become close colleagues and good friends, sharing many dinners together at Trattoria Alberto on Capitol Hill. John said, "There are few things more daunting in politics than the determined opposition of Mitch McConnell, and I hope to avoid the experience more often in the future." This was gracious of him to say and I, too, paid tribute to his resolve. The bill never would have passed without him being as tenacious as he was. It was a terrible bill, but boy, was he tenacious about it. And that's a quality I deeply respect.

When it was all said and done, even at times of differences like these, John and I, and all of our Republican colleagues, were united as a conference in the beliefs that united us as a party, and acting as a leader among my colleagues in the pursuit of those principles was a true honor. The only thing I didn't like about the job of whip was that it was the second most important position in my party and I still had my heart set on getting the top job. Bill Frist, the current leader, had pledged to serve no longer than two Senate terms. If he kept that promise, the position would be open in another three years. I hoped that the work I was doing as the assistant leader of my party—trying to keep everyone together to enact the best legislation we could—was helping to prove beyond a shadow of a doubt that I had the qualifications to be elected to replace him when the position opened. And according to the card I kept in my pocket, on which I was once again recording the number of votes I had secured for the position, it very well seemed that I was on my way to achieving my goal.

CHAPTER FOURTEEN

A Thick Hide

I f you were to stop by my office in the Russell building, you'd see that on a wall to the right of my desk, I have on prominent display a few dozen political cartoons that I find particularly amusing. One of my favorites depicts an entrenched DC politician who has chewed the meat clear off the bones of his critics. In others, he's drawn as a prostitute to big money, the king of earmarks, someone beholden to special interests, and Howdy Doody, the puppet from the classic 1950s children's show.

I am the politician in those cartoons.

Not only do they give constituents something interesting to look at when they stop by, but they remind me that in politics, you have to be humble and have a thick hide. As Harry Truman supposedly said, if you want a friend in Washington, get a dog.

It's no secret that being a member of Congress has always ranked up there with used-car salesmen in the affection of the American people, and every American—political pundits and cartoonists included—have the right to say what they want about us. I view it much like the experience of going to a ball game: you bought your ticket, and you're entitled to scream at the umpires if you want. Though it might sting, hardy criticism of the people we've elected is a reflection of the health of our democracy. So today, when a political cartoon in which I appear strikes me as particularly comical, I call the cartoonist to ask for a signed copy to hang on my wall. (Those conversations are, themselves, often quite amusing. *This is who and you want what?*) I now have quite a robust collection.

That's not to say that I quietly accept the point these cartoons are often trying to make, and I've exerted a fair amount of effort hitting back. More than once, after the *Courier-Journal* published a poll declaring how unpopular I was, I released the results of a poll of my own, showing that most of the paper's readers found the paper to be out-of-touch and irrelevant, its political coverage biased. Perhaps my favorite article ever published in the *Courier-Journal* was one reporting the results of another poll we'd taken. It had found that readers of the *Courier-Journal* were actually less likely to vote for a candidate the paper endorsed.

I attribute my healthy attitude toward criticism to an important lesson I learned from, of all people, Ronald Reagan. He was often ridiculed during his time. We all remember Clark Clifford, an adviser to four presidents, calling Reagan an "amiable dunce." But Reagan, seemingly impervious to the criticism, continued to govern not in a manner to appease his critics, or the employees of left-wing press outfits, but with conviction. Clark Clifford would go on to be charged in a banking scandal. And that amiable dunce? Well, he went on to end the Cold War, develop Reaganomics, help America regain its confidence, and serve as one of our greatest presidents.

In the summer of 2004, I had reason to contemplate President Reagan's legacy with special attention because on June 5, 2004, he passed away at the age of ninety-three. Prior to the funeral, his body lay in state for thirty-four hours in the Capitol Rotunda. I spent a lot of time there, quietly paying my respects. Among the thousands of visitors who came to the viewing, standing in long lines, was a young soldier who'd fought in Iraq, accompanied by Paul Wolfowitz, deputy secretary of defense. The soldier had lost both his hands, which made his salute to Reagan's casket all the more moving.

President Bush declared June 11, the day of Reagan's funeral at the National Cathedral, a national day of mourning and gave what I think just might be one of the most poignant eulogies ever delivered by a US president. He spoke of Ronald Reagan's childhood in a small town, where your neighbor's hardship was your own. He talked about his inherent goodness, which permeated everything he did. He paid tribute to Reagan's boldness, his vision, his courage, and his optimism.

These are qualities that go beyond politics, yet they were also qualities the Republican Party desperately needed as we entered the 2004 election. Bush's approval rating was at about 30 percent, and his critics had brought out their knives, calling him everything from a war criminal to a fascist. As a loyal Bush supporter I believed that, like Reagan, he could crush his critics and win the election and that his legacy, like Reagan's, would stand the test of time. But things were looking bleak, and I tried to find hope where I could, including the fact that the Louisville *Courier-Journal* had endorsed John Kerry.

✩✩✩

On October 13, 2004, I was at home with Elaine, watching the third and final presidential debate between President Bush and Senator John Kerry. We were six weeks from Election Day, and in this debate, Bush was holding his own. This was a relief, because his performance in the first debate had nearly sunk him. Bush has many wonderful qualities. He's astute, decisive, and never wavers from his beliefs. He has a much slyer wit than anyone gives him credit for. But he is not a great debater. During his first debate against Kerry, he'd had a particularly troubling performance, appearing to both smirk and slouch, and he missed many opportunities to hammer Kerry. It was as if he'd run out of things to say.

This night, in a debate moderated by Bob Schieffer, Bush was on point, and Elaine and I were both feeling pleased with his performance. At one point, Schieffer asked John Kerry a question about raising the minimum wage. Kerry took the opportunity to fire a few shots at Bush for opposing these efforts, and the president responded, "Oh, I'm in favor of the Mitch McConnell plan to raise the minimum wage." Well, I nearly fell off the sofa. It wasn't just that I hadn't expected to hear my name in the debate, but I hadn't the slightest idea that the McConnell plan for raising the minimum wage even existed.

I called Kyle. "Any idea what he's talking about?"

"I was wondering that myself," Kyle said. It turns out we had devised an alternative to the Democrats' plan if the issue came to the Senate floor. But because they never offered their version, our amendment never got much further than a stack of papers on my desk.

Other than this amusing experience—and the fact that I spent a day at the Democratic National Convention, acting as a spokesman for my party and speaking to reporters to offer the Republican point of view, all while enjoying the utterly confused looks on people's faces as to my presence there—there was very little that I enjoyed about the experience of Bush running for reelection against John Kerry. Due to the increasing casualties in Iraq, coupled with the scandal of abuse at Abu Ghraib, Michael Moore's film *Fahrenheit 9/11*, and critical television spots from MoveOn.org, the public continued to turn against Bush. Then Howard Dean disappointed us by losing the nomination to John Kerry, and Kerry took the lead over Bush in the polls in August.

The race remained close over the next several months, and both campaigns deserve a lot of credit for their get-out-the-vote efforts. Come election night, voter turnout went from 50 percent in 2000 to 60 percent in 2004, making 2004 the highest turnout since 1960. Going into election night, I had a sense of foreboding that Bush might lose. I saw a political cartoon that summarized the way a lot of other Americans felt at this time. It shows a voter going into a booth. In his head is the word

"Kerry," but in his gut is the word "Bush." In my own head, I was worried about a Kerry victory, but in my gut, I had to hold on to my faith in the American people and the rightness of Bush's policies.

When the results came in, and the president was reelected with three and a half million votes more than Kerry, I was elated. The clear and decisive victory erased the memory of the difficult election of 2000 and gave President Bush and the entire Republican Party the blast of energy we needed. Now, with the mandate of the voters, I could continue with my job and begin to prepare for the biggest role of my career: the leader of my party.

A decade earlier, a special election was held in Kentucky's second congressional district to fill the seat left vacant in 1994 by the death of longtime representative Bill Natcher. The district, which had not elected a Republican since 1865, was thought to be an easy win for the Democratic candidate, Joe Prather, the state's secretary of transportation. Prather went on to lose by ten points. While there were several reasons for his loss—chief among them the fact that Republicans were able to successfully compare him to the very unpopular (at the time) Bill Clinton—Prather had made a stupid mistake that gravely hurt him. About one month before the election, Prather revealed that he had gone to Washington to rent an apartment in anticipation of being elected to Congress. His hubris did not sit well with the voters.

This was a lesson I would never forget. One should never, no matter how sure a victory seems, take that victory for granted. I had to keep this in mind in the fall of 2006. By this time, Bill Frist had announced he was not running for reelection in November. I knew from the tallied votes on my card that I had secured the position, and I anticipated that I'd run without opposition. Not wanting to appear overconfident, I kept this information quiet. But I also had every intention of beginning my tenure as the leader of my party as prepared as I could be, and I began to look for the most talented people in the business to join the team I would oversee as Republican leader. The only question that remained was if Republicans would continue to hold the majority in the Senate.

The night of the 2006 midterm elections, Elaine and I went to the offices of the National Republican Senatorial Committee to watch the results. There was a large crowd in the conference room on the first floor, and dozens of staff members in the war room on the second, but I chose to watch in a small conference room on the third, alone with Elaine and Billy Piper. By this time, Billy had worked his way up from my driver, to my legislative assistant, to my appropriations coordinator, to become the chief of staff for my personal office. Billy sat at his laptop monitoring the results, and he kept his back to us, likely so he wouldn't have to see the look on my face as, one by one, our guys went down. Jim Talent in Missouri. Rick Santorum in Pennsylvania. Lincoln Chafee in Rhode Island. By the time we were through, six Republican senators lost their elections, and with each loss, it was apparent that we were on our way to losing the majority.

I turned to Elaine. "It's worse than I thought," I said. I didn't say much else for a while, allowing Elaine to speak for me. Every time another bad result came in, we all knew Elaine's opinion on it pretty quickly.

We were there until 2:00 a.m., when the final results were in. We'd lost both the House and the Senate, and I felt the sinking disappointment that my hopes of being majority leader had been crushed. I now had forty-nine Republicans in a body that requires fifty-one for a majority and sixty to do most things. If there was ever a time I needed a thick hide, it was now. Before heading home, I picked up the phone and called Bob Corker, the former mayor of Chattanooga, Tennessee. "Congratulations," I said. "You're the freshman class."

The next morning, I woke up around seven o'clock feeling the disappointment of having to play defense to Harry Reid, now majority leader. I like Harry, and even invited him to come speak as part of our distinguished speaker lecture series at the McConnell Center. Reporters may want to believe there's a personal animus at play, but there isn't.

I would never have gotten into this business, much less succeeded at it, if I took political differences personally. But Harry is rhetorically challenged. If a scalpel will work, he picks up a meat-ax.

He also has a Dr. Jekyll and Mr. Hyde personality. In person, Harry is thoughtful, friendly, and funny. But as soon as the cameras turn on or he's offered a microphone, he becomes bombastic and unreasonable, spouting things that are both nasty and often untrue, forcing him to then later apologize. For example, a year earlier, he'd called then–Federal Reserve chairman Alan Greenspan a political hack and later decided to enlighten a group of sixty students by calling President Bush a loser during a speaking engagement at their high school. This lack of restraint goes against what is expected from a party leader, and I was skeptical, at best, about the direction of the Senate under his leadership.

The next morning, given our late night, I was surprised to find Elaine already awake and working in her home office. When I brought her a cup of coffee, she had a contemplative look on her face.

"It's not what you were hoping for," she said. "But you've been working toward this for more than twenty years. I know you'll do everything you can to help govern in a responsible, wise way that will lead us in the right direction and benefit our country. Majority. Minority. Who cares? You'll still get it done."

I went back downstairs. She was right. And yes, while a small part of me may have wanted to spend at least a few minutes wallowing in disappointment over the loss of our majority and that, yet again, my chance of becoming majority leader had slipped away, I didn't have the time for that. After all, the year I was first elected, I was one of just two new Republican senators. And I didn't work my way out of that poorly lit seat in the back corner by wallowing. I picked up the phone. Billy was already at the office.

"We have a lot to do," I said. "What's next?"

The first thing on the agenda was attending the leadership elections a few days later. On November 15, my colleagues and I met in the Old

Senate Chamber—the same room where Henry Clay and Daniel Webster famously debated, and which later housed the US Supreme Court, from 1860 to 1935. It looks exactly as you think it would: richly decorated with crimson drapery, dark wood paneling, and marble columns. Under a domed ceiling and a portrait of George Washington painted in 1823 by Rembrandt Peale, my Senate colleagues unanimously elected me to be the fifteenth Senate Republican leader, and Trent Lott as whip.

Kyle had assembled a great crew to work in the leadership office, identifying a number of talented new hires, like Brian McGuire—an exceedingly smart guy who would be my speechwriter—as well as some seasoned Hill veterans like Rohit Kumar, Meg Hauck, Libby Jarvis, Laura Pemberton, Malloy McDaniel, Mike Solon, Dave Schiappa, and Sharon Soderstrom, who was widely considered to be the best staffer in the Senate. Tom Hawkins made the jump from the Appropriations Committee staff, and most of the whip staff made the move down the hall to the leader's office, including Don Stewart—or Stew, as everyone knows him—who had recently joined my staff as our communications director. John Abegg and Brian Lewis were brought on as my legal counsel. In addition, Billy Piper had an all-star team in the Russell office, including legislative director Scott Raab, communications director Robert Steurer, and my military and defense staffer Reb Brownell. I couldn't have been better prepared.

That night, Elaine and I invited several close friends to help celebrate my election over dinner at the Caucus Room. I felt nothing less than an enormous sense of gratification and an utter thrill that it had, finally, happened. After so many years of preparing for this role, I was ready for the challenge, no matter how great that challenge appeared. We were in the last two years of Bush's presidency and had just lost the majority, due in large part to opposition to the war in Iraq. My job was to support the president in the waning days of his presidency and get as much done as we could as a diminished group.

Little did I know just how challenging this would be.

✩✩✩

Immediately after the election, the resistance to the war expressed during the midterm elections seemed to infuse the air of the Capitol. And Bush knew it as well. In assessing the strategy in Iraq, Bush made several important decisions to immediately change course. Just one day after the elections, he replaced Don Rumsfeld as secretary of defense with former CIA chief Bob Gates and named General David Petraeus as the new commanding general, Multi-National Force–Iraq. In January, just as our session began, in a nationally televised address, the president announced the Petraeus plan, or the so-called surge. It was an entirely different approach to fighting the war that entailed committing more than twenty thousand additional troops to Iraq to clear and secure the city of Baghdad and Anbar Province, and to protect its population.

The announcement created an immediate firestorm. The Democrats' promise to get us out of Iraq had helped propel them to the majority in both houses, and Bush responded by announcing a plan to do the very opposite—to put more troops in. It seemed to many like watching a football game in which your team is losing, and it starts the second half by running the exact same dismal play it had been using, hoping that this time it was actually going to work.

Immediately after Bush's announcement, Harry Reid and many Democrats called on Congress to reject the surge. But the president and Petraeus were convinced that this was our last, best chance at success, and they asked members of Congress and the American public to give their plan a chance—to support our troops in the field, and those on their way. Bush needed someone to carry it across the finish line. As the newly elected leader of my party, I was determined that was going to be me.

That meant, first and foremost, convincing every member of my own Republican conference to support an idea many Americans were dead set against. In February, the House passed a resolution disapproving of the decision to send additional troops to Iraq, but I was able to ensure a similar measure did not pass the Senate. Over the next few months, as thousands of additional troops prepared to deploy, the majority to Baghdad and others to Diyala Province, while four thousand marines in Anbar Province had their tour extended, we were on Iraq almost constantly. The Democrats introduced more than twenty resolutions to force departure from Iraq. Bush was absolutely resolute in his refusal to sign any measure or proposal that set a deadline for withdrawal—a position I strongly supported—and it was my job to keep those bills from landing on his desk.

I relied heavily on Tom Hawkins, my national security adviser, who is also a former marine. He was crucial to this difficult task. Many of our members wanted out. Anyone expressing support for the surge was getting hammered by Democrats and the powerful antiwar left. Every week, I held a meeting of our entire conference where I tried to build unity by making sure my members knew what was at stake, and to create a forum in which they could ask questions and express their concerns. My job here was not only to speak but to listen, and what I was hearing was that many members were wavering in their support. To better address this, I decided to bring in the best person to make the case about why we needed to stick together on this issue: General Petraeus.

I invited General Petraeus to come to the US Capitol to meet with Senate Republicans, especially those who were expressing concerns or were unclear on the strategy. Petraeus agreed, and in my conference room in the leader's office, he sat across from the members and, one by one, patiently explained to them how deeply he believed in this strategy. This was, admittedly, somewhat risky because US officers must walk a fine line to get the funding they need to be successful, while never appearing partisan. Petraeus was convincing. He laid out the facts. What he was after followed a clear logic: There could be no political reforms in Iraq without basic security. And under his plan to bring that security, a greater peace would unfold.

We needed to stick together, to present as a unified minority, because we not only had to block the Democrats' effort to force withdrawal, but also needed to pass an emergency supplemental spending bill to fund the surge. This was by far the heaviest lift, as refusing to fund the surge was the Democrats' best path to stopping it. The most credible opponents were Democrats Jack Murtha, a former Marine Corps officer who served on the House Appropriations Committee, and Jim Webb, the former navy secretary, who served on the Senate Armed Services Committee. With a deep familiarity with the military, they introduced bills that could cause the surge to fail while still appearing reasonable—like stipulating funds only if certain conditions were met, when those conditions were impossible to meet with a military already stretched to its limits.

It was a grueling, constant, day-to-day fight. But it was also where the rubber hit the road. This was about protecting the United States and making sure our troops had what they needed to be successful and safe. Thinking they held the high ground, the Democrats seemed to relish the fight. In April, Harry Reid made the very public statement that the war was lost. Once again, Harry had done it. But of all the insensitive and regrettable things that have come out of Harry's mouth, this has to be at the top of the list. Saying the war was lost—when we had thousands of troops in the field, fighting every day for our country—only conveyed the impression that he was pulling for us to lose. As the Democratic leader, he should have chosen his words more carefully. When we heard Reid make this comment, we pounced on it. Someone on my staff pulled the audio and sent it to a reporter. That story quickly got picked up by the *Drudge Report,* where, within a half hour, it was the lead story.

It was, sadly, hardly shocking. Under Reid's leadership, Democrats were doing little other than giving in to the radical left, to organizations like MoveOn, the Out of Iraq Coalition, and others, many of whom are funded by the unions or George Soros or a combination of the two. And it pulled them very much in that direction, believing that we were supposed to just give up and come home.

The most incensing moment of this struggle was the morning I opened the *New York Times* to see a full-page ad, paid for by MoveOn.org, labeling General Petraeus as "General Betray Us." It was so far out of line. General Petraeus had an astounding record of service. He'd spent four years deployed away from his home and family, with nearly three years of service in Iraq. He led the 101st Airborne with distinction in northern Iraq early in the fight and later improved the way we trained Iraqi security forces after early mistakes by the Coalition Provisional Authority. And he'd served as commander of the US Army Combined Arms Center at Fort Leavenworth, where he developed the army's doctrine on counterinsurgency. He literally wrote the book. He'd proved his devotion to this country, and any suggestion to the contrary, at that time, was totally absurd and demonstrably untrue.

I deeply resented the MoveOn ad, paid for by people sitting comfortably in their air-conditioned offices, thousands of miles away from the firefights and the roadside bombs, trying their Washington best to impugn his name, questioning the character of a four-star general who had the respect and admiration of the more than 150,000 brave men and women serving under his command. This childish tactic was an insult to everyone fighting for our freedom in Iraq. General Petraeus had been honest and forthcoming, telling us that his plan would take time to yield results. He had committed to provide us with periodic updates on his progress and his needs, and he had upheld his end of the bargain.

The morning the ad appeared, I brought it to my office. I wanted everyone on my staff to understand that we were not going to allow this. I called in Brian and Stew. "This is classic, liberal overreach," I said, slamming the paper down on my desk where it would stay, in plain sight, for the next few years. "Democrats have allowed their judgment to be clouded by these people. They are looking the other way while this stuff happens. None of us can lose sight of this. And we need to make an issue out of it. Right now." My staff went to work, and when I spoke on the Senate floor fifteen minutes later, I was prepared. "This is what we're up against," I said of the ad. "This is why we need to stick together."

Impossibly, we did it. We stuck together and got enough Democrats on our side so that of the several dozen votes that came to the Senate to defund the surge or compel withdrawal, only one vote was lost. On April 26, 2007, we approved a bill ordering troops to begin coming home from Iraq by October 1. It was an impractical date Democrats pulled out of the air, tied to no circumstances on the ground. As our troops fought on the ground, we participated in a political charade, sending the president a bill we knew he wouldn't sign. This was just the latest example of the Senate under Harry Reid and the Democratic majority—holding votes they knew wouldn't mean anything in order to make a political point. I'm not saying Republicans never staged a show-vote when we were in the majority or that I don't enjoy a good messaging vote from time to time. But under Reid, it had become much too routine. And not only did that diminish the Senate, but when it had to do with questions of war and the safety and support of our men and women in the field, it was particularly vexatious.

A month later, in May, we passed a $120 billion measure to fund the strategy that included eighteen benchmarks that the Iraqis had to meet for us to continue the funding. Within two months, the buildup was complete and operations began. In September, Petraeus and Ryan Crocker, the US ambassador to Iraq, appeared before Congress to report on the progress of the surge, and they came with good news. Since the implementation of the Petraeus plan, the security situation in and around Baghdad had changed dramatically. Attacks on US troops were down. Civilian casualties in Baghdad were down 75 percent. Iraqi refugees were streaming back over the borders to return to their homes. Outside the cities, local leaders were forging agreements among themselves and with US forces to ensure even greater security, and the surge had allowed Sunni tribes to collaborate with American forces to stand up to al-Qaeda. By the end of the year, US–Iraqi coalition forces would be conducting sweeps through once-violent Sunni neighborhoods with little resistance.

There was simply no question that on the military and tactical levels, the Petraeus plan had been a tremendous success, and as we headed into 2008, US service members were beginning to return home with a sense of achievement—no thanks to the politicians and journalists who had attempted to sabotage President Bush's plans.

☆☆☆

Not long after, I called my staff together for our last meeting before breaking for the holidays. "I finally feel after thirty years I've found a job that fits my skill set," I said. It was true. Despite the extreme challenges of my first year as the leader of my party, I ended the year feeling optimistic. We'd held together on funding the surge, and at the end of the session, the Senate passed our version of the energy bill and another relating to the alternative minimum tax. When I stepped into the job, the party's morale was down, but by year's end, I think everyone in my conference felt more hopeful than we had after the disappointing midterm elections. The appreciation my colleagues showed me in this regard meant a lot. During our last policy luncheon the Tuesday before we broke for Christmas recess, I expected everyone to rush out the door. Typically, these sessions end with people in a bad mood because we've stayed too long. Instead, I received a standing ovation.

What I'd learned during this first year was that dealing with senators sometimes requires a strong voice, at other times a delicate touch. In a roomful of former class presidents, there are certainly a lot of egos involved, and it's not exactly easy to keep that many senators in agreement on anything. I think of it in terms of the old 80/20 rule, which applies to how men choose their ties, or women their jewelry. Of all the ties or pieces of jewelry you own, you're likely to choose the same 20 percent 80 percent of the time. That rule certainly applied to the time I spent with my Republican conference. I spent 80 percent of my time with 20 percent of my members and, conversely, only 20 percent of my time with the other 80 percent.

Why? Because some of my colleagues are, let's say, more needful of attention than others. Those who are inclined to be team players frequently resent the attention focused on those who create the problems. Every once in a while, people I long considered team players would become cantankerous, and I always knew that part of the reason was that they were feeling taken for granted. Their sudden stubbornness was a cry for attention. I understood this dynamic, and I respected it. But I had no respect or tolerance for people who had not, it seemed, learned the simple lesson my mother had taught me as a child: never try to make yourself look good or more important by making others look bad. As a Republican, short of setting yourself on fire, there is no better way to draw attention to yourself than to criticize fellow Republicans. Bad-mouthing a Republican administration or Republican leadership in the House or Senate basically guarantees that even a backbench lawmaker will be relevant in the eyes of the press.

This is why a guy like Chuck Hagel, my Republican colleague from Nebraska, was being anointed by some in the press as a potential presidential contender in 2008 after his frequent Bush-bashing sessions with absolutely no prayer of garnering any Republican primary votes. I told my Republican colleagues during the Bush years that if you have a problem you need to talk to Karl Rove, President Bush's right-hand man, not Carl Hulse, the *New York Times*'s senior congressional reporter.

But while there have always been a few senators willing to throw members of their own party under the bus for some press recognition, Senator Jim DeMint from South Carolina took the practice of shooting inside the tent to another level. As a rank-and-file congressman with a relatively moderate record for the conservative South Carolina district he represented, he was regarded as thoughtful enough to make a good Senate candidate in 2004 when the seat opened. I had invited him to Louisville for a big fund-raiser supporting his campaign and found him personable and someone I thought was grounded enough to be a successful senator. For the first four years, he was.

But then DeMint or his staff, I could never figure out which, became something of an innovator in Republican-on-Republican violence. He figured out how to capitalize on criticizing his colleagues not just with the press, but the American people as well. Of course, Jim wouldn't dream of actually confronting a colleague. He was almost submissive in our weekly lunches, preferring to eat in silence rather than inject his point of view. But outside the doors of the Mansfield Room, where we ate, it was another story. Almost daily he would complain to the press about the insufficiently conservative views of his colleagues. In all the years I worked with Jim, I can't remember him ever initiating a confrontational conversation with them. He rarely if ever attempted to persuade a single senator of anything. But he wouldn't blink at the opportunity to bad-mouth them behind their backs to the press.

I dealt with Jim the same way I dealt with the other frustrating parts of being Republican leader, applying what I had learned by studying those who had come before me—party leaders like Mike Mansfield. Remain composed and focused on what really matters. One of the things that really mattered at this moment was that we were headed into an important election year, a presidential one, and the year I'd be running for reelection of my own, to my fifth term in the Senate. I knew we were going to have another disgruntled electorate. The question was, Who were they going to be discontent with? The Democratic majority had set itself up to be the issue in the election. Historically, a new majority can sometimes misinterpret its mandate and overreach, creating a kind of buyer's remorse on the part of the electorate. Going into 2008 I thought there was an outside chance things might just swing our way. Our biggest hurdle remained the situation in Iraq, but Iraq was improving.

And then the financial crisis hit.

CHAPTER FIFTEEN

Bad News

A quiet settled over Speaker Nancy Pelosi's conference room as all eight of us seated around the table stared at Ben Bernanke, the chairman of the Federal Reserve, seated beside Secretary of the Treasury Hank Paulson.

"Let me say it one more time," Bernanke said. "If we don't act now, we won't have an economy by Monday."

It was September 18, 2008, at seven o'clock in the evening, and this meeting of the congressional leadership had been called at the president's request. Like my colleagues in the room—Speaker Pelosi, Barney Frank, Chuck Schumer, Chris Dodd, Harry Reid, John Boehner, Richard Shelby, and a few of our key staff members—I was stunned. They weren't kidding around. "It's bad news, and we need Congress's help," Bernanke continued. "Immediately."

At the core of what he was speaking about was the urgent and unprecedented financial crisis facing our nation. As a result of lax lending practices earlier in the decade, millions of Americans now found themselves either delinquent or unable to cover their mortgages. If this were the only problem, we could have addressed it individually by helping those who were victims of fraud and letting those who made bad judgments or who lied on loan applications pay for their mistakes. But what began as a problem in the subprime mortgage market had spread throughout the entire economy. And the crisis had hit home.

Banks had begun to sell the risky mortgages they'd made. The institutions they sold them to then shopped them around the world. These troubled—and now frozen—assets were on the balance sheets of the businesses that Americans rely on to buy everything from dishwashers to new homes. I had been hearing how the crisis had impacted Americans from the letters I was receiving from constituents. While the crisis had its roots in the actions of a few, the consequences were having an impact on every home in America.

The economic rescue plan that Bernanke and Paulson were suggesting, and which Bush was supporting, was mind-boggling: acquiring $700 billion worth of mortgage-backed securities. Bernanke explained this as necessary—a way to protect the vast majority of Americans from the misdeeds of Wall Street. And my colleagues and I understood. Doing nothing was not an option.

Harry Reid spoke up. "When do you need this?"

"In three days," Paulson said.

Reid scoffed. "We can't go to the toilet in three days around here."

I leaned toward Reid and patted his forearm. "Harry, we can do this."

When the meeting ended, I walked with Kyle, who had attended the meeting with me, down the back hallway that leads from the Speaker's suite to my office. We were both quite shaken.

"I'm obliged to say this to you," Kyle said. "But this is going to be really unpopular. And we're just weeks away from reelection."

"I'm aware of that," I said. No voter was going to like the idea of giving money to the entities that had caused this mess. I could already hear the word "bailout." I also knew what inaction would mean. It would be impossible to take out loans for college tuition, cars, and new homes. That would trigger a corresponding collapse in manufacturing and services that could wipe out savings and lead to massive job losses.

I stopped and looked at Kyle. "I don't think this will take me out," I said. "But I do understand this is a huge problem. We can't afford not to act. It's too big. This is a crisis, and in a crisis, leaders are supposed to step up and confront things. We don't have the time to act like we normally do—to take our time and deliberate. We can't afford to wait."

"All right," Kyle said. "What do you want me to do?"

"Get a team together. Let's get to work on this immediately."

For the next few days, with the task we faced, my office had the atmosphere of a wake. I called on the help of my policy director, Rohit Kumar. At just thirty-three years of age, he was one of the smartest guys I knew, especially when it came to getting a handle on what we were facing here. By the Saturday after that meeting, the White House and Treasury had drafted language for the legislation they wanted Congress to consider, and then a marathon session began; the goal was to shape the final bill that all parties could agree on. The work was approached in a truly bicameral, bipartisan way. In these meetings, there was an overwhelming sense of anger at the forces and decisions that had gotten us here, and a determination that we would do everything to stop it. When there's a fire threatening to burn your neighbor's house down, you don't go and lecture him about the hazards of keeping gas cans in the basement. You help him put the fire out before it destroys his home and then spreads to the next. Everyone understood the stakes, and there was a general agreement that we had to do what needed to be done to save our economy.

A team of staff met every day, all day, and well into most nights. By the end of the week, we had drafted a bill that satisfied everyone in the room. It was called the Troubled Asset Relief Program, or TARP, and it did what was necessary to bring us back from the brink of financial collapse, authorizing the purchase of $700 billion in troubled assets by the government. Ironing out the details had been no easy matter. Though we had all agreed to put our own political needs aside, objections to the bill still split along predictable ideological lines. The Republicans thought there were too many restrictions, and the Democrats wanted more oversight. We knew it would be called a bailout, and we would need both parties on board for it to pass.

John McCain's decision a few days later to suspend his presidential campaign to return to DC surprised everyone and heightened the sense that things were falling apart pretty quickly. His opponent, Senator Barack Obama, then said he'd come back too, and Bush set up a meeting to discuss the financial crisis with members of the administration and congressional leaders at the White House.

We gathered in the Cabinet Room at the White House, seated around the large conference table, in front of windowed doors offering a view of the Rose Garden. President Bush welcomed everyone, and following the protocol that dictates meetings such as this, he invited Speaker Pelosi to speak.

"Thank you, Mr. President," she said. "But Senator Obama will be speaking on behalf of us today." For several minutes, and with no notes, Obama laid out an understanding of what we faced, and a promise to deliver the votes we needed to get TARP passed. Everyone in the room was spellbound. Not only because Obama had so masterfully shown how well he understood the issue—delivering what sounded like third-draft prose without any notes—but because the Democrats, in breaking protocol by turning over the floor to him, had shown how much they were behind him.

McCain said he was also on board. When we left the room, I was sure of two things. Even though support for TARP would be bipartisan, we Republicans would largely take the electoral hit come the November elections. And the other, having just watched how that meeting unfolded: come election night, we were in a whole lot of trouble.

☆☆☆

Three days later, in a move that stupefied the entire Senate, if not every American who'd been reading the newspaper, the House of Representatives rejected the bill we'd created. It was an act of stunning defiance. Some members of my staff like to say that I go through the five stages of grief—from denial to acceptance—in about one nanosecond. In many ways this trait has been a blessing in my work, as it allows me to make clear-eyed decisions at times when others are overcome with emotion. The flip side, however, is that my equanimity while others are experiencing anger can make it appear as if I don't care, or care a lot less than those who are so mad they're kicking chairs or slamming their fists against tables (or, because this is the Senate, shaking their heads and frowning quite aggressively). This was just one of those times. Inside, I was furious. Doing nothing, as the House seemed intent on doing, was not a sustainable course of action. Anyone questioning that just had to look to the US stock market, which had begun to plunge as the vote went down. By the end of the day, the Dow Jones Industrial Average had fallen more than 5 percent, and other indexes fell even more sharply. That night I felt so unsettled I had trouble sleeping. While the House vote came and went, the threat to our economy had not.

But my anger was not what people saw the next morning, when I calmly got off the elevator at the Capitol. Brian McGuire was waiting with my morning remarks, but I didn't need them, because I already knew exactly what I wanted to say. I went to the Senate floor and, speaking off the cuff, I delivered my thoughts. I assured everyone that Congress would act swiftly and decisively to protect millions of ordinary Americans from the aftershocks of a credit crisis they had no hand in causing, but which threatened to reach into every single household in the country. I assured them that the members of the congressional leadership were continuing to assess the legislative path forward, and that one thing was clear: we would work together to create a bipartisan solution. And we weren't going home until we got to yes. We'd failed the day before, but I wasn't going to let us fail on this day. I assured them that Harry Reid and I both understood that we had to work together on this, to get this rescue plan passed. And we intended to do both.

I returned to my office. Later, Stefanie Muchow knocked lightly on my door. "Boss?"

"Yes, Stef."

My parents, A. M. and Dean McConnell, on their wedding day, September 20, 1940. They had met in Birmingham, Alabama, and my dad was persistent in their courtship, convincing Mom to call off an engagement and follow him to Houston, where the photo was taken.

Age four, having come through my ordeal with polio happy and healthy, all thanks to my mother.

With my dad in front of Mom's sister's house in Five Points, Alabama, 1944, where I would soon be stricken by polio and from where I would regularly travel the fifty-nine miles to Warm Springs, Georgia, for treatment. Dad was home on leave from basic training at Fort Bliss, Texas. He entered combat in March of 1945 and remained in the fight until the end of the war in Europe—VE Day, May 8, 1945.

Fifth-grade class photo at James L. Fleming Elementary School in Augusta, Georgia, where my dad had been transferred after the war. Note the "I Like Ike" pin affixed to my collar. Four years later I would watch both party conventions gavel to gavel, including the one that renominated Ike.

With the baseball glove I bought partly with money made mowing lawns in Augusta in 1955. (Dad and I split the cost.) Together, my father and I attended no fewer than thirty-five Augusta Tigers games that summer. This was also the year my favorite team, the Brooklyn Dodgers, won its only World Series title. I would later attend the same Louisville high school that Dodgers captain Pee Wee Reese graduated from some years before.

My 1960 high school graduation photo from duPont Manual High School, then the largest public high school in Kentucky. At the time of the photo I had been elected student body president after a come-from-behind win powered by endorsements I'd lined up from cheerleaders and jocks.

Originally published in *Thoroughbred* 1963

With Barry Goldwater at the University of Louisville in the fall of 1962. As president of the College Republicans, I was stunned when Goldwater accepted my invitation to speak to the U of L student body, but then realized that as head of the National Republican Senatorial Committee (which I later ran myself), Goldwater was likely already planning to be in town to campaign for Republican senator Thruston Morton. Years later, Goldwater and I would overlap in the Senate during my first two and his last two years in office.

Louisville *Cardinal*

As an intern for Congressman Gene Snyder in the summer of 1963 after my junior year in college. The highlight of the summer was witnessing Martin Luther King's "I Have a Dream" speech from the steps of the US Capitol. I couldn't hear a word, but the moment was unforgettable.

Ceremonial swearing-in by Vice President George H. W. Bush for my first term on January 3, 1985, with my parents and daughters. From left, Elly, twelve; Claire, nine; Dean; AM; and Porter, six. I have used the large family Bible acquired in 1904 by my grandparents, Mamie and Big Dad, each time I've been sworn in for a new term.

With my role model Senator John Sherman Cooper during my first term. I won Cooper's Senate seat two decades after interning in his office. A close friend and Georgetown neighbor of JFK's, Cooper was appointed to sit on the Warren Commission by LBJ.

Answering questions in El Salvador with an election oversight team I chaired at the request of President Bush in 1989.

SENATOR McCONNELL DISPENSES WITH HIS CRITICS

A 1996 cartoon from my hometown paper. Many of the most cutting cartoons about me over the years now hang on my office wall in Washington. This one relates to a response I published attacking a columnist for criticizing Elaine.

US Senator Mitch McConnell Archives

Greeting President Reagan with Elaine Chao sometime during our courtship and toward the end of Reagan's second term.

Richard Ellis

With Senator John McCain debating campaign finance reform on *Meet the Press* in 1997. McCain and I were bitter foes on the issue, but had become close friends over the years and had teamed up on many other important issues since.

On the West Front of the Capitol prior to the swearing-in of President George W. Bush. As chairman of the Joint Congressional Committee on Inaugural Ceremonies, I was the first person to officially introduce Bush to the nation as America's forty-third president.

In Afghanistan in the fall of 2003 with members of the Kentucky National Guard and the Kentucky state flag. This was the first of nine trips to Afghanistan and six to Iraq since the 9/11 attacks.

With General David Petraeus in my Capitol office around the time I enlisted him to help sell President Bush's surge strategy to a new Democratic majority. It was a tough sell, since Democrats had just claimed the majority, they believed, for opposing the president's actions in Iraq.

With Ted Kennedy at the McConnell Center in Louisville in 2006. Kennedy added a personal touch by bringing a framed photo of his brother Jack and Senator Cooper. On it he wrote, "To the McConnell Scholars, With great respect and warmest wishes to the past, present and future McConnell Scholars in their pursuit of leadership, statesmanship and service. I know how much President Kennedy admired John Sherman Cooper in the Senate, and so did I. Mitch McConnell is part of that great Kentucky tradition of public service, and it's a privilege to serve with him today (not that we always agree on the issues)."

Speaking at the annual Fancy Farm Picnic in far western Kentucky in 2010. A Kentucky tradition dating from the 1880s and a must for aspiring statewide politicians, Fancy Farm has featured two vice presidential candidates and countless other politicians over the years. Hosted by a local Catholic church, it was once described by the *Guinness Book of World Records* as the world's largest picnic.

With my tailgating buddies outside Papa John's Cardinal Stadium watching Louisville play Syracuse in 2011. Louisville won the game 27–10.

Meeting Nobel laureate Aung San Suu Kyi in person for the first time in early 2012 at her home in Rangoon after two decades of indirect communication. Suu Kyi would visit the McConnell Center later that year.

With columnists George Will and Charles Krauthammer in the Fox News studio in Washington, DC, having one of our frequent discussions about the Washington Nationals. Few things mix better than politics and baseball.

Shane Noem

At the Campbellsville, Kentucky, annual Fourth of July parade with Elaine on a typical Saturday during my 2014 campaign. A fantastic campaigner, Elaine has become a source of strength and encouragement on the trail and a fixture around the commonwealth.

The moment when we learned Joni Ernst had won her race in Iowa and I would be majority leader. Pictured from left are Kyle Simmons, Stef Muchow, Terry Carmack, John Ashbrook, and my campaign manager, Josh Holmes. Josh's wife, Blair, snapped the photo at just the right moment.

President Barack Obama outside the Oval Office on the West Colonnade with the new majority leader of the Senate, November 7, 2014. As usual, the president is doing most of the talking.

"Just thought you'd like to know that your speech seemed to work. The markets are rebounding."

I felt the weight lift, at least lightly, from my shoulders. "Well, I've had some good responses to floor speeches before," I said. "But that's certainly a first."

Over the next few days, we were back in all-night sessions rewriting the bill to appease the members of the House. On October 3, 2008, just a few weeks after that meeting with Bernanke and Paulson, President Bush signed the Troubled Asset Relief Program into law. It had been a very difficult process, but when it was over, we had done our job. We had saved the economy from complete peril (and in fact, the money given away through TARP has since been repaid with interest). At the same time, the general election was just six weeks away. I knew that my work on getting TARP passed had been necessary, but it was also politically risky. While everyone involved vowed not to politicize the issue, within twenty-four hours of the bill's passage, ads were running on Kentucky television lambasting me for my role in giving away taxpayer dollars to big banks. I didn't question what we'd done. TARP was absolutely essential, and I had done what I'd come to the Senate to do more than two decades earlier—make decisions based on what I believed was best for the country, not my own political future. But, admittedly, I couldn't help but worry about my chances of reelection. Around this time, just before returning to Kentucky to wrap up my campaign for reelection, I gathered with everyone in my office for our annual staff photo. I'd just received the news that after my vote on TARP, I had gone from a thirteen-point lead to a four-point lead.

"I sure hope this isn't a farewell photo," I said, just before the blink of the flash.

☆☆☆

I might sum up my race for reelection this way: In both my 1996 and 2002 campaigns, there were approximately four million people living in Kentucky, I was not the Republican leader, and we spent about

$6 million in each race. In 2008, there were still about four million people living in Kentucky, I was the leader, and we had to spend over $25 million.

Why? Because four years earlier, a very talented former South Dakota congressman named John Thune took on Tom Daschle, the Senate Democratic leader, and for the first time since 1952, a sitting Senate party leader was defeated. Prior to this, there was a sense of détente that guided the reelection campaigns for party leaders, likely stemming from the extremely difficult and expensive work required to even try to unseat one. But since Daschle's loss, elections against party leaders have become highly competitive, all-out battles that, with respect to the money spent and the length of the campaign, are more reminiscent of presidential campaigns than runs for the Senate.

One significant obstacle I—and every Republican running for office—faced that year was the overwhelming disapproval of outgoing President George W. Bush. He had the same standing as Harry Truman in 1952 and Lyndon Johnson in 1968, who were each in the White House at the time of unpopular wars that drained their political capital. Even though they weren't on the ballot, America's opinion of the job they'd done had affected their party's outcome in the next elections. I feared the same would hold true for Bush. Not only was he about to leave office with low approval ratings, but his unpopularity had enabled the opposition, creating, in 2008, a groundswell of dissatisfaction.

Despite public opinion in the last days of his presidency, I think George W. Bush was an outstanding wartime president. This era of instant news makes keeping public opinion on your side while sustaining a prolonged military action a very difficult thing to do. Imagine if you were Eisenhower on D-Day. The parachutes are falling over northern France, you're getting pinned down on Omaha Beach, while back in the studios at CNN and Fox News, retired World War I generals, the Wesley Clarks of their day, are second-guessing every move you make. Had we operated then the way we do today, let's just say I likely wouldn't have been wearing my "I Like Ike" button back in 1952.

But when it comes to the war on terror that Bush was forced to confront, the measure of success has to be the level of security here at home. And Bush's decision to go on the offensive, in both Iraq and Afghanistan, and to create the programs and policies to combat al-Qaeda, is the number one reason there have been no successful mass casualty attacks on American soil since 9/11. His strategy didn't always go perfectly, but that can't be expected, because there is no perfection in armed conflict. There can't be, because the other guys shoot back.

In political combat, the other guys shoot back too, and my own fight for reelection was starting to feel less like strategic warfare and more like mortal combat. My opponent Bruce Lunsford was a wealthy businessman who could afford to self-fund and write himself million-dollar checks when needed—which is awfully helpful. As I always say, the three most important words in politics are "cash on hand." The campaign itself seemed interminable. Not only did we spend a whole lot more than previous years, but we started a lot earlier and faced a much more aggressive deluge, especially, for the first time, from out-of-state forces. Well-funded groups like MoveOn.org, which has raised several million dollars for Democratic candidates, and VoteVets.org were on television as early as February of 2007—one and a half years before the actual election—accusing me of everything from killing soldiers to denying kids health care. The Democratic Senatorial Campaign Committee (DSCC) spent a significant amount in Kentucky alone. The attacks on me became so absurdly personal that one morning, after we aired a TV spot about my experience overcoming polio, I opened the *Courier-Journal* to see an article suggesting that I was lying about having been a Little League all-star. It was a concentrated, major, and well-funded attempt to soften me up for the election while trying to break my spirit.

And it hit home, literally. You might call the Highlands neighborhood where I live "the Berkeley of Kentucky." Elaine's and my votes are among the few I get in my precinct. But during this campaign, I felt particularly beleaguered. In the six years the war had endured, hundreds of thousands of people had taken part in antiwar marches in cities like New York, San Francisco, and Chicago. The protests in Louisville were more modest but also more targeted. Instead of gathering in the center of the city, they took to my own front yard. The first group of picketers arrived with their signs the week of the Kentucky Derby, held in Louisville the first Saturday each May. Later that summer, hundreds gathered one night at Bellarmine University, a few blocks away, and marched from there to my house, bellowing and screaming. They took over my front yard and blocked our street. The police eventually came, and the group peacefully disbanded, but smaller groups were present on and off throughout the following months. Not only did Elaine and I worry about being confronted by protesters hanging out on our small front lawn, but driving home from the airport each weekend, we passed signs on lawn after lawn in my neighborhood, all saying the same thing: "Ditch Mitch."

The bad news didn't stop there. In the summer, as I was preparing for Fancy Farm, the venerable Alaska senator Ted Stevens, the longest-serving Republican senator, became embroiled in a corruption case and was eventually indicted on seven charges of making false statements about lucrative gifts he'd received from corporate executives in the remodeling of his house in Girdwood, Alaska. (Stevens would go on to be convicted, just before the election, and defeated. He would later be exonerated, saving his reputation if not his seat. Years later, in a conversation with Brendan Sullivan, a noted white-collar defense lawyer in Washington, Sullivan told me this was the worst example of prosecutorial abuse he'd seen in his entire career.) Meanwhile, the recession we suffered was having ill effects throughout the globe, and John McCain was taking a battering in the polls.

I stopped reading the news, and every morning, seeing the blinking red light indicating a new e-mail on my BlackBerry, I knew it was likely an update from someone on my staff reporting the results of the night's tracking polls, and I was almost too afraid to read my new messages. One morning I decided to leave them for a while, and after breakfast, I called Kyle.

"How are the numbers?"

"Haven't looked yet," he said. "Can't quite bear it."

"Me neither."

"Sad," he said. "Two grown men living in fear of a BlackBerry."

☆☆☆

On October 20, 2008, I embarked on a two-week, four-thousand-mile, sixty-eight-stop bus tour that ended November 2, just two days before Election Day. Elaine came along for the first leg of it, and as we climbed onto the bus that first morning and headed out, I was once again struck by the breathtaking beauty of Kentucky. I'd had tough races before, but this one was, at its best, a pure toss-up, the outcome very much in doubt. The first stop was in Greensburg, a town of just a few thousand residents about eighty miles south of Louisville. As the bus slowed to a stop, we saw the crowd gathered for our rally in the town's public square.

I turned to Billy Piper, who was at my side. "What am I going to say?" I'm not sure whom the question surprised more, him or me. I'm never happier than when I'm on the campaign trail, meeting people, talking Kentucky issues, and I've never had to ask a staffer for talking points before addressing a crowd like the one gathered that day in the cold.

Billy made a valiant effort to answer my question. "Well, sir, you could talk about the energy crisis and our plan. You know, 'Find more. Use less.' And then, you know, how Lunsford—"

I stopped him. "Do me a favor. Clear the bus for me."

"Clear it?"

"Yes. Ask everyone to leave, even the driver. Give me a few minutes alone in here."

After the bus doors shut, I took a seat, relishing the silence. There were just two weeks left in the race, and all eyes were on Kentucky. The national press was standing in wait. They smelled blood in the water, and if I was going down, they wanted to be there to see it. The pressure was enormous, but so were the stakes. Barack Obama seemed likely to take the White House. The platform on which he was running included some of the most far-left policies I would ever have to face as a senator. I had been working for the last twenty-four years to protect the nation from exactly the type of changes I knew he'd be eager to enact. And I had been working hard for the last two years leading my party. It was now my job to work as hard as I could to win this fight. There was simply too much riding on this. It was not the time to retreat.

When I opened my eyes, I saw Billy's head appearing and disappearing in the front window. He was jumping up and down, trying to see inside the bus to figure out what on earth I was doing. Standing up, I felt absolutely sure of what I was doing. I pushed open the bus door and walked into the chilly, late-October air. I saw Elaine shaking hands, and the stage from where I'd speak, and the people and families who had come to offer their support and share some stories of their own. As I walked toward the crowd, I was greeted by the sound of applause.

Billy stopped me and leaned to speak in my ear. "Sir, just to let you know, the tracker is here." He was referring to the young man from Lunsford's campaign who would follow us, coming to every event to film me, in hopes I would make a mistake they could exploit. "I got a volunteer ready to block his camera."

"No need," I said. "Let him film."

"Sir?"

I started up the steps to the stage. "Let him. I won't be making a mistake."

I didn't that day, or any of the days that followed, because I didn't allow myself to get distracted or down. Instead, I knew that I had to bring the two qualities to this race that had guided me throughout my life, from my decision to methodically build my skills before taking on a Democratic incumbent in a state like Kentucky, to my decision against a run for Senate majority leader at age sixty knowing it may be years before I had another shot: patience and perseverance. They had been the hallmarks of my career, and for the last few weeks of the election, I employed both.

On the night of the election, I rented a suite at the Galt House in downtown Louisville. I arrived a few hours before the polls closed to a whirl of activity. In one room, staff members were setting up phones so they could call into the precincts for the latest results. Others were plugging in computers, and someone was setting up equipment so we could project the results on a wall. At about 5:30 p.m., just before the night got started, I found Stef. "Gather the staff," I said. "I want to say a few words."

"You sure you don't want to wait until after? Until we get the results?"

I knew she was trying to give me an out, to protect me from having to go down and face my staff when we were all still so unsure if I was going to win. Three days earlier, I had called Brian McGuire, my speechwriter, to ask him to do something I'd never asked of anyone before: write me a concession speech. I'd told him not to share this request with anyone else, as I didn't want to discourage the others. But I also wanted to be prepared in the case of a loss—especially with regard to expressing, more than anything else, how deeply grateful I was to the people of Kentucky. They had allowed me to do the one thing I've wanted to do more than anything else, and for a very long time. My sense of gratitude to them wouldn't change based on the number of votes I received that night, and the same was true about my feelings toward my staff.

"My message to them is going to be the exact same, whether we win or lose," I said to Stef. "I'll see you in fifteen minutes."

There were about a hundred people waiting in the Segell Room when I arrived, many of them seated at one of the round dinner tables.

"Everybody put your BlackBerrys down for a minute. This won't take too long, and I want you to hear what I have to say." This announcement got their attention, as my staffers are rarely asked to put down their beloved BlackBerrys. "I know we're looking at a potential loss tonight," I continued. "But no matter what happens, I want to thank every one of you for your work. And for your dedication to what we're trying to do here, and for everything we—not me, but we—have accomplished these last few years. Now stay in your seat, please, as I'd like to come and thank each of you personally."

It took a long time to stop and personally tell each member of my staff how much I appreciated them. By the time I got to Billy, I was no longer able to hold back my tears. If it had been a year of bad news for me, it had been a particularly hard year for him. His mother had been diagnosed with lung cancer, and she'd died in the midst of his work on the campaign. He'd been with me since he graduated from college, and I knew what losing her meant to him. We were both only children, and Billy's dad had died in 2000. I considered him as much a part of my family as my daughters, and with little success, I tried to keep it together as I told him how much not only his work, but he personally, meant to me. It was equally emotional for him, and I could see how uncomfortable he felt as he wiped away a tear.

"Okay, boss," he said. "Can I go now? I gotta go upstairs to see if we're winning this thing."

CHAPTER SIXTEEN

Professor Obama

I t was a proud moment for our country, given our original sin of slavery, to witness Barack Obama elected president of the United States. His victory demonstrated one of the finest qualities of our country: here, all things are possible. I called Obama to congratulate him, and when he returned my phone call a few days later, I was standing in the cereal aisle of a Kroger supermarket in Louisville.

"Hello, Mr. President," I said as the people around me juggled children and picked out their Cheerios. We had a friendly and cordial conversation during which I told the president I was eager to work with him. I was glad he didn't gloat, which he had every right to do because the results of the election were devastating for Republicans.

Brian's concession speech landed in a garbage can at the Galt House. I won my reelection handily, by over 100,000 votes and a comfortable six points, and in fact, it was my third-largest victory, winning 86 out of 120 counties. I was, along with Susan Collins from Maine, the only Republican incumbent targeted by the DSCC to keep my seat.

But, with eight seats going to Democrats, the good news stopped there. We were down to a minority of just forty-one in the Senate. Meanwhile in the House, Democrats increased their majority by eleven. Not long after my win, Hillary Clinton called to congratulate me.

"Thanks for the visit to Hazard," I joked, referring to the at least half a dozen campaign trips either she or her husband, or both, had made in support of my opponent. "You and Bill sure did everything you could to make sure I didn't win." Hillary laughed—but I would later, during her term as secretary of state, successfully convince her to come speak at the McConnell Center by reminding her of these efforts to unseat me.

I suppose the one salve was that I was reelected without opposition to my second term as Republican leader, and with a Democrat in the White House, I was, for all intents and purposes, considered the most powerful Republican in the nation. But with the Democrats holding at least fifty-eight seats (possibly fifty-nine—the race in Minnesota between Al Franken and Norm Coleman would not be decided for another few months), effectively, I had very little power at all.

I invited President Obama to join the members of our conference for lunch at the Capitol soon after he assumed office. After a long and rough campaign season, it was essential to begin the session, and Obama's first term, acknowledging that there were some areas where we were in broad agreement. After sharing a meal, President Obama spoke a few words, and I then opened the room to questions. Johnny Isakson, my colleague from Georgia, rose to speak. "Mr. President, I just want you to know that every night before I go to bed, I pray for you, your family, and your success." It was an incredibly simple and powerful thing to say. The president's election was a stunning American success, and Senator Isakson's words beautifully summed up what all of us in the room were thinking.

On a policy level, however, in the wake of his landslide victory, I was very worried about the direction of our country. I knew from history that a combination of a troubled economy and one-party control of the White House and Congress often results in an explosion of legislation and government control, such as we saw in the New Deal and, later, the Great Society. I worried we were headed in that direction.

It wouldn't take long for Obama to prove me right. A lot of people ask me what President Obama is really like. I tell them all the same thing. He's no different in private than in public. He's like the kid in your class who exerts a hell of a lot of effort making sure everyone thinks he's the smartest one in the room. He talks down to people, whether in a meeting among colleagues in the White House or addressing the nation. And he's simply a very liberal guy who is determined to move the country toward the kind of progressive ideal that Western European societies embraced decades ago. He has a bold progressive agenda, and if he can't get what he wants through the legislative branch, he'll work to do so through the bureaucracy. For someone who came up through the Senate, the president's indifference (or hostility, depending on how you look at it) to Congress is curious. Knowing I could do little to change his perspective on things, my goal has been to stop him when I think he's pushing ideas that are bad for the country.

And to do that, I needed everyone in my conference to stand firmly behind that mission. Since becoming leader, I have, every January, hosted a one-day retreat for the members of my conference. The purpose is to come together, look ahead to the year facing us, and decide on our priorities. This year, the retreat was held on January 9 in the Library of Congress, and the weather was perfect for the occasion: cold, dreary, and rainy. As I welcomed my forty colleagues, sheets of rain hammered the windows, obstructing our view of the Capitol. Nobody was in a good mood.

What we were facing was best summed up by Obama's new chief of staff Rahm Emanuel, who said, soon after his election: "You never want a serious crisis to go to waste." What he meant was that Obama and his team were going to exploit the financial crisis still gripping our economy to enact radical changes. With Democrats in control of both houses by large margins, he could do pretty much whatever he wanted.

And yet I believed there was still reason to hope.

Here's what I knew: in 2008, the American electorate was eager to turn the page on the Bush years and go in a new direction, and Obama was an exciting pick. But it was also true that Obama was so far to the left—in 2007, the *National Journal* released a study finding him the most liberal politician in the Senate—that his policies might not be as popular as he thought. Yes, Americans wanted something new in the short term, but our country is and has always been a nation that is to the right of center. While Obama may have satiated the need for change in the moment, when it came to what Americans wanted in the long term, it was not the far-reaching government control that he championed. At the retreat, I counseled my colleagues, first and foremost, to have patience. I was a young man in the Watergate era, and had been around long enough to know there's no such thing as a permanent majority, despite the joyous proclamations to this effect by the mainstream media, who were all but predicting the imminent demise of the Republican Party. *Newsweek* even ran a cover story declaring, "We Are All Socialists Now."

But this was a very short-term perspective on things. I reminded my colleagues that Americans, fatigued after eight years of Bush, voted for change, but the country itself had not changed. We hadn't suddenly become France. There were still a hundred million Republicans in America who were counting on us to represent them. To do that, we had to stick together. Starting immediately.

On the day Obama was sworn in, he announced his intention to close the detention facility at Guantánamo Bay by the end of the year. This was hasty beyond belief, and with grave implications for our nation's security, decisions about what we were going to do with the prisoners were decisions we needed to get right. Obama had no plan. And folks in Kentucky didn't want these guys living in their backyards any more than people in the rest of the country did. Then, a month into his presidency, Congress enacted a stimulus package of almost $1 trillion—a figure that still boggles the mind. In Clinton's first year in office, he proposed a $19.5 billion stimulus that Congress easily rejected for being too expensive. Obama's package was going to cost taxpayers more than fifty times that, and when coupled with the economic rescue package, could add as much debt in one year as about half the federal budget.

As abysmal as this idea was, it paled in comparison to Obama's plan to take on the great, unfinished task of all American liberals: government takeover of the health-care system. Our one salvation was that the Democrats were one vote short of the sixty-vote supermajority that would enable them to do whatever they wanted. I kept reminding myself and my colleagues of this, urging us all to remain focused. Forty-one wasn't a lot, but when it came down to it, it was enough if we all stuck together. These were the thoughts on my mind one morning, just as spring arrived. It was going to be a good day. The cherry blossoms were in bloom. I was scheduled to speak at the unveiling of a bust of Sojourner Truth, the famous abolitionist, recently installed at the Capitol. Later in the afternoon, I would welcome Howard Baker and Bob Dole for a meeting with a few other senators. I was preparing to head to the Sojourner Truth ceremony when Stef buzzed to tell me I had a phone call.

"Take a message, please, Stef," I said.

"It's Senator Specter," Stef said. "He says it's important."

☆☆☆

"Shut the door," I said to Kyle.

"Am I fired?" Kyle joked as he closed my office door and took a seat across from me.

"Arlen Specter is changing sides."

"What do you mean?"

"He just called. He's leaving the party. He's going over to their side. He said he can't win his reelection in Pennsylvania as a Republican," I said. "He's facing a challenger in the GOP primary. He took a poll and found he can't beat him. They're killing him for his vote on the stimulus. He's switching sides to try to win as a Democrat."

"He said that out loud?"

"Yes. He took a poll."

"What did you say to him?"

"I told him that he's had a long and distinguished career. But that if he did this, it would be the only thing he would ever be remembered for." I buzzed Stef in. "I need you to call a meeting of leadership," I said.

"Yes, sir," she said. "And you're expected now at the unveiling. There's about five hundred people there waiting."

"Fine. Tell leadership to meet here in thirty minutes."

Stef looked at me. "You know you won't be done with the ceremony by then."

I headed out the door. "Come and get me in twenty-five minutes."

I sat onstage at the awards ceremony, beside the First Lady and Speaker Nancy Pelosi, amazed at my own composure. This was devastating. The race in Minnesota between Al Franken and Norm Coleman was still being decided. If that went to Franken, which was looking increasingly possible, Specter's decision would get the Democrats to that magic number of sixty. I was lost in my thoughts when I saw Stef, her face blushed crimson, trying to remain unnoticed as she tiptoed across the stage, in front of a crowd of hundreds, and handed me a note that simply read: "It's time."

Although I didn't relish the task, it was my job as leader. I had to go speak to my colleagues. The news had already gotten out, and as I stood in front of the quiet room, the shock and disappointment was nearly palpable. Unfortunately, the feeling of being demoralized would persist for weeks. In May, Richard Holbrooke, Obama's special envoy for Afghanistan and Pakistan, conducted a classified briefing for senators on the situation in those countries. After Holbrooke held forth on the mistakes of the previous administration, I had to speak up.

"I've been around here awhile and I have to be quite candid with you," I said. "Those were the single most partisan comments I have ever heard from a US official in a classified setting in twenty-four years. We haven't been attacked here in seven and a half years and some of us think it isn't an accident, and you all better hope nothing happens on your watch. It's time to turn the campaign machine off. This is governing, and it's difficult, and this kind of partisanship is completely inappropriate." As I walked out of that room, feeling utterly annoyed, I couldn't help but think, I know when the bad news started: Hurricane Katrina.

But when was it going to stop?

☆☆☆

On June 30, 2009, Al Franken, the comedian and former cast member on *Saturday Night Live*, was declared the winner of his race against Norm Coleman by a margin of 312 votes. He was sworn into the Senate a week later, thus giving the Democrats a supermajority of sixty and making Obama's plan to take over health care all but inevitable.

I did what I like to do in times of great stress or annoyance: I went to watch baseball. The Nationals were playing at home, and I invited Brian McGuire, my speechwriter, to join me for a game. Brian had an interest in baseball that rivaled my own, and he'd been an integral member of my team since I'd become the leader. I wanted to thank him for his efforts. One area in which he'd been particularly helpful was what I considered to be the most important speaking responsibilities I'd had since becoming leader: offering eulogies. Being asked to deliver a eulogy for colleagues like Senators Robert Byrd and Ted Stevens was a request I took very seriously. I also, very sadly, offered eulogies for people who were close to me not professionally, but personally. People like Mary Gabriel Carmack, the wife of my aide and good friend Terry Carmack, who died far too young. And—although this one would come a few years later—my dear friend Judge John Heyburn. I'd met John in 1971, when we were both young men working on Tom Emberton's campaign for governor. He and his wife, Martha, were two of the people closest to me in the world. Having to say good-bye to people like him and Mary Gabriel, to honor the lives they'd led, was not something I could have done without Brian's help.

When Brian and I arrived at Nationals Park and took our seats, I saw columnist Charles Krauthammer in a nearby section. I like Charles, as a friend, and as an intellect. He's certainly overcome a fair amount of adversity—he was paralyzed after a diving accident during his first year at Harvard Medical School—and he provides those of us in the trenches with inspiration through his writings.

"What do you think?" I asked, assuming he knew I was speaking about Franken's election, and what that meant for Republicans.

"I think we should pass a Senate resolution saying the Nationals can't trade Nick Johnson."

I would far rather have taken up that issue than what I knew was coming down the road: Obamacare. Everybody knew there were problems with the current health-care system. Costs were out of control and too many people were being squeezed out of the market. But there were intelligent paths to reform. We could end junk lawsuits against doctors and hospitals, which drive up costs. We could encourage healthy choices such as prevention and wellness programs, which hold costs down. We could further lower costs by letting consumers buy coverage across state lines and allow small businesses to band together for lower insurance rates. But the fact of the matter was that when it came to the real problems with the system, Obama's health-care bill didn't solve any of them. Rather, it used them as an excuse to undermine the very things that people around the world admire most about the American health-care system—the wide array of choices, the constant innovations in technology and treatments, and the high quality of care.

The proposed Affordable Care Act, which quickly became known as Obamacare, was awful. This so-called cure—to overhaul the entire system—was worse than the disease. The cost would be staggering, and it was extremely unwise to ask the government to take this on when it was straining under the health care it was already responsible for, Medicare and Medicaid. And few Americans believed that allowing the folks in charge of the IRS to take over all of American health care, as the Affordable Care Act set out to do, was a step in the right direction.

My goal was clear from the beginning: Because this was the worst bill to come across my desk in the nearly three decades I'd served in the Senate, and because this was not anything like a bill we would have enacted, I didn't want a single Republican to vote for it. It had to be very obvious to the voters which party was responsible for this terrible policy, and I wanted a clear line of demarcation—they were for this, and we were against it. The best we could do was to ensure there was no confusion in the public's mind come the next election that this was in any way a bipartisan proposal, because it didn't deserve bipartisan support. I counseled my colleagues: "Don't muddy this up." Just one Republican choosing to support it—wanting to appear to be on the yes side of a law that was all but inevitable—threatened to bring others along, and allowed the other side to then label the measure bipartisan. So the strategy, simply stated, was to keep everybody together in opposition.

If only its execution were as simple. Over the next several months, this task consumed nearly all of my time. Early on, the administration reached out to members of our conference who were deeply involved in health-care issues, like Chuck Grassley, who was ranking on the Finance Committee; Mike Enzi, who was ranking on the Health, Education, Labor and Pensions Committee (two committees that have major health-care jurisdiction) and, of course, Olympia Snowe, who had often voted with Democrats in the past. In addition to having one-on-one meetings with them to encourage them to stay with the party on this, I was also meeting every Wednesday afternoon with my entire conference, trying to build the view that we were all in this together. I brought in experts to help us make sense of what was a very complicated bill (one that would end up being 2,074 pages long). One of the things I've discovered about being leader is that people do, at least most of the time, pay attention to what I say, so every morning in my remarks on the Senate floor, I was out there pounding away on the bill. Good politics is repetition, and just when I started to bore myself to tears, I knew I'd begun to drive the message home.

Conduct in the Senate Chamber has always been guided by rules of decorum. Regardless of the intensity of disagreement on any matter, senators are expected to speak to one another with respect. It has always been this way, since the Senate's inception, and very rarely throughout history has anyone acted with insolence. (One notable exception, of course, was the day in 1856 when Representative Preston Brooks of South Carolina nearly caned to death Senator Charles Sumner of Massachusetts after Sumner had insulted Brooks's state during a debate about slavery. But that's another story.) The majority party presides over the Senate, and the role of the presiding officer is often assigned to relatively new members. It's not a great job to sit in that chair for an hour, but it helps the newer members get a better handle on how the place operates. During one of my speeches on Obamacare, Senator Al Franken was presiding. As I addressed him, which one does when speaking on the floor, Franken, clearly not approving of what I was saying, in a room that once hosted the likes of Robert Taft and Mike Mansfield, began making silly faces and rolling his eyes to mock me. It was distracting and disrespectful. When I finished, I walked up to the chair and whispered in his ear.

"Al," I said. "Let me remind you that there are rules that guide the way we interact here. You may disagree with what others are saying, but this is not the set of *Saturday Night Live*."

To his credit, Franken later delivered me a letter of apology, and with it, I hoped he had learned a valuable lesson.

✩✩✩

If I had to pick the key moment of the health-care debate, it was when Olympia Snowe of Maine, the most liberal member of our conference who'd expressed some reservations about voting against the bill, and who was the last member whose vote I thought we might lose, came to tell me she had decided to oppose it. By this time, the administration knew that she was their last shot, and it had been a full-court press by both sides to get her to vote our way. Among the arguments helpful in making our case was that, according to poll data, Obamacare was not even popular in her liberal state. We now had every single one of our members on board. I felt an enormous sense of accomplishment and relief.

As we prepared to take up the vote, President Obama said, "I think it's important for every single member of the Senate to take a careful look at what's in the bill." This was a ridiculous and misleading statement, because there was no bill to read. The version we would consider was not the one that we would vote on—because the final bill was still being worked on in private, behind closed doors. Even Senator Dick Durbin, the assistant majority leader on the Democratic side, admitted he hadn't seen the details of this bill. The only thing we knew for sure about it was that it would raise taxes, raise premiums, and slash Medicare by $700 billion to pay for a vast expansion of government into health care that an over-whelming majority of Americans opposed. The only argument Democrats were left with was a call to history. Well, history was going to be made either way. And this much was clear: passing this bill in the way Obama, Reid, and the others were trying to pass it—ramming it down the throats of not just Republicans, but all Americans—would be a historic mistake that those who supported it would come to regret.

The first opportunity to defeat the bill was on Saturday night, November 21, 2009, when we voted on cloture on the motion to pro-ceed to it, which is the first step toward beginning debate. If I could convince even one Democrat to vote no, Senator Reid wouldn't have the sixty votes he needed to even begin the debate. That November evening, I did everything I could to convince just one of my Demo-cratic colleagues—just one—to keep the country from making a huge mistake. I made sure they knew the bottom line: we were voting on a bill that was little more than a massive monument to bureaucracy and spending. At a moment when more than one in ten working Americans was looking for a job, and the Chinese were lecturing us about our debt, the bill cost us trillions, money we didn't have and could not afford.

That was the incredibly sad irony of this whole debate. The problem that got us where we were was that health-care costs were out of control. Yet the neutral, nonpartisan Congressional Budget Office, the scorekeeper on matters such as these, said that under the bill, health-care costs were actually going to go up, not down. So 2,074 pages and trillions of dollars later, this bill didn't even meet the most basic criterion for fixing the system—to lower costs. The Affordable Care Act was a big old oxymoron. It would actually make care less affordable. And yet every single Democrat voted yes on that first vote. And every Republican present? We all voted no.

If I had been the guy in charge of all this, I might have paused at this moment to consider what this meant. I might even have taken a look at the vote tallies of some of the most far-reaching legislation of the past century. Medicare and Medicaid were both approved with the support of about half the members of the minority. The Voting Rights Act of 1965 passed with the votes of thirty out of thirty-two members of the Republican minority—all but two. Only six senators voted against the Social Security Act. And only eight voted against the Americans with Disabilities Act. In no case had those votes happened by throwing these bills together in a back room and dropping them on the floor with a stopwatch running. It happened through a laborious process of legislating, persuasion, and coalition-building. It took time and patience and hard work, and it guaranteed that every one of these laws had stability. So maybe we needed to rethink what the future was going to hold for a bill of this magnitude to be enacted with literally *no support whatsoever* from the minority party. The mess to come was inevitable. Anyone with a sense of the long term could see that. But Democrats plowed forward anyway.

Knowing how precarious support from his own party was, Reid made the decision to keep us in session until the bill passed. He didn't want to let his members return home to their states, where they'd inevitably hear from their constituents about how much they hated this bill.

Losing even one Democrat's vote would mean that the bill was dead. Reid's timing was particularly inconvenient. Majority leaders are always threatening that if something doesn't happen, we'll have to stay over a weekend, or postpone a recess. It reminds me of the way a parent threatens a child—if you don't behave, we're turning around and going home this minute. Nine out of ten times they don't actually go home because Mom wants to stay out just as much as her child. The same often goes in the Senate. But not this time.

We went into session on the bill on November 30 and stayed in seven days a week until Christmas Eve. It was a lot to ask of our staffs, but I knew everyone on my team would do whatever we could to stop this thing. One morning, I called everyone together to let them know that I was going to do the same. "Look," I said, "I like Thanksgiving and Christmas as much as anybody. But we have to try to stop this, and I'm prepared to be here until hell freezes over to kill this thing. I am completely determined, if possible, to kill this bill, no matter the extraordinary lengths they'll go to."

The reason Reid and his colleagues went to such extraordinary lengths, and employed these strong-arm tactics, was that the damn thing was so unpopular that if they let anyone out, they wouldn't get their votes. Even with sixty Democrats, it was hard for them to corral the votes, and Reid was forced to keep us there, cooped up in the Capitol, driving it forward, and making unseemly deals along the way. When Reid announced he would unveil the final bill on Saturday, December 19, and then force a vote in the middle of the night about thirty-six hours later, the whole thing started to feel absurd. One of the most major and far-reaching pieces of legislation in decades and *this* is how they wanted to approach it?

To make the situation even worse, during these already interminable days, DC was hit by the infamous "Snowmageddon," a record storm that brought nearly sixteen inches of snow the weekend before Christmas Eve. On Monday, with federal agencies and schools closed on account of the storm, we showed up for a vote at 1:08 a.m. People couldn't get home afterward and a few staff members who lived within walking distance of Capitol Hill invited other staff members to stay with them. In the morning, they all trudged together through a few feet of fresh snow to get back in time for another vote at 7:00 a.m.

Knowing they weren't going to get one of our forty votes, the Democrats were in trouble. To get to sixty, the number required to break a filibuster, they began to engage in a rather aggressive effort to get everyone on board, catering to absurd demands from the more moderate members of their party. We knew from our experience with the stimulus that when the Obama administration and their allies on Capitol Hill were worried about getting the votes, they frequently turned to the practice of inserting into bills seemingly innocuous language that actually granted huge giveaways to the lawmakers they needed to vote for the bill. The legalese often made it very difficult to pick up, and to make matters worse, they never allowed time for anyone to actually read the bill. Going into the final week before the bill was to be presented in all its morbid glory, we set up an elaborate system of lawyers, wonks, and communicators to identify legislative anomalies that could be special deals for Democrats who were on the fence. The trick was to get these anomalies out to the public as quickly as possible because the entire bill would, within hours of its unveiling, be branded as a success by an increasingly compliant media.

My health-care team, led by Meg Hauck and Scott Raab, tasked the Senate Finance Committee with identifying the potential kickbacks. Meg and Scott would then vet them and send the most egregious examples to Josh Holmes in my communications shop. Josh would quickly brand the item and pass it along to our press secretary, John Ashbrook, to pitch to the press. This system identified a special deal for Louisiana that Josh labeled the Louisiana Purchase, and a special deal for Florida senator Bill Nelson that he called the Gator Aid. Their biggest victory came at the expense of moderate Nebraska Democrat Ben Nelson, who traded his vote for federal Medicaid dollars, a deal Josh dubbed the Cornhusker Kickback. This one was particularly infuriating, and no one was going to let it lie.

"What's the plan?" Brian asked Josh after we got news of Nelson's vote.

"We're gonna make this bill as popular as an internment camp," Josh said.

Within hours, the Cornhusker Kickback took on a life of its own and became emblematic of an entire process that made the American people absolutely disgusted. Undeterred, Democrats continued to hold the line in support of an indefensible bill that was drifting toward political toxicity.

But, as hard as it may be to believe, despite the anger we all felt about these tactics, and that the Democrats did not care one iota that this bill hadn't even a shred of bipartisan support—not to mention the inconvenience to our families and dealing with holiday plans in chaos—in some ways we were enjoying ourselves. There was a wonderful feeling of camaraderie. My office manager, Julie Adams, made sure the office was well stocked with food. Every few days she'd run to Costco and return with enough fruit, soft drinks, coffee, and snacks to feed everyone stuck there along with us. Stef would order take-out Chinese or pizza in the evenings. Members and their staffs would come in and we'd all sit around the table in my large conference room, getting to know one another better.

Toward the end, all forty of us Republican senators gathered in the LBJ Room for a caucus lunch. I tried to keep these as uplifting as possible, allowing us a space to come together and take a breath. At one point John McCain stood up, commanding the attention of everyone in the room.

"Colleagues, I don't know why this comes to mind right now but I want to tell you a story about a Christmas I spent at the Hanoi Hilton." John is someone whom everyone in that room had a great deal of respect for. As our presidential candidate, he was the best-known member of our caucus. If this were the Constitutional Convention, he'd be our George Washington. And while, of course, we were all well aware of his service to our country, and the nearly six years he spent in captivity in North Vietnam, his experience as a POW was not a topic most of us had ever broached with him. I think we all felt the lumps forming in our throats just at the idea of what John was going to tell us.

As the son of an admiral, John had been offered early release as a way for the guards to break the spirit of those who had been there longer and whose turn was due to come before his. John refused, and over the next several years he suffered unfathomable torture at the hands of the guards. There was one guard who seemed to particularly enjoy torturing him. One morning, this guard came to get John. He led him out to the dusty courtyard, where he loosened the ropes binding his arms. "I had no idea what was happening," John said. "And I thought this was it. He was taking me outside to kill me."

He directed John to a patch in the dirt and pushed him to his knees. Then the guard took his foot, and in the dirt in front of him, he drew a cross. It was the morning of December 25. Christmas.

"I think this story is on my mind today because we're all here together," John said. "I know we're going to lose this, but I believe that in staying together for a principle, we are also making it our finest hour. And it's made me think of the camaraderie and friendship I felt with the guys I had around me those years. I thank every one of you for keeping up this fight."

When he had finished speaking, I don't think there was one person around us who wasn't staring at their plate because nobody wanted to look up and see a room full of teary-eyed senators.

Later that day, John's words stayed with me. And his positive outlook infected my own. We were experiencing a moment where we could've picked up our toys and gone home to pout about what had befallen us. As Democrats gathered for their final press conference in the Capitol's Ohio Clock Corridor to announce they had the votes to pass Obamacare in the Senate, I knew that the members of my conference, my staff, and

I were going to make sure the public understood, come the next election, who was responsible for this mess. And I couldn't have agreed more with something Josh Holmes said later that day.

"What you're witnessing right now is the resurrection of the Republican Party."

✧✧✧

On December 24, 2009, Obamacare passed the Senate in a 60–39 vote. Every Democrat voted for the bill, and every Republican voted against it. (Jim Bunning, who retired the next year, missed the vote, but it would not have changed the outcome.) If you'd been given no background information about the fight we'd been through over the year, and had walked into the Senate Chamber at the time of the vote, you would think, by the pride we clearly exuded for having stayed together on this, that the Republicans had just won a big victory and the Democrats had lost. Of course, we were all appalled by the vote, but we'd given this fight everything we had. We were completely unified as a conference but also completely divided as a government.

It merits repeating: Obamacare is the worst bill in modern history, and I still can't fathom why any Democrat found it enticing enough to vote for. When it was all said and done, not only was the rollout of the plan a complete mess, but it didn't do what Obama had counted on: further endear him to the public. By the end of the year, his approval rating was below 50 percent.

The problem with the bill wasn't simply the substance, but the arrogance with which it had been enacted. I was reminded of an experience I'd recently had, a chance encounter with LBJ's daughter, Luci Baines Johnson, in the Capitol Rotunda, to celebrate the hundredth anniversary of LBJ's birth. I had never met her, but I approached her that day.

"Luci, I was there the day your dad signed the Voting Rights Act."

"I was there too," she said. "I remember it so well. Daddy told me to come with him. He said it was an important day. On the way to the Capitol, he told me that Senator Everett Dirksen was joining him at the signing. I asked him why he was having a Republican there with him. 'He had a lot to do with this getting passed,' Daddy said. 'And I think the country is going to be a lot more likely to accept this by knowing it was done in a broad bipartisan way.'" The lesson was clear: Americans believe that on issues of great importance, one party shouldn't be allowed to force its will on everyone else. Yet that's exactly what the Democrats did, and for his part in it, Obama squandered a great deal of political capital.

I was not surprised to see the public sour on the president and his plan. It was tremendously shortsighted. Our forefathers came here looking not for security, but for opportunity, and Obama's blatant attempt to Europeanize the country flies in the face of what America is all about. By pushing this far-left agenda, all the Democrats had done was to explode the government, bringing along a coinciding mountain of debt. The deficit for this year alone was bigger than the last four years of the Bush administration combined. *Combined*. It reminded me of what Margaret Thatcher once said: The problem with socialism is pretty soon you run out of other people's money. Policies like this could not be sustained in the long term and all we were doing was leaving a whole lot of problems our children would have to deal with. So were people angry? Yes. And for good reason.

Anyone doubting the political temperature of the country in the wake of Obamacare had only one place to look: to the special election playing out for Ted Kennedy's seat in the bluest state of our union, Massachusetts. When I was an intern for Gene Snyder and John Sherman Cooper in the early 1960s, Ted Kennedy was already a well-known senator. He served in the Senate for forty-seven years, under ten different presidents. His gregariousness was legendary and his passion and intensity as a lawmaker reached near-mythic proportions. Even though he and I were on opposite sides of issue after issue, I always admired the focus and fight Ted brought to every debate. In 2006, Ted came to the McConnell Center to speak, and he was one of our most popular guests. In a very thoughtful gesture, he brought me a framed photograph of his brother John F. Kennedy with John Sherman Cooper. On it he wrote, "I know how much President Kennedy admired John Sherman Cooper in the Senate, and so did I. Mitch McConnell is part of that great Kentucky tradition of public service, and it's a privilege to serve with him today (not that we always agree on the issues)." When I heard on August 25, 2009, that he'd passed away, I had a hard time imagining the Senate without Ted thundering on the floor.

A special election was held to fill his seat, and it was almost certain to go to the Democrat, Attorney General Martha Coakley. No Republican had been elected to the US Senate from Massachusetts since Edward Brooke in 1972, thirty-eight years earlier. The Republican candidate was Scott Brown, a state legislator, and his entire strategy was to run as the man who would take away the Democratic supermajority and enable us to defeat Obamacare. With the entire nation paying close attention, Scott Brown shocked everybody and won. By 110,000 votes. The Massachusetts election was a referendum on Obamacare, and I sure hoped it was just the first sign of things to come.

CHAPTER SEVENTEEN

You Can't Make Policy
If You Don't Win the Election

T he single most important thing we want to achieve is for President Obama to be a one-term president," I told a reporter from the *National Journal* on October 23, 2010. I then went on to explain that if Obama did what Clinton had done—decide after the elections that he was willing to move toward the political center and meet Republicans halfway on some of the biggest issues facing our nation—we'd do business with him. "I don't want him to fail," I said. "I want him to change."

During the course of the interview, the reporter and I had been speaking about the number of presidents who lost part or all of Congress during their first term in office. As any student of history knows, it's not uncommon for voters to choose divided government—it's happened more often than not since World War II. It's a trend, I believe, that reflects Americans' skepticism about giving one side too much power, and when a president is elected with his party controlling both houses, the voters often show their remorse come election night two years later. I was there when that remorse was expressed under Clinton in 1994, and I was looking forward to see it happening again in 2010 under Barack Obama.

But, once again taking the long view, history has also shown that winning midterm elections doesn't mean the fight is over. In the last hundred years, three presidents suffered significant defeats in their first term but went on to win reelection: Harry Truman, Dwight Eisenhower, and Bill Clinton. With Obama's race for reelection just two years away, I'd been reading up on these matters, hoping to learn some useful lessons. I mentioned this to the reporter, saying that the 2010 elections were just the first step in giving Congress back to the Republicans, and then it would be up to us to keep working, to finish the job. What was that job? the reporter asked me—and I had answered.

Well, I've been taken out of context in the past, but never more relentlessly than with regard to this comment. Over the next few months it seemed that every Democrat was handed the same talking point: remind people Mitch McConnell said his greatest legislative goal is to make Barack Obama a one-term president. People falsely claimed I'd made the statement immediately after Obama was first elected—framing my statement as proof that before anything else, I was out to obstruct the president and cause him to fail—when the truth was that I made it after he had jammed through the health-care bill and the stimulus. Even Obama would exploit this comment, using it as one of the main riffs in his presidential campaign two years later. But to me, this reaction was nothing more than false outrage and political grandstanding. Name a Republican who didn't want another Republican answering the phone in the Oval Office come January 2013.

The real scandal was not Republicans who wanted Obama voted out of office, but Republicans who talked about fighting for conservative principles while obstructing the only constitutional channels available for protecting those principles as best we could. Passing good legislation while dealing with these political forces in addition to an arrogant and uncooperative president posed a challenge that might prove impossible.

☆☆☆

To my great delight, it seemed as if we were moving in the direction of holding Obama to one term: the 2010 midterm elections went as I had expected. After two years of Obama's far-left policies, Republicans gained six seats in the Senate and regained control of the House. We had the president himself—and his role in inspiring a grassroots movement of energetic, conservative voters—to thank, especially for the Republican revolution in the House. Resentment over Obamacare and his trillion-dollar stimulus package, the national punch line that had done little more than reward liberal constituencies and add a Mount Everest of debt to the national balance sheet, had planted the seeds for the Tea Party to emerge. The goals of those aligning themselves with this movement was to repeal Obamacare, take control of the out-of-control spending by the administration, and generally advance conservative ideals, all of which sounded good to me. More than thirty Tea Party candidates were elected in the House. In the Senate, Rand Paul, an eye surgeon from Bowling Green—the son of libertarian presidential candidate Ron Paul, and one of the earliest proponents of the Tea Party agenda, who later became a friend and ally—rose from relative obscurity to win in Kentucky.

The growth of the Tea Party was great for base enthusiasm, and was widely believed to have generated more votes for Republicans in the House elections. But much to my irritation, this movement was being hijacked by a few groups for their own mercenary purposes. The worst of the worst was the Senate Conservatives Fund (SCF), which had been founded in 2008 by Jim DeMint, the senator from South Carolina. For a self-proclaimed conservative organization, it had a particularly interesting way of handling itself. It raised the vast majority of its money from well-intentioned conservatives who sent in small contributions when informed by mail or e-mail that their dollars would ensure a conservative agenda. The pitch was essentially that if only the leaders of SCF had a few more dollars, a "true conservative" Senate would implement their agenda (without the president of the United States evidently). What was left unsaid is that the hard-earned dollars these donors sent to SCF were used exclusively to attack Republicans, to the great delight of liberals across the country.

As more dollars from patriotic Americans rolled in, SCF staff would direct those resources exclusively toward campaigning against the most electable Republicans from the comfort of their townhome on Capitol Hill. For the first four years of his presidency, if Barack Obama didn't have these guys working on his behalf, he would've had to invent them because they would go on to elect more Democrats than the Democratic Senatorial Campaign Committee. While SCF was outfitting its town-house offices with luxurious amenities like a hot tub and a wine cellar, it cost us at least two Senate seats in the elections of 2010, in Delaware and Colorado, and possibly a third in Nevada. In Delaware and Colorado, unelectable candidates backed by SCF unseated established Republicans in primary elections, but they lacked both experience and a message, and were promptly trounced in the general elections by liberal Democrats. In Nevada, where Majority Leader Harry Reid was vulnerable enough to be unseated by a viable candidate, he was able to portray his opponent, Sharron Angle, as too extreme. This was maddening on so many levels. Not only because SCF was misleading Americans, but it was also hurting the conservative movement because, as I frequently say, unless you win the election, you can't make policy.

☆☆☆

With the House back in control of the Republicans under newly elected Speaker John Boehner, a top-notch guy, every Republican in Congress was looking forward to finally doing more than playing defense to Obama, Harry Reid, and Nancy Pelosi. If government spending was the answer to an economic slowdown, we'd have been in a boom. Instead, our debt had skyrocketed 35 percent and our annual deficit was three times greater than the highest deficit the previous administration ever ran. Despite massive spending increases by Democrats, one in ten Americans was still looking for work. It was time that Democrats were forced to make the same kind of tough choices about

Washington's budget that most American families had been forced to make about their own.

At the top of our agenda was tackling the most pressing issue we faced: the need to cut taxes and reduce spending. Getting any bipartisan measures passed during Obama's first two years on these measures had been all but impossible. Since being elected, his idea of compromise was: you capitulate and do what I want to do. As we went into 2011, this much was clear: if Obama and the Democrats wouldn't agree to tackle these issues on their own, it was our job to try to force them to the political center and see if we could find some areas of agreement.

At the beginning of the year, we began to look for areas where we might have some leverage with the president to address government spending and the debt crisis, and we found it in the president's upcoming request to authorize an increase in the debt ceiling, or the amount of money the US Treasury may borrow. Periodically, in what is typically little more than a formality, Congress approves the president's request to raise the debt ceiling. But after two years of historic spending, leading to equally historic debt, it was irresponsible to raise the debt limit without trying to do something about spending. It was our moment to force our pro-spending president to the table.

In June, I sat down with President Obama at that table to explain our position. We wanted discretionary spending reductions, both now and in the future, and a long-term entitlement fix to prevent Medicaid, Medicare, and Social Security from tanking. Obama quickly came to recognize how serious we were, but his solution to reducing the debt was, unsurprisingly, to raise taxes. That was not something we would agree to.

Nothing came out of that meeting or the many subsequent meetings between the White House and members of Congress. Why? Because they went exactly like most meetings with Barack Obama go. Almost without exception, President Obama begins serious policy discussions by explaining why everyone else is wrong. After he assigns straw men to your views, he enthusiastically attempts to knock them down with a theatrically earnest re-litigation of what you've missed about his brilliance. The topic at hand rarely matters—what to do on the debt limit or what to get for lunch. I've never felt the need to lecture a colleague about the merits of his or her opinion during a negotiation. If they've been given the power to make a deal, they're entrusted with deeply held convictions that must be respected, if not appreciated. Re-litigating the failures of liberalism during budget negotiations has never struck me as a particularly productive approach, as much as I'd love to explore that topic with some of my colleagues. In addition to being a little disrespectful, it just wastes time. However, this is not a theory shared by our forty-fourth president.

Never was this more evident than during these tumultuous weeks of trying to tackle the debit limit. Our discussions over the phone went something like this:

President Obama: Mitch?

Me: Yes, Mr. President.

And then I'd listen. The conversation would last as long as it took the president to feel satisfied that his soliloquy had outlined the issue well enough for me to understand. Speaker Boehner famously put the phone on his desk and carried on a separate conversation during one of these exchanges with the president. I never put the phone down, but on one occasion I did watch at least an inning of baseball.

As summer wore on, I came to the unfortunate conclusion that no grand bargain was going to occur. The hundreds of billions in tax increases the Democrats were proposing under the auspice of "reform" wouldn't have solved the problem. On August 2, 2011, the government's borrowing authority would be exhausted, and as the deadline approached, and talks were stalled, the situation became more tense. Christine Lagarde, the new head of the International Monetary Fund, issued a warning: If the United States failed to act before the August 2 deadline and defaulted on its loans, the impact would be felt not just in the US economy, but globally.

John Boehner and I began negotiations with Harry Reid, which lasted several days, and seemed promising. Throughout the negotiations, I wanted to be perfectly clear that Obama was going to sign the deal we were coming close to finalizing. "Don't let me waste my time, Harry. We have to know Obama's gonna sign this." The deal we were discussing would enact discretionary spending caps, increase the debt limit by about $1 trillion, and create a so-called supercommittee to identify an additional $1 trillion in cuts. If the committee was successful in identifying those cuts, the debt limit would automatically increase another trillion dollars. But if not, we'd be back at the table when it came to authorizing another debt limit increase.

"The president's been clear that he doesn't want to deal with another request to increase the debt limit before the next election, Harry," I said. "This deal makes that a possibility. I don't want us spending all of our time working this out if he won't sign it."

"He will, he will," Reid said. "I'm keeping him in the loop. He knows what we're doing and he's fine with it. I can deliver his signature."

We finally came to an agreement less than two weeks before the deadline. I felt good about where we stood, and was relieved that we'd gotten this done and averted a financial disaster. But a few hours after we'd finalized the negotiation, Stef appeared and told me that Harry was waiting to speak to me in my conference room.

"He won't sign it," Reid said. "The president won't sign this deal."

"Why not?"

"The debt limit increase. He refuses to agree to anything that might make this come up again. We have to start over."

Once again, I knew I had no choice but to allow the anger I felt to quickly pass. What this situation called for was not emotion, but an almost athletic determination to keep my cool and figure out what was next. But one thing I knew for sure. I was done dealing with Harry Reid.

In the week before the deadline, the hope that we might resolve this issue continued to deteriorate. The House, under Speaker Boehner, developed a bill that would have made a debt limit increase contingent on huge cuts in spending and the adoption of a balanced budget amendment. The bill passed the House, only to be rejected by the Democrat-led Senate. The next day, the House rejected a plan drawn up by Harry Reid. On Saturday, I received a call from Joe Biden.

"I think it's time we talk," he said.

Over the nearly twenty-five years we served together in the Senate, I'd gotten to know Joe a little. As my dad would have said about the vice president if they'd ever met: if you ask him what time it is, he'll tell you how to make a watch. I'd learned this pretty clearly a few years back, during a flight to Raleigh, North Carolina, to attend the funeral of Senator Jesse Helms. I'd been asked to deliver a eulogy for Senator Helms, and I flew to his funeral on a small plane alongside Bob and Elizabeth Dole, Ted Stevens, and then-senator Joe Biden. Well, Joe started talking the minute we got on the plane, and he didn't stop until the moment we landed. I think this quality of Joe's is endearing, but this day I was nervous about speaking at the funeral, and tried my best to review my notes during the incessant chatter. We got to Raleigh, the funeral went fine, and when we got back on the plane, Joe started talking again and talked nonstop all the way back. It was vintage Joe Biden.

Not only did I like Joe, but in the last several months I'd also learned that he didn't only talk, he also listened. He was, therefore, someone I could work with. A few months earlier, he and I had successfully negotiated a means to address the imminent rise of taxes, with the scheduled December 2010 expiration of the Bush-era tax cuts. Allowing these cuts to expire would have meant a significant tax increase for every American taxpayer. After others had tried and failed over months to negotiate a solution, Joe and I had been able to do so in a matter of days. The reason we could get a deal done—and that I could work with Joe—was that we could talk to each other. I could tell him how far we could go, and he would reciprocate, unlike Obama. The president's way of interacting and "negotiating" was utterly unproductive. Joe, on the other hand, made no effort to convince me that I was wrong, or that I held an incorrect view of the world. He took my politics as a given, and I did the same, which was what allowed us to successfully negotiate when it came to our discussion on taxes in 2010. The administration and congressional Democrats agreed to a two-year extension of all the Bush tax rates, and we agreed to a temporary cut in the payroll tax and the extension of unemployment benefits. As far as Republicans were concerned, the deal was terrific, as evidenced by the fact that come the day of the bill signing, I attended, while Harry Reid and Nancy Pelosi were conspicuously absent.

Now, with the debt limit deadline looming, and with a government we didn't control, I understood there was a limit to what we could achieve. Given the cards we were dealt, what we needed to do—what was in the best interest of our country—was to forge the best compromise we could to avoid a default. Not only would a default plunge the economy back into a recession, but it would also likely result in a spike in unemployment and a risk of a global depression. And the blame for it would fall largely on Republicans. With the 2012 elections coming up, that was a foolish gamble to take.

When Joe and I spoke that Saturday night, three days before the deadline, we agreed to see what we might work out. Sharon Soderstrom, my chief of staff, and I called together the key members of our policy staff to explore how to bring about the best possible deal. We worked late into the night over pots of coffee and take-out Chinese food. Rohit Kumar, my policy director, was key to these negotiations. "Listen to this," he said, pulling the thin piece of paper from a fortune cookie. "'You may be spending too much money.' I think we got the White House's order."

The next morning, I appeared on CNN and *Face the Nation* to voice my confidence that we were nearing a compromise, and then I returned to my office at the Capitol. That afternoon, I had several discussions with Biden, while also stopping by Boehner's office—which meant following the smell of cigarette smoke down the hall—to make sure he was on board. We mapped out a deal that would become the Budget Control Act of 2011: we'd reduce discretionary spending by $900 billion over ten years and appoint what became known as the supercommittee, consisting of six Republicans and six Democrats, to come up with $1.2 trillion more in savings by November. We would not raise any taxes at a time when our economy could least afford them. And by raising the debt limit, we would avoid a government default.

I was proud of the deal we'd struck. In April, four months earlier, the president was asking us to raise the debt ceiling with no spending reductions whatsoever, and here we'd locked in more than $2 trillion of savings, the most significant spending reductions since right after the Korean War, without raising taxes. In 2005, when we'd had control of both the White House and Congress, we'd only been able to manage— and with a great deal of effort—a deficit reduction bill of less than $40 billion. Getting this measure enacted at a time when nobody could get anything out of this administration was particularly satisfying. After the vote, many senators, including a number who voted against the proposal, shook my hand and thanked me. Jim DeMint was among them. "That was the best we could do," DeMint said.

This exchange perfectly illustrated the hypocrisy of DeMint and his whole enterprise. People like him were depending on me to pick up the pieces by brokering deals. He'd say it was the best we could do, privately, and then fund-raise by blasting me for the same deals. I found the fact that DeMint would shake my hand after railing against this deal both jaw-dropping and revealing, and I didn't remain quiet about my frustration. "Jim," I said to him one day, after calling him to my office, "if you want my job, run for it." This time, he had very little to say. But regardless of what he might have been saying about how terrible the deal was, I agreed more with what Representative Charlie Rangel, a Democrat, said after the bill passed—that the Republicans "mugged the president but let him keep his wedding ring."

The day after we passed the Budget Control Act, an article appeared in the *Huffington Post* claiming it was "Mitch McConnell's moment" and that it likely wouldn't be the last. Why? Because chances were good that with the upcoming elections of 2012, I would become the Senate majority leader.

I was prepared, and more than a little eager. After six years as the leader of my party, I was looking forward to the chance to finally assume the position I'd been working toward for the last twenty-eight years.

✩✩✩

As I learned long ago, it's not wise to allow your highs to get too high, because you just might then have to face some pretty serious lows. So it was for me on election night of November 2012. Obama was reelected and, defying expectations, not only did we not flip the Senate, we lost two seats.

There were a few reasons we failed to meet expectations. One was Obama's tremendously successful campaign. He was able to revive the energy of his base, leading to Republican losses in several battleground states like Ohio, Virginia, and Florida. In Massachusetts, which Obama carried by twenty-three points, Scott Brown was defeated despite enjoying a 60 percent approval rating. We also simply had bad luck, especially in North Dakota and Montana, the single biggest disappointments in the cycle. While we ran better candidates who executed superb races, we still lost. The third factor was that, reminiscent of what happened in 2010 in Delaware, Colorado, and Nevada, thanks to groups like SCF, we threw away two seats with unelectable candidates, this time in Missouri and Indiana.

The election results were, on a personal level, extremely disappointing as it began to appear that I might never actually meet my goal of becoming majority leader. I was reelected as minority leader, and John Cornyn of Texas was elected as whip. I was very happy, knowing how much I would be able to count on this very talented colleague as my deputy, and I would not be disappointed. But the election results also mattered nationally and even globally, because we were about to encounter a perfect storm of problems. Just weeks after the election, on January 1, 2013, the two-year extension of the Bush-era tax cuts that Biden and I had negotiated in 2010 was set to permanently expire, creating more than $500 billion in tax increases. At the exact same time, the supercommittee we'd created during the debt ceiling negotiations locked up. Because of the Democrats' desire to raise taxes as a condition of any long-term entitlement fix, we couldn't come up with the $1.2 trillion in savings, which then triggered budget sequesters and deficit reduction measures. This confluence of factors, which, combined, could paralyze the US economy, was what Federal Reserve chairman Ben Bernanke referred to as "the fiscal cliff."

Failing to act was not an option. The combination of higher taxes for nearly every American—an estimated $2,000 to $3,000 per family—coupled with cuts in most federal programs, would be too much all at once for our still-weak economy. The cuts to the deficit included a $55 billion reduction in the Pentagon's budget and across-the-board spending cuts. The question was not if this would be bad for the economy. The question, once again, was what to do about it.

Speaker Boehner and I were prepared to fight for the Bush-era tax cuts to extend to all Americans on a permanent basis, but we also had to be realistic. A cornerstone of Obama's reelection campaign was the promise to increase taxes on the wealthy. It was not possible that the Democratic-controlled Senate would pass the bill we wanted—a bill that was in direct opposition to Obama's promise—or that Obama would sign it. Knowing we couldn't get our preferred policy enacted, we needed to determine how to give the White House the least amount of revenue possible while still maintaining as much of the tax cuts as we could. And all by midnight on New Year's Eve.

The House and the White House once again deadlocked. Obama

was insisting that the Bush-era tax cuts should not apply to those who earned more than $250,000 a year. By allowing taxes to rise on those making more than that, Obama believed we'd help cut the deficit. But we wanted the tax cuts to extend to everyone. Taxing the wealthy hurts job growth, and under the administration's proposal, there was far too much of a cut to the military.

For several weeks I stayed behind the scenes while others tried, with little success, to find an acceptable compromise. Just before Christmas, Boehner presented his conference with the so-called Plan B, which included raising taxes only on those earning more than $1 million annually. But he couldn't get the votes to pass it, forcing him to withdraw the bill and abandon negotiations.

During the Christmas weekend, Elaine and I attended a family wedding in New York before returning to Louisville to spend a quiet Christmas with my daughters. It was a welcome break from work, but I have to admit, I felt distracted and uneasy about where things were headed in the face of no compromise. The day after Christmas, I knew it was time to call Sharon Soderstrom, who'd gone home to visit her family in New York.

"I think it's time to get involved here," I said. "Nobody in DC is talking to anyone else. If we don't act, taxes are going to go up on everyone in just five days. What do you think?" I trust Sharon so much that if she had said this was the wrong move, I would have largely reconsidered my plan.

"I think I'm coming back tonight," Sharon said. "And I'll get everyone else back as well."

For the next few days, as most people in the country were enjoying the holiday break, my staff was back to working marathon sessions. On the afternoon of December 28, Obama called a meeting of the congressional leadership at the Oval Office. The meeting, which lasted about two hours, went exactly as I had expected. We—me, Nancy Pelosi, Harry Reid, John Boehner—all received a lecture from Professor

Obama. On this day, however, Obama's condescending attempts to lecture us about why everything we were negotiating for was wrong were particularly annoying, given that we were seriously under the gun. Even if he had, by some magic stroke of argumentative furor, been able to convince Boehner and me that we should raise taxes on every American, and that we should increase the death tax—the unfair tax the government levies on the transfer of an estate after its owner passes away—we surely weren't going to sell any of it to our colleagues. He knew that, and he had to have known how much time he was wasting.

The same was true for Nancy Pelosi. Her role in these meetings (as with most meetings) was to come with one talking point and repeat it again and again. On this day, the talking point she'd been handed must have said "Don't forget the children." She must have uttered this phrase a dozen times in her attempts to get us to change our thinking on the death tax.

Obviously we got nowhere, and at the end of the meeting, Obama offered a closing suggestion. "Mitch, Harry," he said. "Why don't you guys talk and try to figure this out?" In other words, a meeting that took up two hours' time of the leader of the free world and the four leaders of the US Congress ended with a suggestion that we talk. Those two hours would have been more productive had I spent them napping.

Despite my frustration, we still had to find a way to strike a deal to keep our economy from tanking. The next day, on December 29, instead of being at the U of L vs. UK basketball game as I had planned, I called Harry Reid at 7:00 p.m. and submitted an offer, telling him it was time to get this done and that everyone in my office was willing to work through the night to find common ground if necessary. Reid assured me I'd hear back from him by ten o'clock the next morning, but by 2:00 p.m. I hadn't heard a thing. It was clear he either didn't want to deal or was waiting around for somebody else to tell him what to do. Either way, with just thirty-six hours until the deadline, people were, understandably, growing uneasy. The Defense Department was preparing to notify 800,000 civilians who help keep our military moving that some of them might be forced to take unpaid leave. The IRS had issued guidance to employers who would need to begin withholding more taxes from paychecks beginning Tuesday.

When it became clear that nothing was going to happen with Reid, I picked up the phone and called Joe Biden. He was in flight at the time, so I left him a message.

"Is there anyone over there who knows how to make a deal?" I said. "I need you to get up to speed on this, Joe. Get off the plane, think about things, and call me in an hour."

In case I wasn't making myself perfectly clear that I was not going to allow our country to pass the deadline the next night and face the consequences, I went to the Senate floor. "I am concerned about the lack of urgency here," I said, referring to Reid's failure to get back to my proposal. "There is far too much at stake for political gamesmanship." I then revealed that I had just placed a call to the vice president to see if he could help jump-start the negotiations on his side. There was no single issue that remained a sticking point. The only sticking point was the willingness—and the courage—to close the deal. "I want everyone to know I am willing to get this done," I said. "But I need a dance partner."

Biden had heard me loud and clear, and we finally spoke at 12:45 a.m. on Monday. And then again at 6:30 a.m. And then multiple times throughout the day. At one point, the talks looked like they might be headed toward a stall.

"I think you should call the president," Biden suggested. I called in Rohit and we set up the call. Obama was as helpful as I had expected.

"Rohit is being a real jerk about the spending offsets," the president said, to my surprise, and my frustration. Personally criticizing a member of my staff hardly seemed like the way to negotiate a deal.

"Well, let's keep trying to bridge this divide," I said, and then hung up the phone. "Are you being a jerk, Rohit?"

"No, sir, I don't think so," Rohit said. "All the suggestions I'm making are coming from the president's own budget, which hardly seems like a crazy place to start." He paused. "But it's not every day the president of the United States calls me a jerk."

That conversation went nowhere, but by the afternoon, Biden and I were able to work out our final differences and reach a deal. I briefed my conference and by 8:45 p.m., New Year's Eve, we were ready to announce the news to the media and the American people. With all food services at the Capitol closed for the holiday, my staff was left to fend for themselves. As I returned to my office that evening, I thought I detected the smell of a campfire. Stef snuck by, surreptitiously carrying a stack of paper plates into my office.

"You hungry?" Sharon asked me.

"Very," I said.

I followed her to the back room. Gathered around the fireplace—a fireplace that may have been as old as the Capitol itself—stood the members of my staff, grilling hot dogs.

"Why didn't you tell me about this earlier?" I asked.

"We thought you might be mad," Stef said.

"Why would I be mad?"

"We forgot to get mustard."

☆☆☆

The bill I'd helped write passed the Senate at 2:00 a.m. on New Year's Day—the first time the Senate was in session between Christmas and New Year's since 1948. Most of my members met this bill with a sense of relief, as did I, partly because I was able to make my flight to New Orleans a few hours later. That afternoon, as the members of the House gathered to vote on the bill, Elaine and I sat with some friends at one of my favorite Cajun restaurants, eating black-eyed peas for good luck in the new year. They worked. The bill passed the House and my beloved Louisville Cardinals crushed the Florida Gators in the Sugar Bowl the next day.

Did we get everything we wanted? No. And while I would, of course, have preferred that we had, I take my lead on these matters from the fortieth president of the United States. Ronald Reagan struck many deals throughout his career and often said that getting 80 percent was good enough. He knew when to hold firm, and when it was time to forge a compromise. In this moment, given the government we had—the Democrat-controlled government the American people had elected—we had done very well.

But it's not possible to please everyone. Some people were not happy with what I had achieved in the deal, or with me. My 2014 campaign for reelection was on the horizon, and within days of striking this deal, an ad appeared on Kentucky television, urging voters to help unseat me in 2014. Soon after, a political action committee announced they were willing to spend seven figures to ensure my defeat. I had no doubt: I was going to enter the race with a bull's-eye on my back.

What was most unsettling about these efforts was that this bull's-eye was drawn not by Democrats, but by some members of my own party.

CHAPTER EIGHTEEN

Courage

If the elections of 2010 and 2012 taught Republicans anything, it was that no challenge should be discounted. In each of these cycles, we'd made the grave mistake of following the strategy championed by many political consultants: to ignore primary challenges by inexperienced and seemingly weak candidates championed by groups like the Senate Conservatives Fund. When you poll a primary between an incumbent everyone knows and a candidate nobody knows, the incumbent is inevitably going to poll way ahead. So candidates were advised to lie back and not engage, to trust the poll numbers, let the primary take care of itself, and stay focused on the general election. And again and again—in Nevada, Colorado, and Delaware in 2010, in Indiana and Missouri in 2012—the candidates who followed this advice lost. From the beginning, I had argued this was a false premise and the wrong strategy. Come 2014, I wasn't going to allow that to happen again, because this year, we were going to do things my way. In my race, and in every Republican race across the nation—in Texas, South Carolina, Mississippi—we were going to be supremely prepared for every fight.

I'd been preparing for my own race in 2014 for the last few years, tapping the best people to come on board and building a war chest for what I anticipated would be the toughest fight of my career. Never one to start late or agonize publicly about running, I never pretended I had any other intention. In December of 2010, I gave an interview to *Politico* to address any questions about whether I'd run again. "I'm not planning on running," I said. "I am running." And from day one, my campaign staff had a clear mandate: we were going to run the best campaign for the US Senate in the history of our country.

By the time I opened my campaign headquarters in February of 2013, in the same building I'd used in every Senate race since my first in 1984, I was ready. I would rely heavily on Josh Holmes, who I think has one of the greatest political minds of his generation. He'd been working for me since I'd become leader, helping to build a top-notch communications center that was considered a large part of our success, and was also key to my 2008 race. To manage the campaign in Kentucky, I hired Jesse Benton, who had managed Rand Paul's 2010 Senate race.

Before I even had a declared opponent, the fight was on. A few names were floated as to who the Democrats were thinking of recruiting to run against me, and we were primed for every one of them. Once you become an incumbent, everybody who challenges you thinks you're going to be the issue, but every potential candidate has a record. One of the earliest names being considered was Ashley Judd, the Hollywood actress, and there were just a few things one needed to know about her: she had extremely far-left views, her own grandmother, a Kentuckian, had called her a Hollywood liberal (and had also said I'd done a good job as senator), and she lived in Tennessee. In other words, some on my staff said, she would be a dream candidate. But I wasn't totally sure.

My friend Woody, who works at the local Kroger in Louisville, and who I see almost every weekend, couldn't wait to talk about Ashley Judd. I relish the fact that Woody and I talk about almost everything other than politics, but this weekend he traded the sports page for politics. He knew everything that was written about our potential race. Good lord, I thought, if Woody is talking about Ashley Judd, maybe she will be tougher to beat than people thought. I didn't like the idea of running against somebody as unpredictable as a Hollywood star. I knew if we ran a good campaign I could beat a Democratic politician, but what the heck happens when *TMZ* shows up on the campaign trail? My team assembled a research document on Ms. Judd's public statements, which quickly put my mind at ease. Hollywood star power or not, Ashley Judd was not a serious candidate for office in Kentucky.

In March, Judd announced she wouldn't be running, and soon after, Alison Lundergan Grimes, Kentucky's secretary of state, announced she would. She had been heavily recruited by the Democratic Senatorial Campaign Committee, and their choice made sense. Grimes was just thirty-four years old, and as the daughter of the state's former Democratic Party chairman, Jerry Lundergan, she had deep ties to Democratic politics. Her announcement brought quick endorsements and contributions from Hollywood's liberal elite, and not long after, Jeffrey Katzenberg, the CEO of DreamWorks Animation, hosted a fund-raiser for her in Los Angeles. Her donors read like the guest list at the Academy Awards: Barbra Streisand, Jerry Seinfeld, Woody Allen, and Leonardo DiCaprio.

But I was well aware that efforts from the Left would very well be the least of my problems. The cottage industry of so-called professional conservatives that had sprouted a few years earlier had by this time taken full bloom. Prior to 2010, the energy of the grassroots conservative movement was entirely focused on unseating Democrats, but now certain so-called conservative groups were determined to unseat Republicans they deemed insufficiently conservative. With the "true conservative" facade in full effect, I had become their main target.

The kindling these groups used to fuel their operation was the discontent of conservatives across the country over the deal we'd struck on the fiscal cliff. These groups convinced people that the only acceptable outcome was getting exactly what they wanted, when those things were, at a time when Democrats held the White House and at least one house of Congress, impossible to get. The divide that was growing between grassroots and conservative lawmakers was not a question of beliefs, because in the end, we were all for the same things. But when the American public chooses divided government, a purely conservative agenda is impossible to enact into law. Suggesting otherwise amounts to making a promise that can't possibly be kept. Barack Obama wields an important instrument—the veto pen. So telling Republican primary voters they should settle for nothing less than ensuring that Obamacare is repealed was selling an impossible idea. He was not going to allow it to happen. I was reminded of something Phil Gramm said after I'd invited him to address a GOP lunch after our vote on the Budget Control Act of 2011: "My daddy always told me when you're hitchhiking, that you go as far as the first car that picks you up will take you. Take this victory and pocket it."

Given how draining it was to be fighting a battle from both sides, I tried to look for good news wherever I could find it, and the very best news at the time was that on April 8, 2013, I was there in Atlanta when the University of Louisville men's basketball team took home the NCAA championship. This was just the day before U of L's women's basketball team became the lowest-seeded team ever to make it to the NCAA title game. It had been an exciting few weeks and a welcome respite from my work of trying to lead my conference while dealing with the intensity of the campaign. The morning after the men's win, I arrived at the office feeling pretty good about things. Until Josh Holmes walked into my office.

"Boss," he said. "We gotta talk."

✫✫✫

Someone on our communications team had spoken with a reporter from *Mother Jones* magazine, Josh informed me. "He was asking a lot of questions about a meeting we held at headquarters the day it opened two months ago," Josh said. "The details he has about what we talked about are striking."

"What do you make of it?"

"I'm not sure. But it's enough to concern me."

"Is it possible somebody in the room talked to the reporter?"

"I would trust everyone in that room with my life."

"What's the plan?"

"I'll call counsel. If they have a recording we may have legal recourse and at that point this would be a legal story, not a political one."

Josh was right to be concerned. The next day, *Mother Jones* published a story on its website, alongside audio of a secret recording that had been made of a meeting we'd held two months earlier. It appeared to have been recorded by someone standing in the hallway, outside the door of our headquarters. Not only was this a dirty trick, it was also arguably illegal. Kentucky is a one-party consent state, which means that conversations can be recorded only if at least one person in the room agrees to it. This clearly hadn't happened. The FBI got involved and later found the guys who'd done it—members of a left-wing group out of Louisville. The Department of Justice would decline to prosecute, a decision it never bothered to explain. My staff was quite upset, but frankly, I thought these shenanigans were just more of the same, highlighting the level of scrutiny I was under—a level one might be more inclined to expect in a presidential campaign than a run for the Senate in Kentucky.

And it certainly wouldn't stop there. In March, members of the same group connected to the secret recording sent out racist tweets about Elaine, suggesting the fact that she had been born in Taiwan dictated my stance on China's trade policy. This infuriated me. The Democrats have long accused us of being the party of intolerance, and here they were, attacking my wife for the supposed crime of being born in another country.

It's hard to underestimate just how ruthless the attacks were, and as they escalated from both sides, my staff dubbed this race the Paint Shaker—like the machine that mixes paint at thousands of bangs per minute. If it weren't so exhausting, it would almost be funny: those on the Left and many in the mainstream media were calling me the Senate's chief obstructionist—claiming I was solely responsible for orchestrating 442 filibusters since Obama took office—at the same time a coalition of Kentucky Tea Party groups were lambasting me for my apparent liberal voting record and my willingness to roll over and cede power to Obama. Both sides were going to stop at nothing to force me out, to convince voters that this race was one race too many.

And I have to admit, I was beginning to wonder if they had a point.

✩✩✩

Winston Churchill once said, "Courage is what it takes to stand up and speak; courage is also what it takes to sit down and listen." In the three decades I've spent in the Senate, I've learned the value of patient listening. When looking to achieve an outcome from a group, you're more likely to identify the solution by hearing others' points of view than in reiterating your own position. My tendency to prefer listening to talking is one of the things Elaine loves about me. It's also something that has, on more than one occasion, caused a bit of discomfort to members of my staff.

I know it caused discomfort at the beginning of a meeting I had with Bill Gates. I like Bill. He devotes most of his time to giving away billions of dollars (which makes me think he would make a good Democratic senator), and I, of course, greatly admire his very worthy goal to rid the earth of polio. I was eager to hear why he'd requested the meeting, and so when it began, I waited for him to speak. It took a few long minutes of complete silence between us, but I was fine with that, and he seemed to be as well. But the members of my staff were not. I know these experiences make those around me who are forced to endure them uncomfortable. I can sense them squirming, and sometimes, if I am quiet for too long, others will fill the space with chatter. But I'm perfectly fine with the silence because in the end, I know that listening is far more valuable than speaking.

Well, these months, as the campaign wore on, I was listening as well, and by the summer of 2013, it had become clear to me that two story lines were forming. One was that Republicans had a good shot at taking over the Senate in the final two years of the Obama presidency. With the number of seats at play in red and swing states, and the fact we were running the best slate of candidates we'd had in years, there was a very good chance we'd pick up the six seats we needed to regain the majority.

And the second was that the reason we might not make it was because of a particularly weak incumbent running for office: me. In June of 2013, my poll numbers were looking dismal and I was acutely aware of the drag I might represent for my own party. What if I lost and kept us from taking the majority? My first obligation has always been to help the party succeed, and while I never expressed my doubts publicly, I had begun to seriously consider if it was in fact time to find a better candidate.

Three years had passed since Kyle resigned from my staff, but I still relied on his counsel from time to time. This was one of them. Back in 1994, when I first ran into him in that elevator, he didn't have any connections. He didn't have an Ivy League degree. But he sure had a lot of talent. Asking him to join my team was one of the best decisions I ever made. He was always thinking of the one thing that no one else had thought of and was often the calm navigator in the middle of the storm—the one person in the office who never took his eye off the destination we had set. I knew I needed his counsel on this, and on a warm Friday afternoon in July, after Elaine had gone out for the day, I called Kyle at his home in Alexandria, Virginia, and asked if he'd come over.

"Let me tell you what I'm thinking," I said, as we sat in my living room, the house so quiet we could hear the clock ticking. "I've been taking a pounding, and it's taken a real toll on my standing. I'm the number one target of the DSCC, and the top target of the professional right. It could go either way at this point. What if, irony of all ironies, the only thing that keeps us from getting the majority in the Senate is if I lose?" Kyle was silent. "I have spent the last several years preparing us to take back the majority. But what happens if everything works exactly to plan and I lose, thus denying us the majority. It would certainly be an embarrassing conclusion to a long run."

Kyle's gaze met mine straight on. "What are you asking?"

"I have an obligation to my party. Do you think it's time for me to go?"

One of the great things about Kyle is that nothing rattles him. After taking a few minutes to collect his thoughts, Kyle spoke with his trademark calmness.

"First off, I don't think you're going to lose," he said. "Given what you've built in the state, it's not going to be easy for any liberal Democrat to win. And second, name me someone else who at this stage of the game can withstand the same storm. If you step out, the DSCC won't lose interest in Kentucky. They'll just focus on this seat even more, because without you, it'll be easier for them to win. They're trying to spook you." He leaned forward. "Look, I understand how hard this has been, but not making the race now doesn't put the party in a better position to get the majority. You have been working your whole life to become majority leader, and now, finally, it's within reach. Now is not the time to bow out."

After Kyle left, I took a few moments to sit in the quiet, thinking of what he had said. I was facing a very difficult fight, yes. But I'd been fighting my whole life.

When I was diagnosed with polio at the age of two, the chances I could beat it were slim, at least according to what the doctors told my mother. The disease was paralyzing or killing more than half a million people around the world every year, and nobody had any reason to believe

I wouldn't be among them. But I beat it. Well, no, my mother beat it, as determined as she was to do so. Not only did I survive it, but here I was at seventy-one years of age, walking without a limp, keeping regular fourteen-hour days, feeling far more robust than most my age. In Louisville at fourteen, a stranger in a new city and the odd kid out at a new school, I never thought I'd make a friend, let alone become the president of the student body. Even I doubted the next goal I set for myself—becoming a student body president at college, and then again at law school. I then worked my way to Washington, DC, where, in Senator John Sherman Cooper, I saw greatness for the first time. When President Andrew Jackson reputedly said, "One man with courage makes a majority," he was talking about people like Senator Cooper. But did I have enough courage to keep going, to live up to what I had seen in Cooper?

It was a question I had been grappling with since that summer, even after being elected county judge in the largest county in Kentucky, and especially during my first run for Senate, when every odd was stacked against me, and most were rooting for my loss. The papers, the unions, my well-funded opponent. Ronald Reagan called me Mitch O'Donnell just as Roger Ailes admitted he'd never seen anyone come from as far behind as I was to win. Then, even my win was considered some sort of political mistake, and sitting in that back corner of the Senate Chamber, the last among my colleagues, I wondered if they were right.

Yet I kept at it, spending years paying attention, practicing patience, learning everything I could about the institution of the Senate, an institution I deeply revered. And I'd reached my goal. I'd become the leader of Senate Republicans. I felt nothing but an enormous sense of gratitude that I'd been fortunate enough to make it this far. It had not come quick or easy. I'd hung in there, dealing with the inevitable bumps in the road. And not only had I survived, but I'd excelled.

I walked into the silent kitchen, and as I looked toward the backyard, I thought about all of the people who were, at that moment, once again longing for my defeat. Those who had banged their drums on my front lawn, the constant stream of television ads calling me soulless, dishonest, conniving, ads paid for by people from across the nation, who'd never set foot in Kentucky. They were all gleefully predicting, and cheering for, my demise, praying for me to fail.

Could I do this? Did I have it in me? I was fighting the toughest race of my career. This was, according to everyone on cable news, the most important election of 2014. The pressure was enormous. I could allow it to paralyze me.

Or I could be proud of it, relish it even.

They were coming after me because of the position I now held. They were coming after me because they thought I was effective. They were coming after me not because of my failings, but because of what I had achieved.

I decided to get some fresh air, and on my way out the front door, I passed the framed photograph of my parents on their wedding day that hangs on my wall. My mom was just twenty-one at the time, my dad twenty-two. As they stood there that day, my mom in her short fur jacket, the only nice thing she owned, my dad in his well-pressed suit, they were young and hopeful. They couldn't have known the challenges they were about to face. Within four years, they'd have a baby struck with polio, and a world war my dad felt compelled to fight. My dad had volunteered to go even though he didn't have to, and once there, he never retreated. Rather, he gave it everything he had, even, courageously, serving as a scout, going first before the others, checking for danger so that the guys behind him might find victory. And my mom. I'm sure many days she would have preferred to rest, to read, to do anything other than kneel beside me, leading me through hours of aching exercises that, as far as she knew, were futile.

Both my parents had taught me, in both their words and their actions, that the only way to fail in America was to quit or die. I pulled shut the front door and stepped outside. As I walked toward the Capitol, I was struck by a memory from when I was a young boy, and we were living in

Athens, Alabama: the day I followed my dad's advice and mustered the courage to march across the street and fight Dicky McGrew. How I had swung long and hard enough to bend his glasses, and to teach him, under no uncertain terms, that I wasn't going to allow him to bully me anymore. I knew my dad was proud of me that day, and I knew that if he were still alive, I'd want him to be equally proud of me now.

When I returned home later, Elaine was there. She seemed to notice something in the look on my face.

"What is it?" she asked.

"I'm ready," I said. "For this fight. It's time to tell them: Come and get me. It's time we settle this."

CHAPTER NINETEEN

"Making a Point or a Difference?"

In July of 2013, a forty-six-year-old investment manager and Tea Party–backed candidate named Matt Bevin announced he was running against me in the Republican primary. He had no political experience, no familiarity with running for office, and no idea what he was walking into.

I tried to warn him he was making a mistake. When he'd begun to make some noise about challenging me, one of my aides met with one of his to show him how well prepared we were. Bevin didn't listen, obviously, and the day he announced, we were on the air with an ad defining him as Bailout Bevin. He'd received a government loan to help rebuild his family's bell factory in Connecticut, which had been destroyed by a fire, and had written to his clients that he had supported TARP. After he criticized me for my role in passing TARP—a role I was proud of given the cost of not acting—I couldn't allow the hypocrisy. He'd later help us out by making more than a few bad choices, like speaking at a pro-cockfighting rally.

With Josh Holmes overseeing things, and a strong staff in Kentucky, I was feeling pretty calm, optimistic even, and I remained that way through the fall. I was feeling so good, in fact, that I set a clear goal—not only were we going to win, we were going to win big. We were going to take every one of Kentucky's 120 counties. I pressed my campaign staff to remain focused on the work ahead, not to get distracted by anything that could get in our way of meeting that goal. I planned to follow that advice myself.

And then, in October of 2013, a few rogue Republicans decided to shut down the government.

☆☆☆

Every Congress is required by the US Constitution to pass a federal budget for the next fiscal year. In the summer of 2013, a small but vocal coalition of House members had begun to strategize about attaching a provision to the upcoming federal budget that eliminated funding for the implementation of Obamacare. After initially failing to block Obamacare from becoming law, and then several failed attempts by Republicans to repeal it, and then the 2012 Supreme Court case that upheld its constitutionality, they saw it as the last chance to keep Obamacare from being implemented.

It was a strategy that couldn't possibly succeed.

All this plan was going to do was to keep us from passing a budget by midnight of September 30, which would then, in turn, accomplish just one thing: shutting down the US government. As we say in Kentucky, "There's no education in the second kick of a mule." That lesson was lost here because the first kick had come in 1995 when Republicans, under Newt Gingrich, shut down the government for twenty-seven days over federal spending levels. And all that had achieved was injuring our economy, inconveniencing Americans, and hurting our party.

But, apparently, that was a risk some believed worth taking, because in politics, there are two kinds of people: those who want to make a point, and those who want to make a difference. From time to time, we all want to make a point, but at the end of the day, most of us want to make a difference. Not in this case. In late September, a budget bill was sent from the House to the Senate that included an amendment requiring that Obamacare be defunded. To absolutely no one's surprise, the Democratic-led Senate stripped out the defunding measure, and sent it back to the House. The House then responded by sending back a bill with another amendment to delay the implementation of Obamacare for a year. On September 30, the Senate Democratic majority removed this amendment. I was doing whatever I could to avoid a shutdown. On Friday, I made a stop in London, Kentucky, for less than three hours to attend the World Chicken Festival Parade and was back at my desk in Washington by early Saturday afternoon. On Sunday, I was on the phone all day with my staff, the leadership team, Boehner, and anyone else I thought might be interested in responding with some sense about the situation. But ultimately, Boehner refused to bring the revised bill to a vote on September 30. As I left for the day, knowing that we were at an impasse with only one possible conclusion—shutting down the government at midnight that night—I stopped by Stef's desk on my way out the door. "Stef, you don't remember this, since you were only twelve the last time we did this. But this is going to be bad. For everyone." The next day, approximately 800,000 federal employees were ordered to stay home with no idea when they'd next get paid. National parks and monuments were closed. Federal loans to small businesses and homeowners were put on hold, as was government-sponsored scientific research. Tax refunds were delayed. The list went on.

Every American, other than those in Congress who had spearheaded the move, thought that shutting down the government as a means to block Obamacare was a terrible idea. And they were right. We all agreed on the central issue: we wanted to get rid of Obamacare, and if we'd had the votes to do it, we'd have done it in a heartbeat. But as conservative columnist George Will put it, shutting down the government to get one's way could best be described as "the politics of futile gesture." We had a disability—it was called fifty-five of them and forty-five of us. While I might not be the best person in the room at math, even I knew fifty-five Democrats was more than forty-five Republicans and it was utterly irresponsible for anyone to call themselves a true conservative while misleading people into believing we could get an outcome we couldn't possibly get—to think that a Democratic president and Democratic-led Senate were going to abandon their signature legislation.

I don't like the politics of futile gesture—we were not elected to make a point, but a difference—and I also didn't like that some members of Congress were going along with it. Many Americans were being told that if we just stuck it to Barack Obama, he would cave. They were being told by outside groups and television and talk-radio hosts that the reason we couldn't get better outcomes than we'd gotten was not because Democrats were in control of the White House and Senate, but because Republicans had been insufficiently feisty. That simply wasn't true. Shutting down the government just showed that these groups, while professing to believe in the Constitution, ignored the fact that James Madison, its creator, also created the presidency, giving the president the right to veto legislation. And it was downright disgraceful that many of the groups advocating a government shutdown were not only misleading people, but were making a living off it. Critics called this practice "purity for profit."

The only salve was that soon attention was drawn away from the government shutdown mess to the disastrous Obamacare rollout. Americans had already learned about the impact it was going to have on individuals and families—higher premiums, higher co-payments, higher deductibles, lost jobs—and now it was time to learn what life under government-run health care was like. On the same day the government shut down, the health-care marketplaces opened, and the rollout was a complete and utter mess. The website for people to begin shopping for health insurance crashed, making a visit to HealthCare .gov even less pleasant than a trip to the DMV.

My staff agreed to continue to work through the shutdown, unsure if they would get paid for their time. We've had forty McConnell scholars at the University of Louisville since the program launched, and nearly every year, a group comes to Washington, DC, to spend a few days seeing firsthand how government works. Well, several of them came this week to find the US Capitol closed to visitors. On day three of the shutdown, a woman was fatally shot by DC police after a car chase that began at the gates of the White House and ended at the Capitol. Everyone inside the Capitol was put on lockdown. We were asking law enforcement in our capital to protect us, when we were doing little to protect them.

And I had had enough.

☆☆☆

On October 21, 2013, Elaine came to me with a copy of an article she'd printed from that day's *The Fix*, the *Washington Post*'s political blog. "You have to read this," she said, handing me the paper. "This is the most on-point article I've read about you in a long time."

I took it and read aloud. "'Mitch McConnell isn't charismatic. He's not dashing. He's not an amazing orator.'" I put the paper down and looked at Elaine. "Honey, if you're trying to tell me something, there's probably a better way."

"Keep reading."

"'He is, however, the most powerful Republican in Kentucky—and in the US Senate. There's one reason for that: He is his party's best strategic mind.'"

This article appeared four days after the government had reopened, after sixteen long days, through a deal I helped broker. On October 12, with nobody in DC able to fix the mess we'd made, I approached Harry Reid and told him it was time to find a way to get this done. At the time, I felt as if I had been handed the ball on my own two-yard line, with a shaky offensive line. A week into it, not only were we getting nowhere on talks to reopen the government, but once again, we were on our way to default on our debts. As soon as the shutdown went into effect, I had begun to bring together the members of my conference. We'd meet in the Strom Thurmond Room at the Capitol—a small, ornate room that looks down over the lawn of the mall, off a hallway off-limits to reporters—and, elbow-to-elbow, we discussed how we were going to stand firm in our goal to reopen the government.

My argument was clear: Shutting down the government did absolutely nothing to impact Obamacare. While hundreds of thousands of employees stayed home without pay, while families were locked out of national parks and monuments, while people waited in longer lines at the airports, Obamacare was up and running. We were not effectuating anything. And it seemed the only point we were making was that we were willing to watch our numbers tank, a year before many of us faced reelection.

"We have lost the point, and we are now losing the politics," I said. While building unity among my conference, I also worked with Reid to negotiate a deal: a debt-limit increase until February 7, an extension of federal funding through January 15, and no binding strings attached. The Senate and House voted in favor of the measure on October 16, and the next day, after President Obama signed the bill into law, thousands of federal employees returned to work.

I had hardly made it back to my office after casting my vote when the Senate Conservatives Fund denounced me for "negotiating surrender," and they would later announce their endorsement of Matt Bevin. During the course of my talks to reopen the government, this group had finally frayed my last nerve. Brian, who'd been keeping a close eye on my right flank, came into my office and told me about the latest issue that had been building that day. "They're accusing you of sneaking a so-called kickback for a troubled dam project in Kentucky into the budget bill," he said. Not only was it absurd—nobody could "sneak" anything into this bill, as it was reviewed by too many in Congress—but it was patently untrue. The funding for the project had been requested by Dianne Feinstein, a Democrat, Lamar Alexander, and the Army Corps of Engineers.

"They're calling it the Kentucky Kickback," Brian said. "I think we should take it out."

"This is a pretty worthwhile project, isn't it?" I asked. "We're not talking about a museum to Lawrence Welk in North Dakota."

"That's true. But the politics don't look good. I know we had nothing to do with it," Brian said. "But it's gonna be toxic by three in the afternoon. Maybe we should try to get it out of there."

Too many people were recasting themselves to satisfy these guys. Were we going to follow suit? Enough was enough. I looked at Brian. "Let me ask you a question," I said. "Are we afraid of these guys?"

"No," he said. "We're not."

"Well, then—" Let's just say, I used an expression I rarely use, and never in front of staff, but it made my point. "We're keeping it in."

"I'm on board with that," Brian said, and by the end of the day, my staff was on board. As Josh Holmes later put it: "SCF has been wandering around the country destroying the Republican Party like a drunk who tears up every bar they walk into. The difference this cycle is that if they stroll into Mitch McConnell's bar, he's not going to throw you out. He's going to lock the door."

✩✩✩

When the second year of the 113th Congress convened on January 3, 2014, I had a feeling that some of my colleagues were thinking, as I was, back to a vote that occurred fifteen years earlier, almost to the day. Just two months after securing a congressional majority for the first time in forty years, Republicans strode into the Senate Chamber on January 5, 1995, to cast the first vote of the 104th Congress—a vote to limit their own power.

At the time, Democratic senator Tom Harkin had proposed changing Senate rules so that it would take only fifty-one votes to shut down debate instead of the traditional sixty. Though it was clearly in the Republican majority's short-term interest to support the measure, every one of us voted against it, as did then-senator Joe Biden, and senior members of the current Democratic leadership in the Senate, including Harry Reid.

What every Republican senator, and many Democratic senators, realized at the time was that any attempt by a sitting majority to grasp at power would come back to haunt us. Even worse, any rule change aimed at making it easier for one party to force legislation through the Senate with only a slim partisan majority would undermine the Senate's unique role as a moderating influence and put a permanent end to bipartisanship.

All of this was relevant in January of 2014 because a few weeks earlier, Harry Reid went nuclear. In November, Reid implemented a parliamentary move, commonly referred to as the nuclear option. What is that? He broke the rules of the Senate to change the rules of the Senate. What he achieved from it was a change to the rules to allow federal judicial nominees and executive office appointments to be confirmed by a simple majority rather than the sixty-vote supermajority that had been the rule for nearly forty years. He'd threatened to do this before, and for months I had spent a lot of time trying to get Harry's trigger finger away from the nuclear option.

The similarities between the Democrats' decision to go nuclear on nominations and the Obamacare debate were inescapable. They muscled through Obamacare on a party-line vote and didn't take into account the views of the minority. Since Reid took over as majority leader, Democrats employed every gimmick they could exploit to pursue their most prized legislative goals while attempting to minimize the number of uncomfortable votes they'd had to make. Dick Durbin, the assistant Democratic leader from Illinois, liked to say that if you don't want to fight fires, don't become a fireman, and that if you don't like taking tough votes, don't become a US senator. He has always been right about that. Taking a tough vote from time to time has always been the cost of being a senator. We are, supposedly, grown-ups, and we can take it.

As the Democratic quarterback, Reid set records for the number of times he blocked Republicans from having any input on bills, or cut off our right to debate. The committee process had become a shadow of what it had been. Major legislation was now routinely drafted not in committee but in the majority leader's conference room and then dropped on the floor with little or no opportunity for members to participate in the amendment process, virtually guaranteeing a fight. This partisan approach was one of the main reasons Republicans had stuck together over the past few years. In the best traditions of the Senate, we insisted that the views of those we represent not be ignored. The key thing about the US Senate is that more than any other institution in any democracy, its rules are designed to safeguard the rights of the minority party. This has been a key to America's success because it's helped create laws that are durable, leading to stability over time. Changing a law requires at least some buy-in from the minority, which makes laws much harder to undo, and prevents us from having laws that change every few years. Invoking the nuclear option created a precedent that allows a simple majority that gets impatient to change the rules at any time to achieve a totally partisan agenda.

It was utterly depressing to watch what Harry Reid had done to the Senate. The day he'd invoked the nuclear option, Elaine called and asked if I wanted to meet for a late dinner at La Loma. She knew how upset I would be, and when I arrived at the restaurant, she was there waiting for me at a table in the back, my margarita ready.

"How are you feeling?" she asked after I sat down.

"This place is a mess," I said.

Elaine reached across the table to take my hand. "Well, look at it this way," she said, with a hint of a smile. "There's nothing tougher than following somebody who did a great job, and nothing that makes it possible for success better than following somebody who made a mess of things."

"Where have I heard that before?" I said.

"I know it's going to happen. Next November, you're going to win this thing, Mitch. You're going to be majority leader. Then you can turn things around."

I hoped she was right. If I became the majority leader, my first priority would be to restore the Senate to the place the Founders, in their wisdom, had intended—not the hollow shell of an institution Harry Reid had created. I had had enough of his heavy-handed leadership, and in January, soon after we reconvened, I decided to go to the Senate floor and articulate an alternative. Though it was risky to do so, I wanted everyone to know what a Republican majority would mean for the country. I would restore the committee process. The people we represent would be allowed to have a say through an open amendment process. And senators would once again put in a decent week's work on the floor. That's how you reach consensus—by working, and talking, and cooperating, through give-and-take. That way, everyone's patience is worn down, not just the majority leader's, and everyone can agree on a result, even if they don't vote for it in the end. It's been said that the rules governing the Senate are founded deep in human experience. Using the clock to force consensus is the greatest proof of that. And if Republicans had the majority the next year, we would.

But first I had to win my race.

✩✩✩

In March, we were about two and a half months from the primary, and in Kentucky and around the country, things were looking good. I was asked by Carl Hulse of the *New York Times* how I expected Republicans would fare in the many primary challenges we faced. "I think we're going to crush them everywhere," I said. "I don't think they are going to have a single nominee anywhere in the country."

When I saw Brian and Stew back in Washington that week, they tried their best to be good-mannered about their feelings about what I'd said. "I have to admit it," Brian said. "I'm not totally in love with that comment."

Regardless of how my staff felt about it, I believed what I'd said. I had no animosity toward the Tea Party, because we all wanted to achieve the same things. My problem was with the groups who hijacked their agenda for their own profit.

And I did it.

On May 20, 2014, I beat Matt Bevin 60–35 percent. Mine was the biggest margin of victory of any so-called establishment candidate with a primary challenge, and we came close to winning every county in Kentucky, losing just two of 120. (Demonstrating real resilience, Bevin bounced back the following year and was elected governor of Kentucky.) The good news didn't stop there. After following the advice I'd offered to my colleagues facing primary challenges—to better engage in these fights—we didn't lose a single primary to a candidate who couldn't win in November. It was, after all I'd been through, pretty damn gratifying.

Elaine and I had watched the returns at our campaign headquarters in Louisville with some members of my staff. At the end of the night, Stef walked out with Elaine and me.

"Good night," Stef said before heading to her car. "And congratulations. I hope you can get some rest."

"Not yet," I said. "It's now time for the real race to begin."

When I first ran for the Senate in 1984, I knew how little I knew, especially with regard to important federal issues. My unfamiliarity with these matters was a point of great anxiety at the time. My opponent, Dee Huddleston, had served twelve years in the Senate and I feared the idea of having to debate him. I knew Alison Lundergan

Grimes, my thirty-four-year-old opponent with no national experience, was, if she had any self-awareness, likely feeling the same way in her race against me. So I did something that few incumbents ever risk doing—I challenged Grimes to a series of Lincoln-Douglas–style debates. She of course declined, thus setting the stage for us to prove how utterly unprepared she was for prime time.

In addition to her inexperience, I had a few other things going for me. A vote for her truly was a vote for Barack Obama, and the members of my campaign staff had a running contest to see who could get the word "Obama" mentioned more often in news articles about the race. But one of her greatest weaknesses was the point of her campaign: She was running mostly on the fact that she wasn't me. But voters are smarter than that and require more from the people they are being asked to elect. I knew in the end, our race came down to the question of what type of difference I had been making, and would continue to make, for the people of my state. As a freshman senator, Grimes would be attending committee hearings, trying to figure out what was going on, whereas I would be appointing committee members themselves. I'm not one to say it very often, but I'm proud of many of the things I've accomplished as a senator, and not only with the deals I'd brokered during the Obama years. I'd worked hard for Kentucky, especially with regard to the impending collapse of the tobacco market in the late 1990s. During my tenure as whip, I crafted the so-called tobacco buyout, which Bush signed into law. It was highly successful in helping to keep tobacco farmers from financial ruin, while also having a positive impact on public health.

One of the things I was most proud of—something I consider to be among the greatest differences I've made since holding public office—was my work on Burma. Over the past five decades, this Southeast Asian country had been among the most isolated on earth and its government among the most oppressive. No one embodied the peaceful struggle for democratic reform and peaceful reconciliation more than

Nobel laureate Aung San Suu Kyi. I first came to know of Suu Kyi more than twenty years earlier, when I came across an article that told the story of her and her nation's struggle.

Her father, Aung San, was the architect of Burmese independence, and had been assassinated when she was just a toddler. As an adult, Suu Kyi lived in India for a time, worked at the United Nations, and eventually married and settled into a happy and comfortable life with her professor husband and two boys in Oxford, England. In 1988, Suu Kyi returned to Burma to take care of her ailing mother, and arrived to find a revolution already under way. She didn't go to become a leader, but she was her father's daughter, and she was pushed out front to become the leader of the National League for Democracy. She stayed in Burma with her mother, and two years later the National League for Democracy won 80 percent of the vote in a largely free and fair election. But the regime ignored the election results and cracked down on its own people. Suu Kyi was arrested. Scores of other political reformers were jailed and tortured, and the regime continued its brutal campaign against ethnic minorities, driving many from their homes into refugee camps. Among the many groups that suffered extreme hardships were the Karen, many of whom now call Kentucky home.

With Suu Kyi under house arrest in Burma, her husband fell ill with cancer back in England. She could go to him, but she knew she'd never be allowed back into Burma. With her husband's support, Suu Kyi made the difficult decision to stay. Her husband died and she never saw him again. For nearly two decades, she remained under house arrest in her mother's old home on University Avenue on the shores of Inya Lake.

Since first reading her story, I'd felt compelled, in my own small way, to make her cause my own. In September of 1996, I helped pass a bill that included sanctions against the Burmese regime, and seven years later, along with Democratic senator Dianne Feinstein, I worked to get the Burmese Freedom and Democracy Act of 2003 enacted as a way of further pressuring the regime to reform itself. I then led the effort with

Feinstein to renew the measure every year. In 2007, with Senator Joe Biden, we introduced a measure that enacted enhanced sanctions against the Burmese regime, and three years later, good news finally arrived. The government held an election that was widely thought to be just like the others—unfree and unfair. But, to the surprise of all observers, the new civilian government, which was widely expected to be a continuation of the previous military junta, initiated a number of reforms. Days later, Suu Kyi was released from fifteen years of house arrest, and scores of other political prisoners were freed as well.

Since the recent reforms in Burma, which loosened restrictions, Suu Kyi and I were able to speak by phone a few times and I had been hoping to meet her in person as soon as I heard the news of her release. That opportunity finally arrived in January of 2012, when I traveled to see her in Burma. As I pulled up to her house in Rangoon—the same house in which she'd spent a decade and a half under house arrest, cut off from the world—I felt very emotional. And even more so when she hugged me hello. But during our meeting, she was upbeat and optimistic, telling me that Burma had made more progress in the past six months than in the previous five decades. As the lead author of an annual sanctions bill aimed at encouraging its government to reform, this came as welcome and unexpected news.

During our meeting, I asked her to come to Kentucky to speak at the McConnell Center. She agreed, and I hosted her in September of 2012. I'm always grateful for the people who speak at the McConnell Center, and by this time I'd hosted a number of senators of both parties, six secretaries of state, four secretaries of defense, Chief Justice Roberts, Vice President Biden, and President George W. Bush. But welcoming Suu Kyi was especially meaningful. Before making the trip to Kentucky to speak at U of L, and spend the day with Elaine and me, she came first to the Capitol to accept the Congressional Gold Medal— Congress's highest honor. I had been at the vanguard of wanting to bestow the award on her in April of 2008, knowing she wasn't—and might never be—free to come and accept it. Burma continues to face a number of challenges, and the job is still not done. But even so, it was a very, very proud day and one that I was quite sure I would never live long enough to see.

☆☆☆

In the months before the election, I spent a lot of time crisscrossing the state. I'd been visiting the small towns of Kentucky throughout my career, and returning to them these months felt as if I were catching up with old friends. At every stop, I saw what I'd been seeing over the years—the goodness, decency, and warmth of Kentuckians, and I was reminded of a line from a famous poem about my state: "If these United States can be called a body, Kentucky can be called its heart." Often, Elaine and I would board the campaign bus after an event to find that someone had left a plate of homemade food—a tray of sandwiches, a fresh casserole, or my favorite, ham and biscuits. During one stop, on our way to Lexington, Terry Carmack's sixteen-year-old daughter, Anna, arrived with sugar cookies she'd made herself, decorated with frosting letters reading "Beat Grimes" and "Team Mitch."

In Campbellsville, Kentucky, where I'd helped block the closing of a large apparel factory under a plan to outsource the work to prisoners, I was greeted by a particularly large and enthusiastic crowd. People had come by the dozens to thank me for helping to save their jobs. For another part of the tour, we were accompanied by country music star Lee Greenwood. He opened every rally by singing "God Bless the USA," his song that had become very popular after 9/11. After joining him onstage to sing the song fourteen times at fourteen different stops over two days, I'd often find myself back on the bus, humming the song, morning and night.

"I really love that song," Elaine said one evening. "But Mitch, you're starting to drive me crazy with the humming."

Terry was with me through it all. He'd been with me in my first race, nearly thirty years earlier, and it was nice to be back on the road with him. One of our last stops of the campaign was a parade in Hazard, a town of less than six thousand people in eastern Kentucky. When we arrived, several journalists were milling about, waiting for me. "Remember how I joked, nearly thirty years ago, that being your advance man meant getting out of the car before you?" Terry said. "It's sure not like that today. Look at all the media. Who are all these people?"

There were, indeed, a lot of them. At a few earlier stops, I'd learned that among the reporters present were some who'd come from as far away as Japan and Norway. I walked over to a film crew and introduced myself to the reporter. "Where you from?" I asked her.

"Al Jazeera."

Terry looked at me with raised eyebrows. "Nope," he said. "Nothing like thirty years ago."

✩ ✩ ✩

I have a few cardinal rules that I ask my staff to follow—know I'm going to trust you to do your job, let me know if there's a problem I should know about, and never tell me something is a sure thing if there's a chance it won't happen. This last one is particularly important to me. I don't want to formulate a strategy based on speculation.

The Sunday before Election Day, with this in mind, Josh and I called Ward Baker, who was then the political director of the NRSC. I wanted to go over where things stood with every race across the country in the final forty-eight hours. Ward talked me through the races, state by state.

"Things are looking good," Josh said.

"What's the take-away here?" I asked.

"Sir." Ward paused. "You are going to be the next majority leader." I knew Ward wouldn't say this if there were any chance it wasn't true. I allowed it to hit me. Nearly thirty years of struggle and hard work was now just forty-eight hours away. There was so much I wanted to say, but all I had was silence.

"You there?" Ward eventually asked.

"Yeah," I said. "I sure am."

CHAPTER TWENTY

Victory

O n the morning of November 4, 2014, Elaine and I left home to head to Bellarmine University to cast our votes. On the way, as we rounded a bend in the road near the polling station, Elaine grabbed my arm.

"Look," she said. Gathered along the side of the road was a crowd of people holding handmade signs reading "Team Mitch." As we approached, they broke into cheers and applause. I was unspeakably grateful.

Elaine and I got out of our car to a throng of reporters, and as I pushed my way through them toward the building, I was taken by surprise to see a large number of my DC staff, who had, without telling me, used their vacation days to come to Kentucky. They stood with dozens of my former staff, cheering me on. With a growing lump in my throat, I cast my vote. Afterward, Elaine and I stopped and spoke to the crowd. I'm not sure who was more enthusiastic—them or Elaine. I might not necessarily be known as a big hugger, but even I couldn't help myself. Alongside Elaine, I went from person to person, hugging every one of them, thanking them for their hard work, and for showing up for us, in more ways than one.

We returned home to a quiet house and shared some leftovers we'd picked up the day before at Morris' Deli. "I need to distract myself," Elaine said when we'd finished lunch. "I'm going upstairs to work. What are you going to do?"

"The only thing left to do," I said. "Wait."

A few hours later, I met Stef at the Louisville Marriott East, where we'd all gather that evening. We'd rented two adjoining rooms upstairs, where I'd watch the results, and a large ballroom downstairs to hold a party for our supporters. As I walked into the ballroom, I looked at the large stage, knowing that in just a few hours, from this very spot, I would deliver either the most gratifying or most depressing speech of my life. Several platforms had been set up in the back of the ballroom for the members of the press who were planning to come.

"That's far too much room for the press," I said to Stef. "I don't think we need all that space."

"No, we do. Listen to who's coming." She began to read the list—nearly 150 credentialed members of the press. Fifty-one news organizations.

Just as I had before every one of my elections, at about five o'clock, I called together all the members of my staff. Reverend Bob Russell, the former pastor of Southeast Christian Church, began by offering a prayer. One by one, I thanked everyone for their work. Without the people who stood beside me in that room, and others who had supported me in the long months leading up to this campaign—Josh, who had run a flawless campaign; Kyle, who had advised me to bide my time in 2002, and then to run in 2014; Brian; Stef; Billy; John Ashbrook; Terry—I never would have been there, standing on the precipice. I knew there was a chance my dreams were about to come true. I couldn't have had a more wonderful, more committed group of people to share it with.

As Kyle and I headed to the room upstairs to watch the returns, Stef caught up with us. Her face was flushed.

"We got the early numbers out of Floyd County."

"How do they look?"

"They're weird."

"What do you mean weird?"

"Look," she said, handing me her phone. "We're winning there." We never won there. In fact, Floyd County had not voted Republican since the Civil War.

"Yes," I said. "That is weird."

"Oh, man," Kyle said. "If this holds true, this is going to be a huge night."

But I was more prepared for it to be a long one. The polls in Kentucky close at 6:00 p.m. statewide, but because Kentucky is in two time zones, it's seven o'clock in Louisville when voting ends in the western counties. With a tray of sandwiches wrapped in plastic on the table, and a bucket of cold drinks at the ready, we all settled in—me, Josh, Kyle, Billy, Stef, John Ashbrook, and Terry. Elaine snuck into the adjoining room to make phone calls, thinking it would likely be a few hours before we knew anything definitive. In 2008, it wasn't until about 9:30 p.m. that I felt I could trust the results. But at 7:02 p.m., two minutes after the polls closed in Kentucky, before we even had a chance to unwrap the sandwiches, Elaine came rushing back in, in response to the whoops of joy she'd heard from our room.

"What happened?"

"CNN called it," I said, staring at the television, incredulous. "We won. By a landslide."

"Already? Are you serious?"

As those around me cheered and high-fived, I stood motionless. I looked at Elaine. "We did it."

"Oh, Mitch." She came to hug me, with tears in her eyes. "Thank goodness. Honestly, I was not ready for you to be sitting around the house working on your résumé." She laughed. "Now let's get that majority."

At around 8:30 p.m., after Alison Lundergan Grimes called to concede and we'd watched the results from a few other states, I went downstairs to the ballroom to deliver my victory speech before a rowdy crowd of hundreds. As wonderful as it was to step off the stage, knowing I'd earned the trust of my fellow Kentuckians for another six years (I'd later learn I'd carried 110 of 120 counties), I also knew the night wasn't over. Afterward, I went back upstairs to watch the final results come in, to see where the Senate stood. Not long after, back in that room, with the announcement of Joni Ernst's win in Iowa, just before midnight on the night of November 4, at the age of seventy-two, fifty-one years after I first walked into the office of John Sherman Cooper, I became the majority leader of the US Senate.

✫ ✫ ✫

It was well after midnight when Elaine and I returned home. Neither one of us could sleep. Elaine went upstairs to change, and I took a seat on the sofa in the living room. My ears were ringing with the echo of the ballroom, and I closed my eyes and took a deep breath—the first breath I felt I'd taken in two years. Elaine came downstairs and sat beside me on the couch.

"This reminds me of how you always say that the best moment in a candidate's campaign is the day before his announcement," she said. "Because after that, the hard work, and the attacks, begin. Harder days lie ahead but right now, all I want to do is savor this moment."

I'd been thinking the same thing myself. One race was over but another had just begun. To turn the country around. To restore the Senate. I'd been preparing my whole life.

And I was ready.

Epilogue

B ecause I've flown home to Kentucky nearly every weekend since first being elected senator, I'm usually at least vaguely recognized—*Hey, don't I know that guy from somewhere?*—when I'm there. But things were very different on November 6, 2014, two days after my landslide victory over Alison Lundergan Grimes. As soon as I walked into the airport terminal to head back to Washington, crowds started to form around me, snapping photos and taking selfies. People were lined up three and four deep all the way to the gate. When I finally made it to the gangway, I had to laugh. Only in America could a bespectacled polio survivor who started out in this business with no contacts, no credentials, and no money wake up one day at the age of seventy-two to find himself treated like a celebrity.

Although the animal spirits of both the Left and Right had converged in Kentucky in the months leading up to Election Day, even I hadn't expected this level of attention. But suddenly it was now clear that while I had become a kind of vessel for what many people detested about politics, with this win, I was also an unlikely symbol of its renewal. The editors at *Time* seemed to be getting at the same thing with the cover of their post-election issue. Superimposed over the infamous red-and-blue Obama "Change" graphic was . . . me. Four months later, the magazine would name me one of the hundred most influential people in the world. Improbable as it was, Mitch McConnell, a Kentucky Republican first elected to the Senate the year Mark Zuckerberg was born, was now pointing the way to the future.

The first thing I did after winning reelection was to hold a press conference at the University of Louisville, outlining what Republicans would do with our newfound majority. Since the moment I assumed the role of Senate majority leader, I have been absolutely determined to restore the Senate. Now more than ever we need the kind of institution that enabled Henry Clay to forge the immensely complicated deals that forestalled the Civil War, and where LBJ teamed up with Republicans like Everett Dirksen and my own role model and former boss, John Sherman Cooper, to pass civil rights legislation that would cement a new social order in ways that a court decision never could.

At its best, the Senate is a place where the divisions and hopes of our big, messy, pluralistic country are channeled and resolved into something resembling consensus, and it's been my goal to get us there. I believe that consensus among bitterly disputing parties is not only possible but a necessary condition for the tranquil flourishing we aspire to as a people. It is a thing of genius.

I don't know what some of my more disgruntled colleagues thought the Senate would be like, but perfection is not in its mission statement. This means that if you're a purist, being a US senator will be utterly exasperating. It also means that if you're open to something less than perfection, being a US senator can be deeply rewarding. Plenty of others have explained the ways in which the Senate is designed to protect us from ourselves in moments of passion. Far fewer have written about the ways in which that same design, which typically necessitates bipartisan buy-in on major legislation, has helped ensure stability and broad public consensus about our laws. But the latter effect of the Senate's built-in bias toward supermajorities is just as important as the first, and one I have emphasized again and again in the Obama era.

A standard criticism of this view is that it elevates process over policy or, worse, that it amounts to a kind of ideological surrender to those on the political left who view government as a hammer. Yet while I certainly appreciate the impatience and dismay many of my fellow conservatives feel in the Obama era, the relentless intensity of these critiques suggests it's time to relearn a lesson many of us once took for granted: if you want to be a US senator, you need to be at peace with imperfect outcomes. Conservative icon William F. Buckley urged us, if ever faced with a choice between competing Republicans, to opt for the most conservative candidate who could win. The same maxim should apply to our shared legislative goals. The point here isn't to get comfortable with failure. It is to recognize that failure today often carries the seed of tomorrow's success. It's to see the wisdom in the metaphor of the hitchhiker: if the first car that stops is only going halfway to your destination, take it.

I first internalized this lesson from studying the great legislative battles of the mid-nineteenth century, which make today's political fights look perfectly tame by comparison. It's a lesson I then learned firsthand in a decades-long battle of inches over campaign finance reform. And it's a lesson I've relearned in recent years as a restive faction of Republicans have turned their guns on each other in frustration over their inability to halt the latest incarnation of the ideological left.

These shortsighted and self-interested operatives have exploited these natural frustrations by sowing confusion and discord among our ranks, splitting our party's natural coalitions, handing victory after victory to our political adversaries, and enriching themselves in the process. These people not only give a bad name to conservatism, they have had a poisonous impact on our politics. By setting up impossible goals and then decrying those who fail to achieve them, they create an endless cycle of distrust and finger-pointing that empowers no one but themselves and their ideological opponents. They have become a cancer within the Republican Party, and for too long no one was willing to call them out. When I decided to do so, I took a lot of heat. But it was absolutely the right thing to do.

The answer to Barack Obama and the march of the Left is not to rail against one's fellow conservatives, it's to make better arguments, build broad coalitions, win elections, and stick together. The changes we seek won't come quickly or all at once, but they will be more durable when they do arrive because they will have been achieved through persuasion and, ideally, on a bipartisan basis. As Henry Clay once put it: "All legislation, all government, all society, is founded upon the principle of mutual concession, politeness, comity, courtesy; upon these everything is based . . . let him who elevates himself above humanity, above its weaknesses, its infirmities, its wants, its necessities, say, if he pleases, I will never compromise; but let no one who is not above the frailties of our common nature disdain compromises." This is a program for success in a body of a hundred strong-willed men and women, each with his and her own interests and views. It requires deep understanding, an ability to listen, great patience, and a willingness to subordinate one's own idea of perfection for the moment in the interest of achieving long-term goals later on. It means viewing the legislative process as the best means we have for making good decisions collectively.

I say all this not only because I believe in the Senate, but because I believe in my party. Not unlike the country itself, the Republican Party is a big, boisterous coalition with a proud history. From abolitionism, to geographic expansion through the Homestead Act, to the vast expansion of educational opportunity through the establishment of land grant universities, to women's suffrage, the early causes of our party were rooted in a profound optimism about our ability to carry out the promise of the Founding Fathers even as we looked beyond colonial-era horizons and constraints. The boat may be unsteady at times, and no one would argue that Republicanism is the perfect expression of conservatism. But no national party can ever be expected to achieve ideological perfection. What the Republican Party is, is the best political expression we have for communicating a set of shared principles to the national audience we will need to remain relevant. A party is not a church; it is a tool for achieving broadly shared goals.

Many today aren't satisfied with this vision of party politics. And while enforced uniformity is not a quality typically associated with conservatism, the irony is that many conservatives today are surprisingly quick to embrace it. Many a Burkean now detests the kind of incrementalism, institutionalism, and realism that once defined them. But we simply cannot let the skirmishes of the moment turn us into a regional party, which is precisely what we will become if we fixate on hunting heretics within our ranks. This challenge is of course not unique to us. Democrats are arguably far more rigorous about enforcing a rigid ideological code than Republicans, and in my view their extremism on an issue like abortion or their reflexive dovishness in an age of terror, to take just two examples, is bound to catch up with them. And while individual Democrats may still believe in the importance of religiously informed values or the right to turn a profit, the contempt that the national party appears to have for both is alarming to big segments of the population and carries its own risks of regionalism. But I'll let the Democrats figure all that out. My concern is with my own party and its future.

Throughout the Obama era, I have tried to do two things well: make it clear to the voters which party was responsible for the worst elements of this president's legislative agenda, and, once we had resumed control of both houses of Congress in the elections that followed, responsibly wield the tools the voters had entrusted us with. Legislatively, that meant achieving whatever was still possible, and worth doing, as long as Barack Obama continued to wield the veto pen. Given this president's far-left vision for the country, there was not a whole lot we could expect to accomplish together. But my view is that that was no excuse to do nothing at all. I also set out to repair the damage Democratic leaders had done to the Senate over the previous eight years. That meant reactivating the all-but-dormant committee process, allowing debate and amendment on the Senate floor again, and reestablishing the kind of normal budgeting process that had languished under the leadership of my predecessor. In short order, we passed legislation aimed at curbing the scourge of human trafficking, a federal budget that would balance in ten years, a free trade agreement that would enable a president of either party to expand the market for US-made goods, the first five-year high-way bill in nearly two decades, a rewrite of the No Child Left Behind education bill that some have described as the greatest devolution of power from the federal government to the states in a generation, and a bill that permanently prevents states and localities from taxing the Internet or e-mail. Among many other bipartisan legislative achieve-ments, we also passed important legislation that will give us the tools we need to combat cyber-attacks.

Admittedly, none of these things will get average Republican pri-mary voters on their feet. But compared with the legislative graveyard of the prior several years, the new Republican-led Senate looked like an Amazon fulfillment center. This impression was further reinforced when the *Washington Post*'s Fact Checker issued three Pinocchios to Harry Reid's risible claim toward the end of our first full year in the majority that the new Republican majority was "the least productive in history."

All of this was as good for the country as it was for the institution. And it was good for our politics. Those of us who had become too accustomed to partisanship learned we could accomplish some very worthwhile goals by extending a hand across the aisle. And that we could enjoy ourselves and the job of legislating in the process.

The principle was simple: If the voters decide they want one party to run the White House and another to run Congress, it doesn't mean they want you to do nothing. It means they don't want one party to do whatever it wants. They want us to come together and do the things we can agree on. And that's just what we've done. From time to time, we have also passed legislation aimed at making a point. Shortly before our first year in the majority was through, I worked hard to pass an Obama-care repeal bill. I didn't expect the president it's named after to sign it. But it was important for the country to see that in the face of all the calamities this law has wrought, the president remains stuck in cement on the issue.

This is the great irony of progressivism: what is held out as the tonic for the masses is imposed whether the masses like it or not. In the name of equality, any difference of opinion or dissent is either ignored or crushed. To liberals today, true diversity, ideological diversity, is an obstacle to some vague vision of a life without risk or difference.

Difference is not something to be stamped out. It is something to be confronted and mediated in a way that's broadly acceptable to the public. And I think we've come a long way. In the end, the goal isn't a perfectly running congressional machine or a party without blemish or inner turmoil. The goal is to allow the country to work out its differences freely and energetically, confident that the institutions the Founders left us are capable of accommodating the disputes and disagreements that arise in a nation as big and diverse and open as ours.

So much of liberalism seems rooted not in gratitude but in contempt for the past. It's one of the dividing lines between progressivism on the one hand and conservatism on the other. Both sides tend to caricature the other along these lines, often unfairly. But a lifetime in politics has only reinforced for me the importance of preserving what is good about our country and our shared experience as a people committed to self-governance, a process that is fair, open, and free, and the rule of law.

In many years of travels around Kentucky, I have seen the extraordinary work of ordinary people through the kind of civic, religious, and business groups that serve as the tissue between individuals and their government. I have met and been inspired by individuals like David Jones, a man who told me early on in my career that the most important word in the English language is "focus," and who went on to found one of the nation's largest health-care companies in my hometown; Eula Hall, the self-described "hillbilly activist" who has devoted her entire adult life to the medical care and support of the poor in eastern Kentucky; and Dr. Noelle Hunter, a college professor and proud single mom from Morehead, Kentucky, who invited so many others, including me, into a personal crusade to bring her abducted daughter home from West Africa. These are the people who have made my job so rewarding over the years, and they, not the government, are what makes our nation great. We need to make it easier, not harder, for people like them to emerge and to see their dreams and aspirations through.

I love America. And as I look back on my many years in public life, I think the simplest way to describe my philosophy is to say that I have tried in my own small way to preserve those things I find most lovable about my country. Viewed in this way I can now see a line, however faint, running between my long fight for free speech at home and fair and open elections in Suu Kyi's Burma. I see how an early appreciation for the Senate rules, which empowered one young senator without any real connections or influence, would motivate him years later in a battle to preserve them. I can see how early obstacles and conflicts in an otherwise ordinary postwar life in the American South prepared me for later threats to a great political party that has played a crucial and profoundly underappreciated role in the flourishing of our nation and all its people. And I can see how a little boy with little prospects for what the world calls success can find sustenance for a lifetime of battles in a mother's patient hands. I have learned that the story of a nation's success, and the success of each one of us, is a slow awakening to the timeless value of the long game.

AFTERWORD

The Long Game and the Federal Judiciary

Photograph of my friend Antonin Scalia and me following his nomination to the Supreme Court in 1986. The image was originally inscribed at the bottom by me and given to Nino. After the Justice's passing, the Scalia family inscribed the top of the photo and presented it back to me as a gift in 2018. It is a treasured keepsake and proudly hangs in my US Capitol office. My inscription reads: "To my good friend Nino Scalia with fond memories of our days together at the Justice Dept. & high expectations for an outstanding tenure on the U.S. Supreme Court. Mitch McConnell, U.S. Senator, Ky, 9/17/86." The family's inscription reads: "To Leader McConnell, & his legendary foresight. With appreciation, the Scalia family, Nov. 2018."

As Valentine's Day 2016 neared, I was looking forward to escaping Washington, DC, and taking my wife, Elaine, to St. John, in the Virgin Islands. It was a congressional recess period, and even though I enjoy my work in the Senate immensely, I try to allow myself one weeklong vacation a year. Sometimes it happens, sometimes it doesn't. Politics is an unpredictable line of work, and vacations frequently get canceled. Unlike in some prior years, however, in 2016 both Elaine and I were able to secure the time off, and we were on our way. On the afternoon of Saturday, February 13, 2016, our plane approached Cyril E. King International Airport, in St. Thomas, our overnight stop on the way to St. John. The captivating blue of the Caribbean below pushed politics and government far from my mind. Upon landing, the plane door opened and I felt the immediate warm embrace of humidity. At last, I thought, a week of freedom and relaxation.

Little did I know that this tropical escape would be the setting for the most consequential decision of my career.

As I waited with my wife to deplane, I did what everyone does in this situation: I powered up my iPhone. I figured I would just check to make sure nothing major was happening in Washington or in Kentucky. I expected little news on a Saturday afternoon. However, immediately after I looked at my device, I was confronted with the news that Supreme Court justice Antonin Scalia had passed away.

This was upsetting to me on a personal level. I had known "Nino" for more than forty years. He and I had gotten to know each other in the Ford Justice Department in the mid-1970s. He had been the assistant attorney general for the Office of Legal Counsel when I was a deputy assistant attorney general for the Office of Legislative Affairs. In my position at the Department of Justice, I regularly attended senior staff meetings. Around the table most days were Deputy Attorney General Laurence Silberman, Solicitor General Robert Bork, and Scalia. High intellect and dry wit were the order of the day at these meetings. Even though these brilliant lawyers were all affable, the setting was intimidating. Accordingly, at these gatherings, I followed the old adage that it is better to sit in silence and be thought ignorant than to open one's mouth and confirm it!

Nino and I became friends and had remained so ever since. During my first term in the Senate, I had enthusiastically supported Scalia's nomination to the Supreme Court in 1986. (He was confirmed 98–0.) Over the years, Elaine and I had enjoyed occasional dinners with Nino and his wife, Maureen. I was saddened by his passing and my heart went out to his family.

I remained in a reflective mood as Elaine and I got into a cab and headed to our hotel. As we drove through the town of Charlotte Amalie, I thought about Scalia's towering legacy. His laser-like mind, his lively pen, and his irrepressible personality had helped usher in a revitalization of conservative jurisprudence—all based on the quaint notion that the law should be interpreted as it was written. The salutary effect of this judicial philosophy is to return the lawmaking power where it belongs: to the people's elected representatives. Not only had Scalia's brilliant legal opinions changed the way people viewed the law, but he also had been instrumental in the growth of the Federalist Society, which had encouraged and promoted scores of talented, young, conservative lawyers.

Unfortunately, in the age of the Internet, social media, and the twenty-four-hour news cycle, politics quickly intrudes upon grief. When Elaine and I reached our hotel room, I switched on the news. As I watched the broadcast, I soon began to think about what would be an appropriate statement to make about my friend's passing, one that honored his legacy. First and foremost, I wanted to convey my condolences to Maureen and the Scalia family. But, at the same time, I believed another message was also in order.

It seemed to me that if the shoe were on the other foot—if Senate Democrats had been in the majority with a Republican president in office—they would not have permitted a Supreme Court nomination to be confirmed. My intuition was later borne out by three sets of facts. First, in June 1992, when George H. W. Bush was president, Joe Biden, then chairman of the Senate Judiciary Committee, announced that if a Supreme Court vacancy occurred that year, "it would be our pragmatic conclusion that once the political season is under way, and it is, action on a Supreme Court nomination must be put off until after the election campaign is over." If President Bush put forward a nomination, Biden proclaimed, the "Judiciary Committee should seriously consider not scheduling confirmation hearings on the nomination." Second, in the years since, senior Democratic senators had made similar pronouncements. In 2007, the seventh year of the George W. Bush presidency, Senator Chuck Schumer declared that the Senate should not give its advice and consent to any Supreme Court nomination by President Bush in the last *eighteen months* of his presidency. That was a much more expansive position than the one I had in mind. In 2005, also during the Bush 43 presidency, Senator Harry Reid noted that the Senate was not required to vote on nominees for the judiciary. Finally, history reflects the reality of divided government during a presidential election year. One has to go back to 1880 to find the last time a Supreme Court vacancy that occurred during a presidential election year was filled by a president and Senate of opposite parties.

The fact that Congress was in recess and that I was in St. Thomas proved to be an important factor in the way things transpired that afternoon. Since the Senate was not in session, my Republican colleagues were scattered across the globe, either back in their home states or overseas on official travel. GOP senators would not be assembled in one place again for another week. Had Scalia passed away while the Senate was in session, I might have delayed announcing my position until I had had a chance to try and persuade my membership of this course of action at one of our thrice-weekly lunches. However, under the circumstances, consultation with fifty-some senators spread across innumerable time zones was simply not realistic.

The main formal power a majority leader possesses is the authority to essentially determine the Senate's schedule. Yet, if the leader does not have the support of his membership on an issue, as a practical matter, the leader's power is greatly diminished. A Senate party leader who gets too far ahead of his colleagues on a major issue can find himself in a lonely spot if no one supports his stance. For that reason, staking out a bold position on a significant national issue without prior consultation with one's colleagues carries with it considerable risk.

Sitting in my hotel room in St. Thomas with my unopened luggage stacked next to me, I weighed each of these factors. After a couple of hours of reflection, I publicly announced that "the Scalia vacancy should not be filled until we have a new president."

My statement happened to coincide with a number of other fast-moving political events. That very night, there was a debate of the Republican presidential candidates in Greenville, South Carolina. A number of the GOP hopefuls publicly agreed with my decision. In effect, I had given our candidates a place to land on the issue. Apparently, that same afternoon, Donald Trump's then-adviser (and future White House counsel) Don McGahn gave the candidate a list of potential judges to consider mentioning on the campaign trail. Trump made reference to two conservative judges that very night during the debate, evincing his clear commitment to naming people with similar judicial philosophies to the federal bench.

Later in the week, a couple of my Republican colleagues reached out to me. They were a bit skittish about my unilateral decision. In the end, however, almost all of my colleagues supported the decision I had made in St. Thomas.

As one might expect, the reaction on the left was the exact opposite. My statement created a furor. However, Democrats overlooked that the Constitution's advice-and-consent function does not *require* the Senate to act on presidential nominations. Advice and consent is to a great extent what the Senate chooses to make of it. And the Senate's view of advice and consent has evolved over time. I got my first exposure to advice and consent when I was a young legislative staffer for Kentucky senator Marlow Cook, and the Senate was considering President Richard Nixon's nominations of Clement Haynsworth and Harrold Carswell to serve on the Supreme Court. Both were defeated. Not long afterward, I wrote an article for the *Kentucky Law Journal* in which I argued—naively, in retrospect—that the Senate should defer to the president's judicial philosophy and look only at the nominee's qualifications. Following this approach, I argued that Haynsworth should have been confirmed and Carswell should have been defeated; which turned out to be the way Senator Cook had voted.

Over the past half century, I have watched the advice-and-consent function change to fit the sentiments of the Senate and of the public. In 1971, I found myself with some time on my hands after working on Tom Emberton's losing Kentucky gubernatorial campaign. I went to Washington and, on a pro bono basis, helped assist on the nomination of William Rehnquist to be associate justice on the Supreme Court. (I had come to know and admire Rehnquist in prior years, when he and I worked together on the Haynsworth nomination during my time in the office of Senator Cook.) Rehnquist was confirmed by a vote of 68–26.

A decade and a half later, as a young senator, I served on the Judiciary Committee and participated in Rehnquist's confirmation hearings to be chief justice and, of course, those for Scalia's elevation as well. In 1987—though no longer on the committee—I witnessed the nomination and regrettable defeat of Bork's nomination to the Supreme Court. The Judiciary Committee reported out his nomination unfavorably, and his nomination was defeated on the Senate floor, 42–58. In 1991, President George H. W. Bush nominated Clarence Thomas to serve on the high court. The Judiciary Committee deadlocked 7–7 over the Thomas nomination and reported his nomination out without recommendation. The full Senate confirmed him 52–48. I supported each of these nominations. As with Bork's nomination, Thomas's proposed elevation to the court was opposed vigorously and viciously by Democrats and their left-wing allies. Yet, despite the heated opposition by liberals, both Bork and Thomas received an up-or-down vote on the Senate floor; neither nomination was filibustered, which under Senate rules would have required sixty votes to overcome. As Thomas received only fifty-two votes, had a Democratic filibuster taken place, it would have torpedoed his elevation to the Supreme Court. This required only a single Democratic senator to stand up and object to moving to the Thomas nomination. Tellingly, none did. The Bork and Thomas nominations reflected the Senate norm that held that if a judicial nomination made it onto the Senate's executive calendar (meaning that he or she had been reported out of the Judiciary Committee), he or she should receive an up-or-down vote on the Senate floor.

This tradition of not filibustering judicial nominations continued throughout the 1990s. During this period, Majority Leader Trent Lott and Minority Leader Tom Daschle went to great lengths to avoid defeating President Bill Clinton's judicial nominations through filibusters. Once the George W. Bush administration came into office, however, the left grew restive regarding the traditional Senate approach to considering judicial nominees. In 2001, Senator Schumer assembled his fellow Democratic members at a retreat with liberal luminaries Professors Laurence Tribe and Cass Sunstein. The outcome of this meeting was that Senate Democrats decided they would use every tool in their tool kit to block nominations. This came to include filibusters, particularly of circuit court nominees they viewed as potential future Supreme Court nominees, such as Miguel Estrada. Ultimately, a bipartisan group of senators—"the Gang of Fourteen"—reached a compromise, which papered over the cracks of the issue in the short term.

When John Roberts was nominated to fill the vacancy left by the passing of Chief Justice Rehnquist in 2005, he was confirmed without having to face a filibuster. However, when Samuel Alito was named shortly thereafter to replace Justice Sandra Day O'Connor, Democrats— including Senator Reid and then-senator Barack Obama—mounted a filibuster against his nomination. The filibuster was ultimately overcome by assembling the required sixty votes, a process known as "cloture." This reflected a departure from the way the Senate typically had operated; only on the rarest of occasions had Supreme Court nominees ever been filibustered.

From 2009 to 2013, Republicans employed this new standard of requiring sixty votes to defeat judicial nominations only twice: in the case of two circuit court nominations. In addition, Republicans did not attempt to filibuster either Sonia Sotomayor or Elena Kagan. However, in 2013, Senate Majority Leader Reid decided it was time to stack the DC Circuit—often considered the second most important court in the land—with Obama nominees. He pulled the trigger on what has come to be known as the "nuclear option." Senate rules require sixty-seven votes to change the rules themselves. Instead of assembling the necessary sixty-seven votes to change the Senate rules, Senator Reid used a bare majority to change the *interpretation* of the rules to permit fifty-one votes to overcome a filibuster instead of sixty votes, as the rules expressly state. This new interpretation covered all nominations except Supreme Court justices. At the time, I warned Senator Reid and his Democratic colleagues that they might come to regret their decision sooner than they had envisioned.

Despite my February 13, 2016, announcement that the Senate would not take up any Supreme Court nominee that year, President Obama, as I had expected, named a well-qualified individual. That person was DC Court of Appeals judge Merrick Garland.

The president's Garland gambit raised new questions. Should Republican members meet with Garland? Should Garland be permitted a Judiciary Committee hearing? My able counsel, John Abegg, argued against it. His view was that there was no need to string Garland along. John's thinking was that widespread Republican meetings with Garland followed by a Judiciary Committee hearing would only raise expectations for Garland advocates and give his nomination political momentum. Indeed, as noted earlier, until the George W. Bush administration, Senate norms counseled that if the committee reported out a judicial nomination, the individual could expect an up-or-down vote. Why waste Garland's and the Judiciary Committee's valuable time and make matters more difficult for my Republican colleagues?

John's logic made perfect sense to me. Chuck Grassley, the esteemed chairman of the Judiciary Committee, agreed. There would be no committee hearing for Merrick Garland. This, of course, only enraged the left still further.

Let me state for the record that I have nothing against Merrick Garland. From what I can tell, he has been an able public servant. In fact, in 2017, I even went so far as to propose that he serve as director of the Federal Bureau of Investigation.

Predictably, I came in for intense criticism from the left. But when Donald J. Trump became the presidential nominee for the Republican Party, I began to receive criticism from the right as well. Everyone seemed sure that Trump would lose the general election and that the Democratic standard-bearer, Hillary Clinton, would be the one to fill the Scalia vacancy. Clinton declined to say whether she would renominate Garland, and many speculated that, as president, Clinton would name someone younger and even more liberal than Obama's pick. Nonetheless, I stuck to my guns. I not only believed it to be the right decision, but I believed it could ultimately bolster the Republican nominee. After all, if there is one issue that rallies Republicans of all stripes, it is the Supreme Court. One can debate whether or not the high court has too much power, but the reality is that it is a very powerful institution and it makes decisions affecting the entire nation.

During the campaign, candidate Trump had made a shrewd decision in putting out a list of potential conservatives whom he would consider for nomination to the Supreme Court. This was the fruit of Trump's consultations with Don McGahn and Leonard Leo of the Federalist Society. The publication of this list was reassuring to Republicans, leading Trump to win 90 percent of GOP voters, the same level achieved by Mitt Romney in 2012. These voters proved key to Trump's election victory. Indeed, post-election analysis demonstrated that this was the biggest single issue for mainstream Republicans voting for the nominee. At the same time, despite the dire predictions of those on the left, the Garland issue made no discernible impact on any Senate races. Democrats tried to use Garland as a cudgel against Senator Grassley, but to no avail.

As one might expect, on election night 2016, the Scalia vacancy was very much on my mind. My February 13 decision would have been all for naught if the Democrats kept the White House and regained control of the Senate. I was bracing for a bad night for my party. However, as the returns began to trickle in, my mood began to brighten. At 1:27 a.m., Fox News declared that Republicans would maintain a narrow majority in the Senate. That was certainly a welcome relief, from my standpoint. But, at 2:40 a.m., when Fox News announced that Trump had won the presidency, the feeling of relief turned to one of exhilaration. A Republican president would fill the Scalia slot!

By November 2016, I had been fortunate enough to have served as Senate party leader in a number of different settings: as Senate minority leader with a Republican president, as Senate minority leader with a Democratic president, and as Senate majority leader with a Democratic president. Now, at long last, I would be able to serve as Senate majority leader with a Republican president. With a president of the same party and majorities in both houses, this political alignment provided an opportunity for Republicans to leave a lasting legacy for the nation.

Although it was the wee hours of the morning, I began to reflect on the "long game." What Senate priority could do the most to shape the nation in a constructive, enduring, and conservative direction? My mind kept coming back to the same option: the judiciary. The federal courts play an enormous role in our government, and federal judges serve lifetime appointments. Indeed, numerous federal judges have served on the bench for more than a quarter century. Moreover, candidate Trump had made a point of emphasizing judges during the campaign; his and my priorities dovetailed in this respect. The actions of the new administration and the 115th Congress with regard to judges could have positive effects that could carry forward for decades to come. Before I went to bed on election night, I had resolved to make the federal judiciary my top personal priority in the next Congress.

A week after the election, once it became clear that Trump would name Don McGahn as White House counsel, I immediately called the counsel to be. I wanted to see if this was someone I could do business with. The answer proved to be yes. During our phone call, I strongly urged Don to take personal control over the judicial nominations process. As I explained, I had seen numerous instances of the White House Counsel's Office and the Department of Justice struggling for control over judicial nominations, the result being delay, delay, and still more delay. I also told him that I was going to work with Judiciary Chairman Grassley to do away with what is known as the "blue slip" process for federal appellate judges. (The "blue slip" process is a Senate tradition by which senators can informally veto non—Supreme Court judicial nominees from their home states.) I said to him, "Don, just send up the best conservative nominees you can, and as quickly as you can, and Chuck and I will take care of the rest."

As far as the judiciary goes, the Supreme Court gets most of the public attention, as it is the tribunal that establishes constitutional doctrine for the nation. But the Supreme Court decides only a small fraction of federal judicial disputes. Federal district court judges and federal appellate court judges hear and decide the vast majority of federal legal matters in our country. That is why, after it became clear that Donald Trump would be president and Republicans would retain control of the Senate, I set out to confirm as many qualified, conservative judges to the federal bench as I could. These included judges such as Kentucky's own Amul Thapar, who now sits on the Sixth Circuit Court of Appeals. The net result of my collaboration with the administration and with my Senate Republican colleagues was that the upper chamber confirmed thirty circuit court nominees in the first two years of the Trump presidency, the most during the first two years of any administration since the creation of the federal circuit court system, in 1891. Indeed, by July 2019, forty-three circuit court nominees—nearly a quarter of all sitting federal appellate judges—had been named by the president and confirmed by the Senate.

Not long after election night, I spoke with President Trump about the Scalia vacancy. I urged him to name the best-qualified conservative candidate, since filling this slot would almost certainly lead to a showdown over the question of filibustering Supreme Court nominees. Because of the high stakes involved with a potential Senate rule change and with a narrow 52–48 majority, there was little margin for error on the Republican side. If any question existed as to the nominee's fitness for office, it might result in the nomination's defeat and an embarrassing setback for the administration and the Senate majority. It soon became clear that Senate Democrats were not going to support any Trump Supreme Court pick. Within just a few days of his swearing in, to his great credit, the president nominated Tenth Circuit judge Neil Gorsuch to the Supreme Court. He could not have named a more thoughtful, principled conservative jurist. I was overjoyed.

But Gorsuch's fate was far from assured. The left was looking for payback for Garland, conveniently forgetting the "Biden rule" laid out a few decades before and the more recent Schumer and Reid declarations. Democrats opposed Gorsuch with all their might. Given the nominee's undeniable qualifications, it was clear that the Democrats would have filibustered whomever Trump chose. These, of course, were many of the same lawmakers who had supported Senator Reid's efforts to change the interpretation of Senate rules to permit a bare majority to confirm all lower federal court judges.

When the GOP regained control of the Senate in January 2015, some of my Republican colleagues had wanted to return the threshold to sixty votes to invoke cloture and defeat filibusters for nominations. I fully understood their frustration; after all, I had been deeply angered at Senator Reid's high-handed approach. But after two years had passed, I reflected on the effect of the rule change. Looking back at history, it seemed to me that the fifty-one-vote threshold for breaking filibusters on the executive calendar had essentially returned things to the way they had long been in the Senate—that is to say, prior to the election of President George W. Bush. In other words, the new rule interpretation had reestablished the norm that the Senate should not engage in the filibustering of judicial nominees who had been reported out of committee (as was the case, for example, with the Bork and Thomas nominations). Gorsuch's sterling credentials and clear majority support, coupled with the left's frenzied opposition, helped me make the case to my Republican colleagues: it didn't matter who Trump put forward; Democrats would filibuster the nominee no matter what.

I was not about to let Democrats block this extraordinary nominee out of spite. I had warned Democrats not to "nuke" the Senate's rules; they had ignored the Senate GOP's views, and now they would reap the whirlwind. We defeated the Democratic filibuster, completing the work of my predecessor by making Supreme Court nominees subject to a simple majority vote. Neil Gorsuch was confirmed on a 54–45 vote on April 7, 2017.

At the time, it seemed difficult to imagine how the battle over Neil Gorsuch's nomination could be exceeded in vitriol and intensity. But it certainly was. In June 2018, Justice Anthony Kennedy—commonly seen as the Supreme Court's "swing justice"—announced his retirement. Immediately afterward, I spoke with the president about the vacancy. The only point I raised with him was the issue of a paper trail. My concern over a paper trail could be summed up in a single word: timing. The bigger the paper trail, the longer the deliberations and the more opportunity for Democratic mischief. I wanted to get a justice on the court by the first Monday in October, when the court started its term. At the same time, if the nominee was defeated, I wanted to give the president and the Senate sufficient time to consider and confirm a replacement before the end of the Congress. The 2018 midterm elections were fast approaching, and it was quite possible that control of the Senate might switch hands to the Democrats. For these reasons, I suspected that the Democrats would try to intentionally draw out the confirmation process by making unrealistic and unreasonable document requests. From the Democratic standpoint, if they could delay the nomination process past the November elections and then win back enough seats to claim a Senate majority in January 2019, they would have been in a much stronger position. Under this scenario, if the Democrats could have then defeated the nominee in the lame-duck session, the administration and Senate Republicans would be left with insufficient time to confirm a new justice prior to the Democrats taking control of the chamber. With control over the Senate in the new Congress, Democrats could then stymie the president on the Kennedy vacancy. I was determined not to let that happen.

Not long after my conversation with President Trump, he nominated a highly distinguished jurist, Brett Kavanaugh of the DC Circuit, to fill the post. Predictably, Democrats used the nominee's paper trail to try to delay matters. Kavanaugh performed well during his first hearing and seemed to be well on his way to confirmation. Ultimately, however, in their desperation, Democrats and their liberal allies outed a woman, Dr. Christine Blasey Ford, who had made confidential allegations about Kavanaugh from their high school days. This led to a firestorm and a second Judiciary Committee hearing, where first she and then Kavanaugh were to testify.

The president and I were in close communication throughout this time. The night before the second Kavanaugh hearing, President Trump called me to get a sense of where I stood regarding the nominee. I told the president I felt "stronger than mule piss" about sticking with Kavanaugh. I conveyed to him two additional, if less earthy, sentiments: First, that Kavanaugh deserved a vote. And second, that if Kavanaugh went down to defeat, the president needed to be ready with a replacement so that the Senate could confirm him or her before the start of the new Congress in January 2019. It was clear to me that the president didn't need any persuading to stick with Kavanaugh; I think he just wanted to make sure that I felt the same way.

On Thursday, September 27, 2018, like much of the nation, I watched the Judiciary Committee hearing closely. Immediately after Dr. Ford had completed her testimony that morning, the phone rang. It was a familiar voice: the president. Again, he wanted to get my views. He and I both agreed that Dr. Ford had been a compelling witness. I expressed to the president that it was only "halftime," however, and that he should wait until completion of the second half before making any decisions. Again, the president needed no persuading. I then watched Kavanaugh's afternoon appearance before the committee. Immediately after the hearing had concluded, the phone rang again. Once more, it was the president. We both thought that Kavanaugh had done well. With consideration of his nomination scheduled for the next morning in the Judiciary Committee, it seemed as if the Kavanaugh confirmation was back on track.

That was not to be the case, however. To add to an already dizzying array of recent developments, Republican senator Jeff Flake, a member of the Judiciary Committee, made a major announcement at the Friday morning "markup" of Judge Kavanaugh's nomination. After meeting with his friend and fellow Judiciary Committee member Democratic senator Chris Coons, Flake declared that he would only vote to report Kavanaugh out of committee. He would not support the nomination on the Senate floor unless and until the FBI conducted an investigation into the specific allegations made by Dr. Ford.

To put it mildly, this put another fly in the ointment. We were beginning to run out of time to confirm Kavanaugh prior to the start of Supreme Court business in October. And we were running out of time if the Senate had to confirm a replacement before January (assuming a partisan shift in control of the Senate). Following the eventful Friday morning committee markup, that afternoon I convened a meeting in my office. Included were all the Republican members of the Judiciary Committee, plus Senators Susan Collins and Lisa Murkowski. Along with Flake, Collins and Murkowski were now the key players in this drama. Without their support, Kavanaugh's nomination would almost certainly be defeated. At this meeting, I began by saying that the Senate was voting the next week on the Kavanaugh nomination—no matter what. We all soon came to agreement on the scope of the additional background investigation. It would consist of the FBI interviewing everyone Ford had mentioned in her testimony and everyone that a second accuser from Kavanaugh's college days, Deborah Ramirez, had mentioned. My colleagues and I were in agreement that the individuals promoted by the self-aggrandizing Democrat lawyer Michael Avenatti would not be pursued. Immediately after the meeting broke up, I called Don McGahn at the White House and relayed to him what the scope of the investigation was to be and that the probe needed to be wrapped up in a week. The FBI immediately swung into action.

During the Kavanaugh nomination process, especially in the period following Dr. Ford's allegations, the left's behavior was reprehensible. I take a backseat to no one in my defense of free expression: it is the very backbone of our democracy. But the left's approach was something altogether different. It constituted a mob mentality—win at all costs, even if it involved threatening lawmakers and their staff members. Democracy operates on persuasion, not on physical intimidation—that is the stuff of banana republics. Republican senators and their staffs were menaced by mobs of radical activists. Matters had reached a fever pitch.

On each day leading up to the Kavanaugh vote, I spoke on the Senate floor. The nomination so dominated the news cycle that my floor speeches were carried live every day on cable news in their entirety. I repeatedly emphasized the importance of two points: the presumption of innocence and the need not to be intimidated by angry mobs.

By Thursday, October 4, the FBI had spoken with all of the relevant people and had delivered its report to the Senate. Senators Flake, Collins, and Murkowski each read the report and were satisfied that it contained no evidence corroborating what Dr. Ford had alleged. The Democrats, however, had one last card to play. They tried to promote further delay by having the FBI report copied and made public. This was a bad idea. FBI reports contain raw, unsubstantiated, and unsworn assertions that are not meant for public dissemination. Anticipating this move, Senator Grassley and I had already tracked down a memorandum of understanding between President Obama and then—Judiciary Committee chairman Democrat Pat Leahy that clarified that FBI reports are executive branch property and are not to be released to the public. Yet another obstacle overcome.

At 3:06 p.m. on Friday, October 5, Senator Collins requested recognition on the Senate floor. The nation held its collective breath; what she was about to say would likely decide the outcome of the biggest political standoff in recent memory.

Senator Collins and I had had lunch earlier that afternoon. During our meal, she seemed relaxed and fully at ease. As we ate, I did not ask her for her vote, and she did not volunteer it. But, given her demeanor, I intuited that she was going to vote for Kavanaugh.

I was in my seat on the Senate floor when Senator Collins began to speak. It was a privilege to be on hand to witness this historic event. Senator Collins wound up giving one of the great speeches in the annals of the Senate. She discussed in dispassionate terms the issues before the chamber regarding the Kavanaugh vote. In the end, she concluded that he deserved to be confirmed. Through her speech and her vote, Senator Collins displayed to the nation the same traits that her colleagues in the Senate and the citizens of Maine have long known: she possesses a steely determination to do what she thinks is right. This was not an easy position for her: she hails from a liberal state, and she and her staff were subjected to numerous intimidation tactics by the left. Coming on the heels of her speech, Brett Kavanaugh was confirmed the next day.

An epilogue to the Kavanaugh battle was the political fallout. Democrats were incensed at the results of the 2016 election and were gearing up rapidly for the 2018 midterm elections. As is often the case with the incumbent party, Republicans were less energized. The treatment of Kavanaugh, however, galvanized conservative voters, which played a role in the GOP not only retaining but actually growing its Senate majority following the election.

In retrospect, the 115th Congress produced a number of notable achievements: the first major tax reform bill in more than three decades, significant criminal justice reform, and the biggest deregulatory effort since the 1980s. Nonetheless, the backbone of what some have considered the most productive right-of-center Congress since the Reagan era was federal judges. Upon reflection, it seems hard to believe that the genesis of what proved to be such a far-reaching collaborative executive branch/Senate effort took place far from the corridors of power in Washington, DC, but instead in the isolation of a hotel room tucked away on the coast of a small Caribbean island.

Acknowledgments

I t would take more pages than I have to thank every one of the people who have had an impact on my life, but I would like to single out a few. First and foremost, my late parents, A. M. and Dean McConnell. Nothing has meant more to me than their abiding love and support; and it was only through applying the lessons they taught me early in life—how to overcome adversity, tenacity, standing up for myself—that the long game was possible.

I would also like to thank my wife, Elaine. I'm so lucky to have her at my side every day. She has made my life far richer and happier than I'd ever thought possible. Not only is she an incredible wife, she is also one of the best campaigners I've met. I'd be lost without her.

I'm grateful to—and exceedingly proud of—my three daughters and their families: Elly, and her new daughter Rowan; Claire and her husband, Richard; and Porter, Tom, and Charlie. My daughters have enriched my life in so many ways, and have been a constant source of joy and inspiration throughout the years. They're such good kids and mean more to me than I can say.

Elaine's parents, Dr. James S. C. Chao and his late wife, Ruth Mulan Chu Chao, have been a source of tremendous encouragement. Their coming-to-America story is an inspiration to those who come to this country seeking greater opportunities. I'd also like to thank my four sisters-in-law and their husbands: May and Jeffrey, Christine and Jos, Grace and Gordon, and Angela and Jim.

I'd especially like to thank the team behind this book. Not one word would have been written if it hadn't been for Bob Barnett's initial counsel and belief that this was a story worth telling. Brian McGuire was integral in organizing my initial thoughts. Aimee Molloy, an extraordinary talent, brought uncommon professionalism, steely determination, and good humor to what seemed like a monumental task under a grueling deadline. Special thanks also to Adrian Zackheim and Bria Sandford at Sentinel for pushing us all to create the best possible book. And to Deborah Skaggs Speth, the curator of the McConnell Chao Archives at the University of Louisville, and Nan Mosher, who's been a member of my team for almost thirty years, for their help with research.

I'm exceedingly grateful to the members of my Republican conference, especially the class of '14, whose election made me the majority leader; as well as the members of my leadership team, past and present, particularly Jon Kyl, John Cornyn, Roy Blunt, John Thune, Orrin Hatch, and John Barrasso. Additional thanks to Judd Gregg for his strategic vision in the early years of my leadership and Lamar Alexander for his forty-year friendship and shared respect for the Senate.

I wouldn't be where I am today if it weren't for the nearly five hundred members of the McTeam who have worked for, with, and beside me through the years. While I wish I had the space to thank each of them by name, I would like to extend a special word of thanks to a few, including my chiefs of staff, who deserve far more credit than they either ask for or receive: Janet Mullins Grissom, a fighter and a trailblazer whose many personal sacrifices on my behalf early on are not forgotten; Neils Holch; Steven Law, who has been at my side with good counsel and good humor for more years than any of us would like to acknowledge; Kyle Simmons, whose steady hand and uncommon wisdom have been a constant in my life; Hunter Bates, another constant whose intelligence and decency helped anchor and guide us in many early battles; Billy Piper, a friend and trusted companion in many political foxholes; Josh Holmes, whose political smarts and great good nature make him a joy to work with; Sharon Soderstrom, a remarkable woman who (knowing she'll appreciate the sports analogy) is the Willie Mays of legislative staffers; and Brian McGuire, whose versatility and rare gift with the pen have served me well in many ways.

My deepest thanks also to leadership staff past and present. Don Stewart, or Stew, my deputy chief of staff, whose bold personality rules the Senate corridors and whose sound counsel commands respect; John Abegg, the lawyer's lawyer who packs a potent political punch; Tom Hawkins, my national security adviser, a serious leader for serious times; Julie Adams, a grace note in the Senate. Thanks also to Rohit Kumar and Hazen Marshall, alike in their keen negotiating skills and affable personalities; Meg Hauck, the valiant-hearted warrior against Obamacare; and Scott Raab, who continues that fight and is one of the best all-round players on my team. Thanks also to Neil Chatterjee, whose gift for relationships fostered legislative wins. I deeply appreciate the contributions of David Hauptmann, Matt Kenney, Rebecca Fleeson, Brian Lewis (whose knowledge of campaign law equals my own), John Ashbrook, Dan Schneider, Moon Sulfab, Lanier Swann Hodgson, Mike Brumas, Denzel McGuire, Libby Jarvis, Malloy McDaniel, and Brandi White—all of whom are among the most talented people to work on Capitol Hill. More recent additions to the leadership office deserve thanks as well, including Brendan Dunn, Erica Suares, Brian Forest, Jon Burks, Terry Van Doren, and Antonia Ferrier. And to Stefanie Muchow, a keeper of confidences and a source of strength. Stef is the first and last person I've talked with at work for more than a decade. She not only keeps me on my toes, she makes it fun.

I have been lucky to have the knowledge and help of two extraordinary floor tacticians as well in Dave Schiappa and Laura Dove.

Over the years, I have been fortunate to have incredibly talented legislative and press staff in my personal office too, including recent departure Russell Coleman and current staffers Jennifer Kuskowski, Phil Maxson, Katelyn Conner, Elizabeth Strimer, Stephanie Penn,

Justin Jones, and Daniel Cameron. Robert Steurer, my communications director, has been an anchor and a valued adviser for decades, and Reb Brownell has been an invaluable help in ways large and small.

Robin Cleveland, my foreign affairs adviser extraordinaire from the early days, taught me about the courage of Aung San Suu Kyi. Tam Somerville guided us through the early campaign finance reform battles. Paul Grove has been a great help at the Appropriations Committee. Mary Suit Jones has been a trusted and longtime friend.

Thank you to my team in Kentucky, including Larry Cox, an indispensable help and rock of support from the beginning; Terry Carmack, my state director and longtime confidante; longtime state staffers Patrick Foster, Sue Tharp, and Angie Schulte. And also to the director of the McConnell Center, Dr. Gary Gregg, whose intelligence and creativity were on full display at the Intercollegiate Studies Institute before the McConnell Center was lucky enough to pluck him away; Sherry Allen, the beloved den mother of the McConnell Center; and the 160 graduated McConnell scholars, the overwhelming majority of whom have chosen to remain and work in Kentucky. This group of young men and women have helped make me feel very optimistic about the future.

As I've said more than once, you can't make policy if you don't win elections. When it comes to winning mine, I need to first thank Roger Ailes. Without his creative genius, I'd probably be an unhappy and unsuccessful lawyer in Louisville, Kentucky. Thanks also to Larry McCarthy and Rob Hennings, worthy successors to Roger on the creative side, who've been absolutely invaluable during my hardest-fought battles. Laura Haney, my finance director, has trekked with me from Pikeville to Paducah, and around the country, to make sure I had adequate funding to run my campaigns. Jan van Lohuizen has skillfully managed the polling in all of my Senate races. Special thanks also to Joe Schiff, who ran both my campaigns for county judge, and Larry Steinberg, who has flawlessly (and on a wholly volunteer basis) managed every penny raised in every one of my campaigns.

My Saturday afternoons in the fall would be far less enjoyable if it weren't for the dear friends who've been joining me at our tailgate parties for many years: Dave Huber, with whom I went to college, and his wife, Kelley Abell; the late Judge John Heyburn and his wife, Martha, best friends of forty years; Jan Karzen, another friend of forty years; Rich and Dee Kern, friends of thirty years; John and Bridget Bush; Jim Adams and his wife, State Senator Julie Raque Adams; Rachel and Shep Schrepferman; and Gary and Krysten Gregg.

Very special thanks, of course, to Dr. Alan Speir, who I met on arguably the worst day of my adult life, when he told me I needed triple bypass surgery. He saved my life and subsequently became a close friend.

I'd also like to thank David Jones, an inspirational community and business leader and the founder of Humana, and Jim Patterson, another longtime friend and an extraordinarily successful entrepreneur. Both have been with me since the "Mitch who?" days. And special thanks to two good friends from my college days, Judge Chuck Simpson and Dr. Larry Cook.

And, finally, my special thanks to the magnificent people of Kentucky who have stuck with me. In resisting all of the arguments for my removal over the years, it's they who have made the long game possible, allowing me to do what I love on their behalf for a very long time. For that, I will always be exceedingly grateful.

Index

About the Author

Mitch McConnell is the longest-serving US Senate Republican leader and longest-serving senator from Kentucky. He has represented the Commonwealth in the upper chamber since January 1985 and has been Senate majority leader since January 2015. Prior to that, he was leader of the Senate Republican minority for nearly a decade. Senator McConnell has been described by Frank Luntz as having "had a bigger impact on the United States Senate than any senator in my lifetime" and by one journalist as being "arguably the most influential Senate majority leader since Lyndon Johnson." Twice he has been selected by *Time* magazine as one of the 100 Most Influential People. He has three daughters and is married to Elaine Chao, the secretary of transportation.